He believes that the nation's greatest challenge is not from international communism, but from internal selfishness. He calls for drastic political reform, urging the adoption of a system of complete party responsibility, a cabinet form of government, an eight-man inner executive group to make the President's work more effective, and a career service of men and women from which leaders will continue in high office from one administration to the next. He favors the decentralization of federal functions that could be turned back to state and local governments or to voluntary groups, and offers an original proposal for the establishment of regional governments in the United States.

THE NEW AMERICAN POLITICAL ECONOMY, with its bold and imaginative operational plan, will stir thoughtful controversy among leaders in industry, finance, government, and other public-spirited citizens.

MARSHALL E. DIMOCK has served three Administrations in Washington in important policy-making posts. He is presently Head of Department of the Government, New York University.

THE NEW AMERICAN POLITICAL ECONOMY

BOOKS BY MARSHALL E. DIMOCK

Administrative Vitality

Business and Government

A Philosophy of Administration

THE NEW AMERICAN POLITICAL ECONOMY

A SYNTHESIS OF POLITICS AND ECONOMICS

BY MARSHALL E. DIMOCK

GOVERNMENT CONSULTANT AND HEAD OF THE
DEPARTMENT OF GOVERNMENT, NEW YORK UNIVERSITY

HARPER AND BROTHERS · PUBLISHERS · NEW YORK

THE NEW AMERICAN POLITICAL ECONOMY. COPYRIGHT © *1962,* BY MARSHALL E. DIMOCK. PRINTED IN THE UNITED STATES OF AMERICA. ALL RIGHTS RESERVED. NO PART OF THE BOOK MAY BE USED OR REPRODUCED IN ANY MANNER WHATSOEVER WITHOUT WRITTEN PERMISSION EXCEPT IN THE CASE OF BRIEF QUOTATIONS EMBODIED IN CRITICAL ARTICLES AND REVIEWS. FOR INFORMATION ADDRESS HARPER & BROTHERS, *49* EAST *33*RD STREET, NEW YORK *16*, N.Y. FIRST EDITION. B–M. LIBRARY OF CONGRESS CATALOG CARD NUMBER: *62–7315.*

CONTENTS

PREFACE *vii*

ONE · BUILDING FOR GREATNESS *1*
Toward national greatness · The universal searching · A unifying con-cept · Argument of the book.

Part I · *THE POLICY BASE*

TWO · AMERICA'S POLICY WEAKNESS *17*
The meaning of policy · Social sympathies · The corrosive effects of group selfishness · Raising our sights.

THREE · THE NEW POLITICAL ECONOMY *35*
The managerial approach · Growth and change · The objectives of the new political economy · A high standard of living · Encourage ambition, discourage indolence · Avoid overconcentrated power and maintain bal-ance · Innovation and entrepreneurship · Stability at home and peace abroad · National heritage as a sacred trust.

FOUR · THE PUBLIC INTEREST *55*
A main concern of political economy · Freedom and the public interest · Power of the democratic idea · The whole interest above selfish interest · An American consensus.

FIVE · THE ELEMENTS OF STATECRAFT *72*
Governing is generic · Adjustment between natural and artificial man · Maintaining structural balances · Cohesiveness and a sense of belonging · The content of power · The poverty of manipulation.

Part II · *THE APPLICATION OF POLICY*

SIX · REVITALIZING THE DOMESTIC ECONOMY *95*
The new frontier · Elements of a plan · Problems of decentralization Economic decentralization · People are too crowded.

SEVEN · COMPETITIVE BALANCE *114*
The case for competition · The conditions of success · A positive program for laissez faire · The tax remedy · Values and competition.

EIGHT · GUIDELINES OF FOREIGN POLICY *135*
Political economy as the base · Suggested policy lines · International competition · Coexistence · World government.

NINE · HUSBANDING RESOURCES *154*
A sacred trust · Taking stock for the morrow · A positive program.

Part III · THE NEED FOR GOVERNMENTAL REFORM

TEN · THE CHANGED ATTITUDE *175*
An Achilles Heel? · Personal skills needed · Energy from challenge.

ELEVEN · A MINIMUM PROGRAM *187*
Outline of a plan · Determining priorities · Securing better coordination.

TWELVE · SECURING RESPONSIBILITY *203*
The gamble on one man · The party system · That which works · Institutionalizing the presidency · Helping the President with management.

THIRTEEN · TOP-LEVEL ORGANIZATION *221*
Opposing views · A recommended plan · Securing continuity.

FOURTEEN · PUBLIC AND PRIVATE MODELS *237*
How the plan would work.

EPILOGUE

FIFTEEN · EDUCATING FOR GREATNESS *253*
Knowledge is instrumental · Educational responses to stages of growth · The moral philosophy tradition · Teaching political economy · The future of political economy.

NOTES and SUGGESTED READING *275*

INDEX *297*

PREFACE

We stand today midway in a great national debate, a family discussion in which we Americans are trying to determine whether we must give up some of our traditional freedoms in order more effectively to compete with world communism and how to improve our institutional organization in order to stabilize our economy, better our surroundings, and maintain our national well-being.

During the first half of this candid analysis—which has been going on ever since the first Sputnik—we talked in terms of big ideas for a big country, and emphasized goals rather than the means of achieving them. We were treated to a series of essays by some of our most gifted writers: *The National Purpose,* expressing the sober passion of writers such as Adlai Stevenson and Archibald MacLeish; *Goals for Americans,* which was a little more operational but no less devoted to pure philosophy; and the America at Mid-Century series, in which the Rockefeller Brothers study groups topped off their work with *The Power of the Democratic Idea,* reminiscent of *The Federalist Papers* at another crucial juncture in our national history.

So now we are half way through the course, and the second half is likely to be as important as the first. From here on we must turn increasingly to means—how our policies are to work, how we are to get from here to there—keeping always in mind the goals toward which we are headed.

Typical of this phase is the work of the so-called Jackson committee of the United States Senate. Since its creation in the middle of 1959, it has been gathering and publishing down-to-earth testimony and think-group pieces on, for example, how the Soviets and the Chinese organize, on what our most cherished traditions are, and on how we may correct mistakes in our policies and what machinery is needed for their formulation and execution if we are to increase our national effectiveness in the face of severe competition from the communist world. The Jackson committee correctly assumes that we are all partners in this end-means reanalysis—that business corporations, trade unions, farm organizations, women's clubs, the universities—all are part of our democratic process of making and executing national policy.

The present book relates to both halves of this national debate—that is, to the whole of it. If this seems like a large order, the justification is that nothing less is possible, considering the approach that is involved.

The belief that the selfish interest somehow promotes the public interest is probably superior to the dogma that an all-wise government should determine every aspect of the productive process. But neither theory is good enough. The traditional American belief that government is, at best, a necessary evil and hence should not become too effective lest it be tempted to do too much, is preferable to the belief that the political state, through some mystique never fully explained, is capable of Utopian perfection. But again, neither extreme suffices anywhere in today's world.

I have gone back, therefore, to the political economy tradition, which assumes that every aspect of a nation's life ultimately focuses on policy; that policy is made by private as well as by public groups; that business and government must work together if men's basic aspirations are to be realized; that business will not thrive unless government is enterprising; that values and the spiritual life (moral philosophy) are at least as important as institutional know-how; and that by and large, a nation endures and prospers to the extent that it grasps and puts to use the principles of balance and human aspiration on which society rests.

I believe that as a people, we should adopt an approach that makes the whole political economy the test of attitudes and of the public policies that eventually emerge from them. The political economy is all social institutions pulling together to serve the community's needs. The purpose is to fulfill material wants as well as those that are social, aesthetic, cultural, political, and psychological. Political economy is the pursuit of the better life through a wise admixture of institutions and voluntarism. It involves a vivid awareness of the concept of the public interest, which it makes the ultimate regulator of public policy.

The political economy approach seeks to combine the best in private and public interest. It emphasizes the production of superior persons plus the sovereign needs of the group. It neither worships nor idealizes government, but insists that government be treated with respect and that it be made attractive and effective; for its policies and administration occupy a central role in every nation.

America's new political economy is business and government working together on the basis of common aspirations and common principles. These principles have a universal currency and apply to all nations. If men everywhere better understood the basic truths of political economy and acted accordingly, it would go a long way to reduce international tensions and create the mutual accommodations that are necessary in an explosive world.

If I had to say whether this book is more theoretical than practical or more concerned with goals than with means, I should find it hard to answer. I have tried to be concrete. After a discussion of political economy in Part I, Part II focuses on policy decisions confronting the United States. I take a stand on many issues, including economic competition, foreign policy, and the wise use of natural resources; all of these subjects are treated in some detail, as a practical view insists that they must be.

I claim no finality or superior authority for any of the conclusions reached, however. The principles of political economy are not sufficiently well understood nor are the intricate processes from principle to conclusion sufficiently reliable to make such claims valid today. I shall be disappointed, however, if the argument is not clear enough to cause those with opposing views to re-examine some of their own conclusions in a new light.

In Part III I argue for a fundamental governmental reform in the United States if we are to act as a prudent man would when confronted with the possibility that the cold war will last a long time and that the competition with communism is likely to intensify before it relaxes. Believing this and having learned from long first-hand experience the respects in which our government needs strengthening, I propose a drastic decentralization of federal functions that could be turned back to state and local governments or to voluntary groups; advocate the eventual establishment of regional governments in the United States; recommend the adoption of responsible (cabinet) government for the nation; and propose in detail a method of creating an eight-man inner executive group to make the work of the President really effective for the first time since government in Washington began to mushroom, around the time of the depression of the 1930's.

These administrative recommendations are interrelated with the principles of political economy, a body of knowledge based on an organic whole plus intricate balances. The principles themselves do not change; the weighting and combining of them do change as time and new factors require new analyses and new solutions. We are now at one of those turning points in history where the only safe approach is to ask, "What is the situation, and what are *all* of its elements?" We must be hard-headed about every policy, decision, and action.

My observations as they relate to the federal government concentrate on the period before the Kennedy administration took office. The interval between the inauguration and the time this book went to press (six months) was too short to develop any reliable impressions or conclusions. It is interesting to note, however, that some of the measures recommended in my text, such as those relating to natural resources conservation, have already emerged as Kennedy policy.

Finally, a theme that runs throughout the book and is especially dealt with in the final chapter is that American education must face up to the problem of reviving the political economy tradition and producing more well-trained people for policy roles in both government and business. I have no quarrel with economics and political science as they are presently formulated; I do believe that we cannot get along much longer without their being brought into a closer working accord.

It is a pleasure to thank all who have made possible the writing of this book. My employer, New York University, gave me a leave of absence for one year. The early research was commenced with a Ford Foundation grant administered by the Department of Government at the University. During the two-year period that I worked on the book I received substantial research grants from the Alfred P. Sloan Foundation of New York, the Relm Foundation of Ann

Arbor, Michigan, and the Shinner Foundation of Chicago. To all of these I am grateful.

During the entire course of the research I was assisted by Nellie Stavisky, whose early research training was in Canada. Also, at various times I secured research assistance from Diane Monson, Robert Littman, and Carol Tarzian. My wife, Gladys Ogden Dimock, did the editorial work on the final draft.

The general procedure was to digest every publication in political economy, economics, or political science that seemed to bear on my problem. Then I concentrated on the reports of the Jackson committee; studied analogous developments in some of America's largest corporations; visited Canada to study the political economy tradition in the universities and high-level coordination in Ottawa; spent some time in Scotland studying the political economy tradition and the business-government relationship there today; spent a short time in England and France learning about political economy and governmental organization; and wound up with several weeks in Switzerland, where the objects of my interests were the use of the collegial executive for the federal and cantonal governments, the methods used to secure decentralization, and the solution of problems of tax distribution.

The original title of this study was *The Idea of Political Economy: America's Missing Concept.* I am indebted to Ordway Tead, my Harper editor, for the title which eventually emerged.

M. E. D.

"Scrivelsby"
Bethel, Vermont
June 1961

THE NEW AMERICAN POLITICAL ECONOMY

ONE

BUILDING FOR GREATNESS

In the course of its national development the United States has reached a plateau. From this temporary base it can either go forward to greatness or, unable to meet the challenge of being the largest and strongest of the non-totalitarian nations, it can slip into mediocrity. It is possible that in the final reckoning, historians will conclude that by mid-twentieth century a decline had already set in. If so, the trend should be reversed and the forward movement toward greatness resumed.

TOWARD NATIONAL GREATNESS

America has everything to live by except a cohesive faith. Her people have the vitality of pioneers and immigrants. Her land is continental and diverse. She has the biggest businesses, the largest incomes, the highest standard of living of any great nation. She has a faith in education and a belief in universal human improvability. She has in large abundance that rare quality called organizing ability. She has social sentiments that are opposed to snobbery and privilege. America is flexible and innovative.

But with all these advantages something is missing. Business leaders seek power without understanding its dangers. Labor leaders act as if power could be indefinitely concentrated without inviting socialism. Our cities are full of slums, and we have not found financial or civic incentives adequate to demolish them and replace them with decent homes. Much of our social wealth is in a shameful state

1

of obsolescence and inefficiency—many of our schools, for example, or the New York subway system. We have not been able to transfer an excessive opulence in some areas, such as the produce of our farms, into the capital needed to improve our community services, such as homes and schools.

In short, we know more about management than we do about policy, more about production than about balance, more about making money than about the power to govern.

This phrase, "the power to govern," is a shorthand expression designed to convey the idea of a kind of sixth sense based on ability or skill. However, there is nothing mystical or mysterious about it. It is not something that some people have and others will always lack. Rather, it is a subtle combination of brain and sentiment, policy and practical ability, training, shrewdness, and ethical standards. Like the human personality, it is a composite. In part it is what the British call taste, knowing the right thing to do in the right situation, at the right time, and with the right effect. In the hands of the statesman, the power to govern adds up to survival, which means staying alive and strengthening one's institution in the process.

It is this skill, whose ancient lineage runs back to earliest recorded history, that a raw, partially civilized nation such as the United States most lacks and finds so hard to acquire. Hence, in this respect we are in the same relative position as many of the so-called under-developed nations whom we have done so much to help. They would probably contend that the United States has everything, while they have next to nothing, except "our wonderful people," as they will tell you everywhere. What is not so generally realized is that an industrially developed nation can suffer in certain ways from youth and lack of tradition quite as much as underdeveloped nations, many of which are old, suffer from the consequences of age and custom.

Paradoxical as it may appear, therefore, the United States is strong in administrative theory and relatively weak in the power to govern, whereas many older nations have a governing tradition that is superior to ours, but are weak in organizing ability and lacking in the tenets of modern management. In both cases, the deficiency is a serious one.

This suggests the possibility that the power to govern may be a skill stemming from the total state of cultural development in a particular nation. If so, it is possible that the acquisition of the skill comes slowly, is handed down from one generation to the next, like the British class system, and cannot be artificially speeded up. While visiting other countries, I have sometimes thought as much and have been inclined to think, "America is young. Her mistakes are understandable on that basis. As yet, we have no class of men with a developed sense of *noblesse oblige,* men who put the common welfare ahead of their own, who know how to handle authority with skill and circumspection. We have hardly outgrown our city machines, our political bosses, our degrading spectacle of large-scale urban political maneuvering."

But almost immediately I think again: "How much progress we have made, in one lifetime, in cleaning up the seamy side of urban politics. How quickly we respond in times of national emergency. How many able leaders we have developed in American corporations, who compare favorably with the best that older nations, such as Britain, France, or Germany, have produced."

Then the self-confidence ingrained in all Americans comes to the fore. "We are lacking in this governing skill, but we can produce it," I think. "We need only identify it, and we will produce it, just as we produce everything else." The way to produce it is through a thorough understanding, early acquired, of the universal principles of political economy.

THE UNIVERSAL SEARCHING

America is more than a nation. For much of the world's peoples it has been and remains a cause, a dream. In the outcome of the experiment on this continent are involved questions that newly formed and newly emancipated nations and the millions of their people who have recently acquired voting rights are everywhere asking: Is it possible to blend diverse cultures and maintain a durable culture? Can men and women of average intelligence learn to govern themselves in a manner that compares favorably with that of a government directed by the supposedly greater skills inhering in a more narrowly recruited elite? Can a nation that prizes freedom also learn self-discipline?

Historically, America is the testing ground of democracy and is its best champion. Recently, however, our right to claim this role has been brought into question by world communism, by means of a powerful propaganda campaign that presents the United States to emerging nations in Asia and Africa not as the champion of universal man but as the foe of freedom and self-government.

In fact, of course, our record shows us to be more radical than the communists as champions of freedom and believers in equality and the innate ability of the common man. Nevertheless, the communist distortion of our historic image has sufficient truth to make us ask ourselves whether we have not temporarily, at least, lost our way and some of our courage. Do we still believe as strongly as we did in the American dream or do we regard it as a little sentimental? Do our beliefs in democracy and freedom coincide with our behavior or is there a dislocation between the two?

If we are to find the way off the plateau where we have been resting and contemplating for some time now, we need new thinking for these new times. We need new wisdom tapped from old sources; we need to go back and relearn the wisdom contained in the concept of the political economy before specialization divided it into the separate and largely independent fields of politics and economics. If we could put new life into this old concept it would quickly get us off dead center and back into the business of leading emerging nations that want freedom and self-respect. The revived political economy concept would also strengthen our own way of life, which is now threatened more by our loss of courage than by communist propaganda.

The United States has everything a nation needs for greatness except a unifying concept to show us—and others—how to prosper without becoming materialistic; how to cooperate without losing individual initiative; how to build big institutions without becoming frozen into a bureaucratic mold; how to allocate resources without the need of dictatorship by a central intelligence to do the whole job; how to use resources without wasting them; how to secure efficiency without forsaking freedom of choice; how to govern the complicated institutions of business and government in accordance with the right decisions at the right time for the right people, which is *all* the people.

Political economy is concerned with all of these factors, and I know of nothing else that is. Hence, I submit that we must acquire an understanding (which is always an image) of what political economy is, so that the concept will become as real to us and as desirable as bliss in marriage or compatibility in one's work. We must not only revive the old concept of political economy, we must adapt it to new conditions and make it live for us and for the future.

America needs a better relationship between business and government, between Congress and the President, between Washington and local centers of population, between economics and political science, and between skill groups of all kinds, if we are to measure up to the challenge confronting our country. Better relationships would give us better policies, better values, and better morale, through better organization and stronger institutional arrangements. But all improvement depends first on learning the principles of political economy, which we once knew but in recent generations have allowed to slip out of our grasp.

A UNIFYING CONCEPT

What is political economy? As an initial definition, it is business and government working together to produce the good things of life, both material and spiritual, on which human happiness depends.

Men do not live by bread alone, nor do they live exclusively by concepts and ideals. They live by both. Much of the world's tragedy stems from the failure of national leaders to understand this connection. In America, for example, there is a belief in some business circles that we can have profits without competition or capitalism without individual ownership. We talk free enterprise, but in large areas of our economy we act collectivism. Either the idea or the behavior must eventually predominate. If for a long period (and this varies) too great a disparity prevails between belief and behavior, between profession and deed, then first the individual becomes less effective than he was and eventually either his ideology or his behavior must change.[1] Generally, it is the belief that finally changes, since forces are stronger than myths; but often the adjustment comes too late to avoid disaster.

The pragmatic advantage of including all institutions and behavior in a single unifying concept is to provide greater effectiveness in every part of the nation's life. With effectiveness comes high morale. A man with a philosophy works better than a man without one and puts more back into life than he takes out of it.[2] Similarly, a nation whose ethos lacks a unifying concept, combining beliefs, behavior, and the institutions and balances which give more or less consistent expression to this ethos, is both less effective in the eyes of the world and less satisfied in its own domestic tranquility than one that has such an ethos. An all-embracing concept, such as political economy is, promotes consistency and contentment because it is consistently effective.

We Americans are idealistic, in our own peculiar way, and we are notoriously pragmatic. Hence, we must have a unifying concept to guide and motivate us, or we invite one of two main perils, either of which could destroy the American dream:

We could become hypocrites, as already we are made to appear in communist propaganda.

We could become selfish and cynical and hence lose our vitality and our cohesiveness.

What are the possible objections to developing a vivid awareness of the political economy concept? Would we become worshipers of the state? Not as I conceive of political economy. Would we become ideologists? A little ideology might help to clarify our concepts and our values. Would we become less practical? On the contrary, we would become more so if our thinking and our behavior were in the same pattern.

A more serious objection might be that the political economy concept is too inclusive, that it works against rather than toward a proper specialization. Although more will be said on this issue in later chapters, it should be noted here that there are at least two aspects to the question, the academic and the practical. Academic specialization is undoubtedly necessary, but it is possible and, as I will argue, essential to be profound and also integrative. I would further argue that the proper preparation of a nation's future leaders includes a philosophical grasp of many factors and their interrelatedness in a conceptual whole.

As for the practical aspect of the matter, in both industry and government there is an unfulfilled need for men and women in top positions who have the philosophical and human grasp of the practical political economist. Our affluent society is as much exposed to the dangers of excessive bureaucracy as it is to the equal dangers of softness and torpidity. If initiative is to be encouraged and the excesses of bureaucracy kept in check, we need not more engineers, accountants, lawyers, or other specialists, but the principles that the political economy approach can provide, within the framework of which these and other specialists can operate at maximum effectiveness.

On balance, therefore, I see no valid objection to a unifying concept—a political economy ethos, if you please—so long as it combines values and mechanisms plus ideals and institutions so as to further universal happiness in a system where freedom is promoted and not stifled.

The alternative to communism with its dogmatic beliefs, its rigid planning of all phases of life, and its so-called new class, monopolizing all power, is a system of belief under which men may make free choices in free institutions, guided by an over-all concept that squares with universal principles.

Political economy is that concept. Democracy is not the whole of it, although it is an essential ingredient. Government is not the whole of it, although it also is essential; and "the power to govern" is seriously lacking today. An automatic and self-regulating market is not the whole of it, although it is an important part and must not be subverted.

The goal of political economy is the good life. The institutions of political economy are business and government working together in independent and self-respecting roles. The body of political economy consists of universal principles relating to forces and growth and the maintenance of a proper balance between them. Political economy is the practical knowledge of how to produce, distribute, and consume the material things of life and, at the same time, protect the spiritual things of life on which both individual and collective happiness depend.

It is possible that, in time, the applied principles of political economy will cause excessive nationalism and even bitterly contested political systems to dissolve, or at least to cease to be a hazard to world peace. While studying administration at first hand in the Union of Soviet Socialist Republics I saw that even in that rigid framework the system is undergoing constant change, and I am convinced that it will continue to change, even if another Stalin were temporarily to appear on the scene.[3] If the trend continues, as I think it will, then possibly the institutional balances and the prevailing ideas of political economy in the United States and the USSR will, in time, reflect a growing degree of similitude. The reason is that as we learn more about the science of society, we shall hear less about the political differences that divide us.

All political economies are subject to the same forces and the same stages of growth, and putting a political label on an object of contempt does not change this underlying fact. In 1957, for example, the USSR passed a law decentralizing its mammoth economic bureaucracy. In time, as consumer goods are produced in greater quantity, it will be necessary to decentralize even more, even if communist political doctrine is opposed to it. Simultaneously, the United States continues to concentrate operations in banking and in various other fields, such as manufacturing and merchandising (our chain stores are studied by businessmen from all over the world). Such concentration is contrary to our doctrine but allegedly inevitable because of forces that operate at this particular stage of national development. We can, of course, reverse these tendencies, and we probably will. The point is that in both countries, despite opposing political beliefs, concentration seems to be responding to forces and stages of growth rather than to the imperatives of political faith.

I would not push this argument to the point of positing a new kind of technological or biological imperative, causing the USSR to deconcentrate at a time when we tend toward greater concentration. That is not my conclusion. I do, however, believe that certain principles relate to such developments, that they are subject to human understanding, and that they can be disregarded if it is so decided. Nevertheless, if they are valid and the conditions are right, a wrong interpretation will inevitably create stress, social frustration, and social imbalances, which must sooner or later be corrected.

In the social sciences, a universal principle concerns a cause-and-effect relationship compounded of forces and stages of organic growth. But such a principle also concerns people; although people are a part of animal life and are subject to organic forces, their behavior is additionally complicated by strong attachments to symbols and by a seemingly incurable unpredictability, which is present even among those of indubitably high intelligence.

All of which makes political economy a complicated business. If it were merely a question of rationality, the problem would be relatively simple; but political economy is more than that. It is what Adam Smith called sentiment, and what people since David Hume, or earlier, have called moral philosophy. It is what political philosophers since Confucius and Socrates have been saying. It is what Frederick W. Taylor and management experts, with an assist from psychologists, have been finding out in more recent years.

Irrespective of whether a nation is growing, declining, or standing still, it needs the challenge which the political economy approach offers. The reason is that this approach, unlike any other, is organic, managerial, and balanced, which is to say that it is complete, sequential, and responsive. It sets goals and values and at the same time develops institutions and procedures suited to the particular needs of the nation at a particular time. In periods of growth, the wholeness of the plan constitutes a blueprint for action. When decline sets in, the engineers look to see what forces are temporarily out of balance. And when a nation appears to be neither growing nor declining, but is apparently standing still, the search is not only for weaknesses in plans and balances but also for weaknesses in effective incentives, especially those which promote teamwork. In some ways the static period is the most difficult of the three, and it is in this one that the United States finds itself today.

Despite its complexity, the concept of political economy is worth investigating. Anything that will throw light on happiness and the good life and identify nature's own principles of survival must be worth the effort, especially if it gets us out of the bureaucratic grooves in which we now so comfortably reside.

ARGUMENT OF THIS BOOK

In this book I shall argue that what the idea of Manifest Destiny was to the American nineteenth century westward movement, the concept of political economy should be to our twentieth century technological society. During the nineteenth century the American dream emphasized the limitlessness of opportunity and the near limitlessness of human self-confidence. Owing to time, technology, and a vast population, which now fills the continent, these beliefs have lost some of their fire. A new unifying concept would take account of the complexity of a modern industrial civilization, would supply a governing philosophy throughout, and would recognize universal principles that would not only relate us to our environment and to each other, but also to the rest of mankind.

Because our beliefs have failed to adjust to the necessities of the times, already our behavior is out of bounds in many respects. We are losing our natural cooperativeness and our national morale. We have distorted what eighteenth and nineteenth century economists taught, and we now act as though economic activity were the whole of life, calling ourselves "a businessman's civilization" as though this were enough. We disparage the importance of government. We act as though our resources were replaceable. We allow the power aggregations of big corporations and big labor unions to play the game of outsmarting the other fellow, instead of realizing that with power go added responsibilities as stewards of the common welfare.

We take a narrow view of economics, leaving out the institutions, the political maneuvres, the clashes of high policy on which a high-powered civilization depends. We have become so specialized that two of our academic skill groups having the most to contribute to the state of the nation—the professional economists and the professional political scientists—scarcely understand each other's language.

When I speak of a body of knowledge called political economy and suggest that it is capable of providing reliable principles of universal validity that can shape public policy and guide the decisions of the holders of power, I am assuming that the governing process is as much private as it is public.

By business I mean the whole of the economy: trade unions, farm organizations, professional groups such as doctors and engineers—even unorganized groups—in addition to corporations, firms, and the like. Hence, the term "business" is a shorthand expression for all that sizable and infinitely complicated institution in modern life we familiarly call the economic system.[4]

By government I mean not only the organized state and the whole of political activity at all levels, but also businessmen: being wielders of power, they are also makers of public policy and governors of the nation in a legitimate sense. In our free society, policy originates with individuals and with pluralistic groups, of which economic groups are the most influential. Moreover, after policies have been formalized in law, then these same economic rulers at the heads of corporations, trade unions, and farm organizations have a larger combined responsibility for administration than the state itself. Collectively, the decisions of these private officials are more numerous than those of public officials in the political bureaucracy.

When I speak of the governing function in political economy, therefore, I am not suggesting that the organized state is alone involved. Indeed, the organized state might well do less than at present if political economy became widely understood, if business and government pulled together in the same harness, and if the excesses of laissez faire were not the cause of much of government's expanding responsibilities.

To the policy makers, the decision makers, the combined wielders of power in both business and government, the thesis is as follows:

Assume that you are in this together and that you can match the concentrated power of communist planning and strategy only by increasing your social responsibilities. Government officials must know more about economics and business and must be more sympathetic to the businessman. Business leaders must realize that government makes the life-and-death decisions in matters such as war and peace, depression and inflation; hence, business leaders must be more solicitous toward government and must try to develop among themselves the same broad statesmanship that the organized state historically has commanded. In other words, business leaders must acquire statesmanlike qualities and applaud government when it develops outstanding statesmen of its own.

I shall contend, furthermore, that the qualities needed in top business and governmental positions are essentially the same and that the training of these two groups of people would be better done if we were to combine the facilities of economics, political science, and philosophy, rather than keeping subjects and students alike in separate compartments. Further, I shall contend that the point at which economics and political science meet is the apex of the social sciences, for here economic and political theory are translated into policy and into decision making for the nation.

Today's economic rulers will find more wisdom in political philosophy than in economic theory, but neither alone is enough. The two must be effectively combined as the joint possession of both the economic and the political community. As a result, leaders in business and government alike must think consciously and consecutively about the most important concepts on which our common fate depends: the public interest, the general welfare, and the elements of statecraft.

The implications for higher education are clear. We should begin to teach political economy even before young men and women get to college, so that they will have an early understanding of why freedom, self-reliance, and cooperation create a better system than one based on concentrated and autocratic power.

In the universities we should create faculties of political economy, bringing together economics, politics, philosophy, and the other social sciences in a working accord. This can be done in such a way that all who would specialize may still do so. The problem is one of organization and administration. We Americans can justly pride ourselves on our effective grasp of the centrifugal and centripetal forces that, in combination, produce the best balanced result.

The creation of faculties (not necessarily departments) of political economy would have the following advantages, as shown by experience in other countries, such as Canada, Britain, and Scotland.

First, the search for reliable principle would be furthered. To start with incomplete assumptions is to secure incomplete and unreliable results. As things stand today the professional economist, on the basis of his initial assumptions, can tell the policy maker what the decision maker should do, but he cannot be sure it is feasible nor can he speak with assurance about how to implement the recommendation, because this is in someone else's bailiwick. Similarly, the decision maker in government, who ordinarily knows much about administration but little about policy, must decide both, and often he is no better equipped for the task than the economist.

The result is that too often in both business and government the separate processes of policy formulation and administrative instrumentation are inadequately coalesced, so that serious errors occur, various expedients are attempted, and neither business nor government is guided with the sure, safe hand that modern conditions make imperative. These dangers can be and have been demonstrably reduced when the economic and the political, the policy-making function and the administrative function, are brought together in the concept of political economy as taught in Scotland[5] and in some other countries which are still loyal to the political economy tradition.

The splitting up of economics and political science into two separate and largely unrelated departments is a recent development in American education. The lineal descent of the concept of political economy to the American scene was from mercantilism, through the teachings of the physiocrats, the doctrines of Adam Smith and those of the utilitarians (most notable of whom was John Stuart Mill). It proceeded to America in the latter half of the nineteenth century where some notable individuals still championed the political economy tradition. Even the establishment of the American Economic Association was motivated largely, if not almost wholly, by a determination to keep economics and politics together, so as to assure a more effective handling of issues of vital public importance.[6]

It is only in the last fifty years, or even less, that economics and political science in the United States have been divorced, and the results are inadequate to modern-day needs and demands. Fortunately, it is not too late to redress our mistakes and to return to the older tradition, one that is still found in considerable vitality in the countries already mentioned as well as, apparently, in others that I have had no opportunity to study at first hand.

In addition to developing this argument I shall try to indicate, partly by reference to older writers and partly by attempting to combine political and economic theory, what are some of the foundation principles of political economy that are valid in our time. Then, in another group of chapters, I shall apply these principles to certain key issues of current American policy—competition, conservation, and foreign policy—in order to show how all are of a piece and how thought and decision in one area involve repercussions and value judgments in others.

I believe this effort to be germane to the issue of whether America will remain on a plateau or whether we shall find the missing concept that will enable us to respond to the demands of greatness. Furthermore, if we are correct in thinking that the universal principles of political economy may be combined and fitted to the differing requirements of time and condition, then there should be a residue of speculation and analysis that has application beyond our shores. If so, not the least of my hopes is that this book may do something to reinforce the faith of those who have remained steadfast in their support of the political economy tradition.

PART I

THE POLICY BASE

TWO

AMERICA'S POLICY WEAKNESS

What America lacks is a policy base from which to reach sound decisions that are consistently right in the long run. We do not have that assured base at present because some of our assumptions and values are wrong.

There is every indication that the cold war will last a long time, possibly fifty years, possibly more. If we can avoid a shooting war, the best informed guess is that both the liberal-individualistic and the authoritarian-collectivist systems will undergo gradual but significant modification, so that in both cases extremes will tend to disappear, and the values and institutional procedures begot of a combination of technology and institutional necessity will produce a pattern with striking resemblances.

The need of collectivist nations is to relax, so as to promote innovation and spontaneity, while our need as a capitalist nation is for a better idea of what constitutes the public interest, how public and private programs may effectively work together without impairing the virtues of either, and how we can tighten the organizational and policy weaknesses of our rather loosely knit governmental mechanisms, so as to balance freedom and efficiency more satisfactorily than at present.[1]

The basis of a vital economy is voluntarism with its accompanying sense of responsibility and self-generated initiative. The health of any free society may be measured by the degree to which private individuals and groups recognize the needs of society, organize to meet them, and conduct their affairs in a manner that shields them from the necessity of bureaucratic interference.[2] Power is safest when widely distributed among many members of the community. Freedom and competition are the way to individual self-development, the means by which society renews itself.

These are sobering thoughts. The factors of modern life militate against voluntarism and the individual and in favor of compulsion and collectivism. Science and technology are precise disciplines and tend to overwhelm the arts and humanities. Men are characteristically born into and later work in the collectivities of cities and large business institutions and then instinctively try to escape to the suburbs. Powerful economic groups include trade unions and farm organizations in addition to business interests. Government is the biggest business and the nation's largest producer and consumer if only because the inexorable needs of national defense make it so. Ill-conceived advertising techniques and powerfully financed "educational" programs tend to standardize and debase human tastes and values —and it bears repeating here that a nation's future is partly determined by its style and its sense of fitness. In our public policies we have made errors, some of them hazardous in foreign affairs, and we have floundered from one expedient to another, as in our farm program, which allows enormous surpluses of food to accumulate in government bins.

We have done so poorly in recent times because as a nation we are weak in the area of policy. We do not have a proper base of principle on which to formulate sound policy and sound decisions that affect the public interest. In place of flabby creature comforts we need a vision of a better America. In place of stratified knowledge we need philosophical breadth and depth. In place of canned, standardized entertainment we need creative arts and crafts. In place of the growing view that work is to be avoided if possible we need Veblen's and Hobson's concept of workmanship and craftmanship,[3] of work as a stimulus to individual growth. In place of a lazy conformity we need a rebellious and insistent striving for self-determination. Instead of treating values with cynicism we should study them, as our most gifted scientists have done since the discovery of atomic fission and fusion produced the means of total destruction. Instead of parroting the old saw that government is a necessary evil and the plunder of robbers, we should treat government with tender loving care, thus keeping it within desirable bounds conditioned by proper values, rather than made the servant of those who think they have the most to gain.

In this chapter I propose to deal with the bases of policies that will help us to get over our difficulties. First, I shall explain what I mean by policy. Then, I shall try to show how the traditional American credo is as valid today as formerly, despite the corrosive effect of narrow group interests. I shall conclude with a brief discussion of some of the major policy problems that beset us and of how, by raising our sights, we can begin to work toward their solution.

THE MEANING OF POLICY

Policy is more important than organization, more important even than the whole of administration, because policy is the base for all decision making, whether public or private. In both cases, these decisions affect all the interests of society, its prosperity and its survival. This is especially true, of course, in areas of great consequence, such as foreign affairs. Moreover, modern life is so complex and there are tensions in so many areas that many policies are needed for many purposes.

Public policy is a plan of action consisting of ends and means and designed to cope with a particular problem or tension area. It includes analysis, a knowledge of principles, a choice of alternatives, and methods of execution consistent with the ends sought and with the other programs of society. A public policy may or may not eventuate in law, and it is not solely a matter of governmental action. Public policy is molded by public opinion, especially by the opinion of men in positions of power and influence in economic government —business executives, labor union officials, and farm leaders, for example. Hence, I hold the term public policy to mean what private and public officials *jointly* believe the standards and goals of the economy should be.

Policy is a statement of principle and forms the connecting link between purpose and action. Suppose the objective is to stay at peace with the world; the policy might be to establish as many communication links and as many methods of peaceful negotiation as possible in order to reduce tensions. Once this is decided the remaining problems are administrative in the ordinary sense: who is to do what, who is to make final decisions, how are the various activities to be coordinated?

At the same time there might be a parallel policy: under no circumstances to lose territory, lower prestige, or surrender sovereignty. Here is a more difficult terrain because the variables and unknown contingencies are greater. If the policy is to negotiate from strength, there are the usual administrative problems: the influence of the military vis-à-vis the State Department, how to assign functions, how to arrange for final decisions and for coordination.

In most areas, policies are plural because, ordinarily, interests and objectives also are plural. A major problem of policy formation, therefore, is how to arrange organizational framework for decision making, so that the different and sometimes conflicting interests expressed as policies will be given cohesion, symmetry, and consistency. For if the parts are not so coalesced, those who administer the program will do one thing today and another tomorrow. In foreign relations especially, the result is to confuse the home side and baffle the other party to the negotiation. If the uncertainty becomes sufficiently grievous the other party becomes the victim of a chronic state of jitters and is likely to attach the most unfavorable interpretation to the unsettled state of affairs. In the unfortunate incident of the U-2 overflight over the USSR and the subsequent debacle of the summit meeting in Paris in 1960, these factors played a part.

A foremost objective of social intercourse is to build confidence, to give the other fellow a feeling of security by offering him a reliable pattern of policy and the assurance that action now and in the future will be guided by it. This does not mean that policies must not change. They *must* change when objectives change, when the behavior of the other party becomes radically different, or when new factors are injected into the situation. Accordingly, the experienced policy maker will not only seek continuity, he will be constantly alert for needed adjustments. In other words, equilibrium and flexibility must be combined.

In the world of affairs where the stakes are large it is impossible in practice to draw sharp distinctions between objectives, policies, organization, and instrumentation. If objectives are not clear there will be no adequate policy. If the organization is not clear there will be no adequate assignment of roles for decision making, instrumentation, and coordination. And if execution is weak the best of policies has a way of coming to an ignoble end. The larger the institution, furthermore, the greater is the need for skillful organization and management, because without these essentials, policies never seem wholly clear, and execution tends to break down.

Those who suggest that policy is one thing and administration another and that a choice may be made between them are not thinking clearly about what is involved in the total policy-making and decision-making process. Like society as a whole, policy is an organic process which must have some internal unity in order to succeed. Policy must combine the "what" and the "how," the goals and the techniques. These will differ, of course, in various stages of social development and in different historical periods, for society must respond to the challenge of change. At the same time, there are certain basic values and principles which continue from one generation to the next. History is both past wisdom and new adjustments, both stability and change. It is the task of political economy to build its principles and its techniques around all of these factors, not merely one.

Just as policies must be combined within a particular area of activity, so also must they be combined in the institution as a whole. Americans have great difficulty here, especially in the federal government. To take a hypothetical illustration, it would be absurd for the State Department to assure an underdeveloped nation that it would help to build up its agriculture if at the same time an agency of the Department of Agriculture were dumping surplus farm commodities in the same nation.

Thus, there must be some degree of consistency among the various units within the same program, and there must also be some attempt to combine and regroup smaller policies into larger policies for the government as a whole. There are two steps in this process: First, the main areas of the economy, as sources of policy, must be analyzed; and secondly, these separate policies must be compared to determine whether they are consistent, complete, and designed to accomplish the over-all purposes of government. In the solution of a problem of economic policy, for example, the steps are: economic analysis, a study of administrative and political feasibility, and a study of relations to other policies.[4]

Here again, Americans are weak, for despite periodic attempts since 1937 to rationalize the organizational processes for policy decision making at the top level in Washington, we are far from having achieved any real success. This will be shown more clearly in later chapters.

Public policy is not merely a matter of what economics has to say about the economy. There are usually involved other and larger issues that are political and social in that they relate to the kind of life society is seeking. If income tax policy were to be uniformly applied to agriculture in the same manner as it is to industry, for example, so that farmers were required to include as income everything they and their families produced and consumed for themselves, it would force many farmers out of business and speed the trend toward large-scale industrialized agriculture. This might be good economics, but it would hardly be acceptable social and economic policy —the family farm is too important a national asset for that. If loans to small businesses were granted only on the basis of full collateral and the element of character were ignored, the trend toward economic concentration would be stimulated, as the absence of such special credit facilities in the past makes clear. Again, such a policy might be economically desirable, but would it promote the kind of life the nation wants?

In short, there is much to policy formulation that does not ordinarily meet the eye. To determine and then to guide policy wisely is a big order, and we in the United States are far from having mastered its execution. It would help if we had a better idea of the principles on which to base policy in the first place, especially the principles of political economy.

Principle is a different thing from sentiment or even from values, although both are involved. If it is a principle of political economy that government will do less when people are encouraged to do as much for themselves as they can (voluntarism), for example, then certain value judgments are involved in assessing what it is that people seek. Once this objective has been determined, then the methods of encouraging self-reliance are legion. But, of course, they require organization, procedure, and delicate balances between voluntarism and formal action, initiative and habit before they can take form. None of this can occur until the basic policies have been adopted.

Hence, if principle is to be the basis of policy, as it should be, we must think in terms of *everything* that is involved, including values as well as structure, balance, and the administrative process. To be objective, however, we should be as explicit as possible about values instead of trying to slip them in by the side door. The purist may charge that value judgments are "unscientific"; the fact remains that they govern the choice of public programs and constitute the standards by which results are appraised. In the real world in which we are interested and in which sentiment is so large a factor, it is impossible to deal with policy or intelligently to consider political economy without bringing values and sentiment into the picture.

Finally, policy is a generic term. There may be policies for almost every action, including the aims and desires of the individual. In general, however, when we speak of policy we have an institution in mind, either a private or a public one. In the private area, for example, there is what is known as "business policy." The larger the corporation, the greater is the likelihood that it will have carefully formulated policies and that these will be widely advertised, partly to build confidence and morale amongst employees and partly to attract stockholders, but even more to provide a base from which to deal with trade unions and government. The greater the seat of power, whether in a corporation, a labor union, or a farmer cooperative, the greater the chance, first, that the institution will develop policies as consciously and as completely as it can and, secondly that these private policies will shade off into public policy. For every wielder of power is inescapably a public person.

The largest category of policy, which is public policy, as already noted, is in reality a good deal more than that which takes the form of law as decided either by constitutions, courts, legislatures, or the executive officials of government. Many public policies never take the form of law at all, but derive from principle, custom, taste, or the canons of statecraft. Even when unwritten, they are real. The decision maker believes in competition, for example, or economy, or in helping the underprivileged, and although he is under no legal compulsion to take account of these factors, his decisions are based on them because for him they are a matter of ethics and principle.

SOCIAL SYMPATHIES

Although America is on a plateau in her progress toward greatness, I am optimistic about the outcome because our basic social sympathies are right. As Adam Smith remarked in his book *The Theory of the Moral Sentiments,* this is the fundamental need, because social sympathy is anterior to policies formulated to guide the conduct of business and governmental affairs.

Traditionally, Americans have held:[5]

That man is born free and that freedom is a goal as well as a means

That every individual has a right to happiness

That ability is likely to appear among people from the least privileged environment and that hard work and dedication are necessary to its fulfilment

That every individual has the right to equal opportunity, guaranteed by government, that the on-going development of all is a goal of society, and that no one, no matter how inferior his intelligence or his economic station, should ever be treated as a commodity but always as an end in himself

That the common people, with all their shortcomings, have a better idea of what they want and aspire to than any group or government, no matter how much talent it commands

That no group or interest has a monopoly of truth, that every individual is entitled to his own opinion and to the free expression thereof, and that no minority shall have the power through government to prevent this free expression

That man should be guaranteed the fruits of his own labor, that private property is an integral part of the good life of the individual and must be respected as such

That competition is essential to individual growth, encouraging the talented to use their gifts and the less talented to struggle harder to catch up with them

That power in all forms, especially concentrated power, is suspect, for power usually corrupts the user thereof and limits the efforts of those on whom it is used

That with power goes a corresponding increase of responsibility and the need to act morally, patriotically, and with a sense of stewardship vis-à-vis the public

That the government, being powerful, should be the servant of the people and not their master and that powerful individuals and groups should be under similar constraints.

Alexander Pope mirrored these underlying sentiments in a couplet in his *An Essay on Man*.[6]

> Thus God and Nature link'd the general frame
> And bade self-love and social be the same.

And from the same source:[7]

> Self-love but serves the virtuous mind to wake,
> As the small pebble stirs the peaceful lake;
> The centre moved, a circle straight succeeds,
> Another still, and still another spreads;
> Friend, parent, neighbour, first it will embrace;
> His country next, and next all human race.

So long as we can echo these sentiments we need have no doubt of our ability to correct the faults that have appeared in our national life or in the image that America presents to the outside world.

Most Americans still subscribe to most of the credo here set forth. But we have been so busy building factories and cities that we do not think and reflect on the continuing value of our traditional beliefs. We have tended to become cynical, partly because it is the fashion, and to disparage those who express an honest emotion in public. We have seen our institutions grow so fast and so bewilderingly that, without previous experience to guide us, we have been overwhelmed by problems which political philosophers have long recognized as important to national well-being. Politics has become a carnival, with the Big Tent pitched twice at four-year intervals. In the resulting free-for-all, everyone gets as much as he can for himself, and all interests are supposed to be equally legitimate.

We try to call this tolerance "liberalism," when in fact it is merely shallow thinking.

So the nation has developed a split personality. In the eyes of the world we sometimes appear as hypocrites. We still say the right things, for the most part, but we seem often to say them with calculated effect. We behave in a way that, if not directly opposite, is at least inconsistent with our high moral pretentions. Thus, we gave wheat to India's starving millions with a *quid pro quo* requirement attached. After hostility in Latin America became pronounced, in the late 1950's, we grudgingly decided something had to be done about it and appropriated millions for economic development there—and then admitted that we thought it was to our advantage. Candor is one of our better qualities, but in the eyes of most other peoples such a manner of granting the aid seemed like a cynical and callous treatment of peoples who would like to be friends.

I would deny that such behavior is due to a change of heart among Americans. Rather, it is due to weaknesses in our public policies, which no longer accurately reflect the social sentiments of most Americans. Government is not an automatic institution—it does not work by itself. Nor are able men in government all that is necessary. For a variety of reasons our government now operates so clumsily that the State Department and the President sometimes find it necessary to appeal to the lowest motives of an isolationist minority in a jealous Congress. It should be possible, instead, to act from policy positions that represent the best and most responsible views of the party in office.

Rather than despair of our people, therefore, we should move quickly to return to the first principles of the traditional American credo and then remedy the deficiencies in the procedural areas of government which impair America's image at home and abroad.

THE CORROSIVE EFFECTS OF GROUP SELFISHNESS

Because policy making in the federal government lacks a base of principles derived from political economy, America is more exposed than most countries to the pressures of self-seeking interest groups, whose irresponsible behavior must be adjudged one of the main factors from which we are suffering. Narrow self-interest takes many forms in the United States, but none is so pronounced, perhaps, as the attempts of pressure groups to influence government to their own advantage. It is true that pressure groups have a legitimate role to play in the determination of public policy and that they are often helpful to government in reflecting sections of public opinion. At the same time, government must maintain its independence and integrity, for it is umpire no less than servant, and its greatest responsibility is in every case to discover what constitutes the public interest.

The despair of patriots, said Stuart Chase in 1945, is the "me-first boys," the pressure-group leaders who assume that they can "go it alone" and that they have no responsibility as their brothers' keepers.[8] Such people are found especially in the economic areas dominated by big business, big labor, and big agriculture—the Big Three of special interests in the United States. Their servants are the journals of organized opinion and the experts of Madison Avenue.

Pressure groups have become so Machiavellian that they are sometimes too smart for their own good. Wesley McCune, in *Who's Behind Our Farm Policy,*[9] tells how railroads, chambers of commerce, business lobbies, and other non-farm groups often use farm organizations as fronts to promote their own interests. (But, says McCune, "they always exude love and affection for the farmers.") Pressure groups that once fought the farmers now send their most polished representatives to court farm organizations for their political support. Vertical integrations of agricultural industries have been formed in such a way as to include farmers, manufacturers, brokers, wholesalers, and other middlemen. In addition, to use McCune's words, there has been a rash of foundations, councils, and institutes formed in recent years to promote friendly relations between farmers and industrialists, some of them with the unstated goal of combining against a third force, which is organized labor.

The me-first tradition is an old one that comes down to us from David Ricardo as a distortion of what Adam Smith said in *The Wealth of Nations*. According to Ricardo's interpretation, which Adam Smith would have been the first to disavow, business is a matter of getting as much as you can for yourself; the more one serves one's selfish interest the more the public interest also is served; and government should keep its hands off economic affairs because by its very nature it is inefficient and "corrosive." Following this line, extremists even today are heard to say that the best public servant is the worst, to argue that inefficiency in government is preferable to efficiency because "good" public servants eat holes in our liberties,[10] and to rejoice when their most pessimistic views of government are proved true.

The fact is that Adam Smith did *not* say that the "invisible hand" is the only economic regulator that is needed. What he said was that insofar as men are sufficiently intelligent and principled to allow market forces to operate, the result would generally be beneficial. He did *not* say that selfish interest, by some miraculous process, is translated into public interest; in fact he wrote *The Theory of the Moral Sentiments* to prove just the reverse. Smith was first of all a moral philosopher and a political economist and believed that wise public policy and the skills of the statesman and legislator were the principal virtues an enlightened society would seek to cultivate. Smith distrusted businessmen and their motives, he believed that they often conspired to their own advantage, and were too narrow-minded for the country's good; and he made no attempt to conceal his views.[11]

In more recent times—and as competition with the USSR becomes sharper—one hears less disparagement of government and more talk about the social responsibilities of businessmen. Some of the nation's largest corporations have become so disturbed by the apparent weaknesses of government that they have formed departments of government and politics of their own in an attempt not only to deal effectively with the complexities of their relations with government, but also to try to strengthen the foundations of government and of civic consciousness. This is a reassuring development.

Nevertheless, there remains enough of the old antipathy in some quarters to sanction behavior injurious to the nation's effectiveness. As late as 1956 one observer noted that "business comments on government are rarely complimentary; . . . Government, as it is seen in the business creed, is inherently evil."[12] Some powerful leaders of business are unethical in their dealings with government, try to bore from within, and seek special favors and handouts. Others, who are merely shortsighted, fail to recognize that in their own interest government must be made as efficient as our best-managed corporations, if the nation is to prosper in a world that is now so largely ruled by totalitarian regimes.

It is amazing how pervasive this cynical philosophy has become, and how obsolete. Even among political scientists in the universities, it is sometimes argued that the essence of politics is "who gets what, when, and how" and that the unifying principle of government is "access," that is, how one gets inside government to accomplish his purpose.[13] Access is proper and necessary when it signifies representation or responsiveness, for a democratic government must include both. But surely, in addition to representation, government also provides the conditions under which all of society can live a better life in constantly improving circumstances. The role of government is positive and beneficial, providing services and amenities, such as education and public health, offering many forms of protection, including protection from military attack and from economic depression, and assuring a fair-handed justice. If we want industry and the arts to be creative and enterprising, then government also, which provides the environment in which they flourish, must be creative and enterprising.[14]

The danger is not merely that government will suffer from a narrow interpretation of its role, but that we shall all suffer. If we cannot guide ourselves by the concept of the public interest, a despot will fill the void. It is not a matter of more government or less; it is a matter of more *self*-government in all of the governing institutions of society, including corporations, labor unions, agricultural organizations, trade associations, and organized professional groups.

The danger that many observers see is that suddenly we may have to shove huge additional loads of responsibility onto a government that has been criticized and disparaged for so long that an anxious nation will find it unprepared and overwhelmed by its new burdens. To avoid such a calamity, all of our institutions must master the power to govern, as explained in the preceding chapter, not on the basis of a philosophy of selfishness, even if it is called "intelligent self-interest," but on the basis of the public interest and the principles of political economy.

RAISING OUR SIGHTS

What is it that has sneaked up on our blind side and caused us on occasion to act like hypocrites? It is a number of problems that existing specialties cannot cope with, but which political economy could readily handle. They are the problems that C. Wright Mills deals with in *The Sociological Imagination,* that John Maurice Clark discusses in *Economic Institutions and Human Welfare,* and that Overton Taylor traces historically in *A History of Economic Thought.*

Briefly, the problems are these:

How to keep society served by power, without power becoming concentrated and subject to abuse

How to confine big institutions to the legitimate area of technology, so as to safeguard equality of opportunity and permit the rise of the "little" man

How to professionalize management without allowing it to become objectionably bureaucratic

How to expand production without making it an end in itself

How to provide effective incentives for the gifted individual without treating unfairly those of lesser talents

How to guarantee individual businesses all the freedom they need for efficiency and progress without permitting them to be unfair to others

How to foster competition, so as to promote efficiency and growth without allowing it to become cutthroat and destructive

How to help business and agriculture without subsidizing and corrupting them at the taxpayers' expense

How to encourage organized labor and collective bargaining without creating rigid prices and additional areas of economic concentration that will eventually undermine the market system.

Then, as already suggested, there are the crucial issues of how to grant pressure groups all the freedom they are entitled to without allowing them to subvert our institutions with their destructive and anarchical me-first philosophy. Also, how to produce a government effective enough to carry on foreign policy, stabilize the economy, and provide a myriad of services, while an influential minority, particularly in business, criticizes and tries to turn public opinion against it.

Other issues that demand equal attention are these:

How to change the carnival atmosphere of politics, so as to make politics the vehicle for wise decision making

How to make government responsible and to secure cooperation between the legislative and executive branches

How to organize the executive function, including the presidency, in such a way that planning, decision making, leadership, and coordination will take place as sensibly as in our best run corporations

How to conserve and at the same time utilize our dwindling natural resources, so that future generations may enjoy wealth and beauty in their time.

These are not all of the problems that need to be solved, but they are enough to start with.

One difficulty is that although economists understand the basic laws of our system and know them to be valid, few others, including businessmen, do understand them; or if they do, they fail to appreciate how to apply them to everyday management and decision making. An experience in England during the course of a study there brought this truth home to me rather forcefully. I was talking with the Number Two man, formerly a professor of economics, in one of Britain's largest nationalized industries. "You know," he remarked, "the thing I've learned since being in this job is that the economic principles I taught in the classroom are much truer than I realized. The trouble is that so few people understand them, and even the economists quibble over them."

Here then are two other reasons for stressing the political economy approach: to add policy, pressure-group, institutional, and political factors to tested economic principles, so as to broaden the policy base of decision making; and secondly, to make our knowledge of political economy operational, so that when the businessman or the government administrator faces a tough problem and finally makes a decision, he will know why he did so and what the probable effect will be on other areas of policy and on the welfare of the nation.

Our sentiments as a people are still sound. But technology and institutional growth have outdistanced social science in many ways. We have trouble adjusting our concepts and even our word structure to the new conditions. Some of the key words in a mid-twentieth century political economy are power, competition, decision making, policy, cooperation, organization, values, statesmanship. Few of these have been fully accepted in formal economics, and yet, in the modern power structure, which the United States has pioneered, they are basic concepts.

Why do I choose these words?

Power: because we see so much of it; it can do so much social good, and so much harm.

Competition: because it is essential to development and efficiency, and because many businessmen would gladly dispense with it in the mistaken belief that profits alone are the "essence" of our system.

Decision making: because this process is now so complicated that it needs structuring, either voluntarily, which is the American preference, or by iron discipline, which is the communist method.

Policy: because it derives from well-thought-of goals and needs proper operational guidelines to instrument it.

Coordination: because it is the moral superior of totalitarianism and because it is terribly hard to secure in a self-centered society.

Organization: because it is the instrument of policy, and as a technological necessity, it must be kept human and responsive.

Values: because we can expect neither useful goals nor a proper spirit in our institutions unless we put values in first place.

Statesmanship: because the affairs of the economy, as of government, are now so diverse and baffling that without men possessed of the skills of the successful synthesizer, we must despair of remaining both free and efficient.

These key words represent managerial thinking and the managerial approach, but the wisdom needed to implement them comes from economics, political science, and moral philosophy—from that area at the apex of the social sciences where, as Frank Knight was fond of pointing out, the principal concerns of society meet and are decided.[15]

Academically, at least, we are awakening to the challenge. Symptomatic are the findings and recommendations of a comprehensive survey of education for business administration in the United States, entitled *Higher Education for Business,* published in 1959.[16] What do business executives need today and tomorrow? In addition to technical competence, says this report, they need humility, breadth of outlook, and the qualities of leadership. Leaders of the future must have a "well-developed sense of social responsibility," and their talents should include analytical ability and judgment, skill in inter-personal relations, a willingness to accept responsibility and make decisions in the face of uncertainty, a strong personal motivation, a desire to develop subordinates, and the usual administrative skills, including the capacity to lead, to plan, to organize, and to delegate. In the better business schools throughout the country the authors of this survey found a sentiment favorable to capping off a man's education with a concentration strikingly like the idea of political economy presented here.

"If irresponsible self-seeking remains the dominant mood," said one of America's greatest economists recently, "we can have freedom without co-operation—which mean chaos and breakdown—or we can have co-operation without freedom—which means totalitarianism in some form. We cannot have both."[17]

The things America needs if she is to remain strong are not physical or materialistic; they are moral and institutional and, as such, coincide with what political economy has always been concerned with. Economics, which is a comparatively recent subject, finds the laws that control prosperity. Political science finds how groups organize and conduct themselves to achieve political ends. Moral philosophy guides the selection of goals and finds suitable ethical and institutional means of making the good life possible. Hence, moral philosophy comes close to being the equivalent of political economy, combining modern-day economics and political science.

As Overton Taylor has recently pointed out, however, in the United States (unlike Canada, Britain, Scotland, and other nations that have been wiser) progress in moral philosophy and political economy has been disappointingly slow, owing largely to the artificial separation between their economic, political, and philosophical components. In fact, despite a certain amount of ritualistic use of moral philosophy, carried over from the Enlightenment, for a long time now in the United States there has been no fresh, living philosophical endeavor to enrich the fund of knowledge designed to provide creative solutions to novel contemporary problems.[18]

If America's lack is to be repaired, it seems clear that we must overcome our neglect and raise our sights. Instead of assuming, as most of us now do, that citizenship is chiefly a governmental concern and that between business and government there is a wide gulf, we should redefine our citizenship to include business as well as government. Otherwise, we are likely to find government doing too much. For, as Clark has remarked, citizenship is not exclusively or even primarily political. Other institutions also govern. And if they are to govern successfully they must accept the *sine qua non* of all successful rule: duty as well as rights, self-government as well as command, initiative as well as compliance.[19]

THREE

THE NEW POLITICAL ECONOMY

Well-being is more than wealth. Natural forces and managerial principles also are involved. Values are necessary as well as rational calculation. A concept of public interest that becomes operational is required. A government that does the minimum essentials well is equally imperative. As a nation, we expect to be in business for a long time. We need, therefore, a managerial approach to national well-being that emphasizes husbandry instead of manipulation.

Some fifty years ago we ceased to combine private and public interest, what we profess and what we do. Intellectually, we abandoned the philosophical insights of our best thinkers: John Stuart Mill and his theory of private and public interest as a unity; James Madison and his strictures against faction; Thomas Jefferson and his idea of a balanced economy. We turned from political economy to economics and political science, both of which are necessarily specialized and, hence, incomplete as guides to statesmanship, both public and private alike.

There is now beginning to emerge, however, a new political economy which is consonant with the great tradition of the past but adapted to modern times. It is with this new development that I propose to deal in this chapter. It would be impossible to give a complete history of economic thought nor is there any reason to do so. I can, however, indicate some of the elements of political economy that have been constantly emphasized since the time of the mercantilists, the physiocrats, and Adam Smith, and shall do so when these analyses support the synthesis which today seems imperative. Every new synthesis contains many ingredients handed down from older analyses but, having been temporarily neglected at some point, now seem fresh and full of vigor.

THE MANAGERIAL APPROACH

The new political economy is managerial in outlook and proceeds in terms of succinct values and in an unbroken sequence from the projection of a goal to its attainment. The key terms in the new political cal economy, in the approximate order of their importance, are interrelationship, balance, diminishing returns, values, standard of living, structure (organization), policy, public interest, statesmanship, conservation, management, entrepreneurship, competition, market price, efficiency, cooperation, decision making, coordination, power, and control. I shall not at this point try to justify these choices nor to defend their order or their listing. My only purpose is to suggest the key words around which it should be possible to formulate principles that have institutional and human significance.

We Americans admire the connotations of the adjective "businesslike" because they convey an image of consecutive thinking and practicality—of getting things done. Following this lead, we should think about our country as a businessman thinks about his business; a farmer, his land; or a college president, his seat of learning. That is, we should think of our nation as a unity and consider ends and means at the same time.

Every manager has in common with all others the need to consider the role of his institution in the larger collectivity in which it exists, and its relationship to that whole. He must consider goals and values and the policies that will achieve them. Then he must think about the strengths and weaknesses of his institution: What are its assets; what are its liabilities? What needs buttressing; what can be relied on in a pinch? Which part needs an extra push? Where is the weak link in manpower? What about the availability of resources, human as well as material, now and in the long run?

Finally, the experienced manager turns his mind to organization and method. Considering all the resources I have to work with, he says repeatedly to himself, what changes must I make in organization, leadership, supervision, and control?

Like the philosopher of history, the manager recognizes that external and internal tensions are constantly changing and that he must not only adapt his institution to shifting currents but, perhaps even more important, he must try to anticipate them. Survival and influence depend in large measure on how skillfully this job is done. It is this last responsibility that constitutes one of the soft spots in the performance of our national government since World War II, irrespective of the politics of the administration in office. Instead of a husbanding approach to world and domestic problems, there has been brinkmanship and drift.

In a word, the managerial outlook combines program and procedure. It draws on all the specialties of human knowledge and relates them to human need and to institutional functioning. It draws on the principles of economics, developed over many decades, and combines them with other elements to make a useful compound of theory by which to guide reliable policy.

Businessmen and government administrators alike reach out toward statesmanship without, however, neglecting the characteristics that have made ours a "businessman's civilization": the native practicality that gets a job done quickly and efficiently, with an inner drive which sometimes reaches awesome proportions.

The managerial *élan* also stresses policy formation and decision making in the public interest, realizing that men work best if they are guided by principles and policies, but are left free to innovate as to means and as to day-to-day decisions of their own. Thus, self-reliance and cooperative activity are encouraged as equal and necessary goals.

In addition, the managerial *élan* recognizes the rational need for bureaucratic efficiency, but balances it with innovation, initiative, and enterprise. It realizes that there is no asset equal to the gifted individual, but recalls that the most gifted, caught in the web of institutional rigidity, soon becomes warped, emotionally starved, almost subhuman. Clearly then, men are not solely motivated by the invisible laws of the market place, necessary as these are as a guide to policy; men are consciously affected by their choices among conflicting values and by the preferences of the society of which they are a part.

So defined, management is not merely a guild or a syndicate, an elite group, or the exploiter of the common people. It is an approach to plenty and "the good life" and is broad enough to include what are now called economics and political science. The management approach secures a *balance* of forces and factors; it emphasizes values, techniques, and a workable equilibrium.

Some people recoil from the concept of management in the belief that it sounds authoritarian, but this could be so only in a narrow view. Let us be clear, therefore, about what we would avoid as well as what we would accomplish.

Authoritarianism is to be avoided. The administered state, in which goals and values are dictatorially determined and men play out their roles according to rule, could only add to the problems we already have. We need to reaffirm our belief in an open society with its competitive price system, its tests of marginal utility, its freedom of entry into occupations, its mobility of labor, industry, and resources, its freedom of consumer choice, and its reliance on profit making as a main incentive toward efficiency and economic growth.

Nor is the managerial outlook associated with a constant growth of governmental functions. Rather, a vital economy must include large draughts of voluntarism with its sense of responsibility and its self-generating initiative. It is partly by this means that power is shared in society, instead of being concentrated in a few places; and competition and individual self-development are furthered.

Another possible objection to the managerial approach is that by concentrating on the aim of making America great, we might run the danger of becoming autarchical and anti-internationalist. In fact, however, the danger is more theoretical than real. Every nation must focus on its own problems and produce as high a standard of wealth and well-being for its own people as it can. But necessary to prosperity is international trade, drawing on other areas of the world for goods and services that can be most advantageously produced there, in exchange for what is most advantageously produced in the home country. From the managerial standpoint, the encouragement of trade that is as free as it can be made is a mark of administrative statesmanship. Such trade forces on the decision maker a competition that, in turn, forces him to increase his efficiency. This takes self-confidence and courage, and both are essential to progress.

A great nation, therefore, is internationally oriented and at the same time practical, humane, and democratic. It encourages a balanced economy, one midway between "pure" laissez faire, in which the market supposedly supplies all the governance and motivation that are needed, and collectivism, where the government, run by an elite, assumes that it knows best what is good for all the people.

GROWTH AND CHANGE

Yet another argument for the managerial approach to political economy is that managers customarily think in terms of stages of growth, each with characteristic problems of its own. The modern economist, on the other hand, almost has to assume a static condition, which of course is unrealistic.

In any society, three common, basic factors are culture, institutions, and human wants. Institutions are structural patterns in the larger entity of culture. Today, cultural change most often occurs within the economic and political institutions of society. Hence, people's wants are now almost wholly dependent on how management operates in a complex series of interrelated patterns called institutions. To understand economics or politics as such, therefore, it is first necessary to understand the interrelationship of wants and institutions in the total culture of society.

Some of the things that an experienced manager learns about the economy—some could almost be called principles—are these:

The way to understand the complexity of the economy is to study its development through various stages, from the simple to the complex, after the manner of the biologist. At each stage the structure of the economy is influenced by cultural factors, such as history, popular beliefs, and values.

Before industrialization can occur, government must provide certain minimal services, such as law and order, transportation, and credit. Government's role, therefore, varies appreciably in different stages of the nation's economic development. The more the economy advances, the more damage can government do if its values and policies are wrong.

There is a direct relationship between private competence and the scope of required government service. After it has provided basic services, government must encourage private enterprise to invest in industrial development. This is the hardest transitional stage of all. Economic development is largely a matter of fashioning new institutions and processes as they are needed. But structural development is not possible until trained leaders are available; and, hence, a first responsibility of government, especially in underdeveloped nations, is to provide training facilities in this area.

The notion that special problems inevitably arise at particular stages of development is only partly true. The evidences of old age, such as rigidity and inflexibility, may appear in fairly new institutions, and old ones have been known to stay young in behavior. The problem in both cases is to understand the principles of institutional growth and decay and to apply preventive measures before difficulties become acute.

In addition, priorities must be established, because the rate of progress depends on the rate of increase of capital; in the long run, if a nation is to control its own destiny, the capital it needs must be produced within its own borders. A steady economic development depends on the skill with which business and government determine priorities in order to anticipate next steps, avoid waste, and maintain a favorable balance of payments.

Orderly growth requires balance, a factor that leadership must be aware of at all stages of development. Balance is not secured simply by a free consumer choice; it also depends on conscious attention to values and goals and on the wise exercise of administrative controls by both business and government.

Structure is a principal ingredient of political economy, for without the right tools and mechanisms the right things are not done and the wrong ones cannot be prevented. Hence, structure is an area where change is frequent and on which managers must focus much of their attention.

The experienced manager who has dealt with stages of growth and with adjustment to change is understandably bewildered—especially if he has read the history of economic doctrines from the time of mercantilism—when modern economists debate whether the market is a self-contained and self-regulating entity. It *cannot* be, except in the imagination, for like every other aspect of economics, the market is an integral part of a nation's total behavior and growth pattern.

The best economists have consistently realized that economic life is organic and that change is inherent, making decision making and statesmanship the center of the system. I shall illustrate this by turning briefly to the ideas of two economists widely apart in time, Adam Smith and Alfred Marshall.

Adam Smith realized that results are ultimately determined by institutions and by human decisions. Far from men being logical and consistent, they are swayed by emotions and prejudice. Hence, the cement of life is a feeling of sympathy, or what today we call empathy. Smith believed that the skills of the legislator-statesman and the morality of the "sympathetic" citizen constitute the most important bases of community life. He thought that the work of economic statesmen would become easier, however, if they understood the natural balances that nature intended for human as for other forms of life and that are found also in the market system. Increased national wealth depends on the efficiency of *all* the units of production, including government, industry, labor, management, and capital alike. He subscribed to the principle of balance as illustrated by supply and demand, by the reconciliation of private and public interest, and by the right relation between agriculture and industry. If these balances are to be maintained, furthermore, government must fulfill its role as decider of policy and maintainer of competition.

In short, Smith's vision of a good society involved at least four assumptions: first, just laws to govern dealings among men, part of the role of government being to secure such laws; secondly, natural laws that apply to dealings in the economy, as when a competitive market mechanism secures "automatic" responses and adjustments between supply and demand; thirdly, the voluntary improvement by every individual of his own efficiencies and productivity, thus increasing social satisfactions and the common welfare; and fourthly, the determination of prices and individual incomes by efficient methods and effective competition, each factor seeking its own proper level.[1] Smith's was a dynamic view of economy and of statecraft, one in which decision making was inherent and inescapable.

Alfred Marshall, writing in the first quarter of the present century, was similarly sociological in his approach, if by that is meant that he was attuned to forces, institutions, and social change. Money and economic goods are always means to ends, said Marshall, not ends in themselves. Market and price factors are important as the means of measuring the rival desire forces that impel men to act as they do. Pure competition is a figment of the imagination: the real question is whether there is "enough" competition and of the right kind at the right time. Large size is not necessarily efficient; bureaucracy is inherent in all big organizations, and like tall trees in a forest, huge firms mature and die as younger competitors force their way up alongside them. Marshall fervently hoped that competitive institutions might survive but foresaw a trend toward overcentralization, excessive size, a consequent statism, and possibly even socialism if right policies were not effectively pursued.

Even his most celebrated principle, that of diminishing returns, showed his essential orientation toward balance and a managerial outlook. It is balance we seek, not maximization; any good thing can be carried too far—competition, for example, or price, or even efficiency. On this last point Marshall offered as illustration the fact that optimal economies are possible even in such matters as efficient organization, management, and control. And since any element may be overemphasized if surrounding considerations are neglected, he held that in all decision making there is a cut-off point which must be discovered by the manager-statesman, because nothing in life is "pure" or "unlimited."[2]

There are, then, laws of political economy that can be discovered if we search patiently for them. But they are only partly automatic, and, even then, they fulfill their role within a larger framework, involving choice, decision making, and delicate balance. Accordingly, if balance and well-being are to be achieved, we must be clear about what we want out of our economic system.

THE OBJECTIVES OF THE NEW POLITICAL ECONOMY

Just as a manager must think about goals before he can think about or decide other matters such as policy and organization, so here must we be as explicit as possible about the aims of the American economy. There will be plenty of room for disagreement and discussion, of course; and, in addition, time and circumstance will make occasional changes and adjustments necessary. In general, however, the basic aims of political economy as expressed in business and official government policy may be said to be these:

1. To create a high standard of living
2. To encourage ambition and discourage indolence
3. To avoid an overconcentration of power and to maintain balance
4. To create an environment in which invention and entrepreneurship are stimulated
5. To work constructively toward stability at home and peace abroad
6. To look upon the national heritage as a sacred trust

Objectives such as these can be pursued under any political system, including some that are socialist as well as those that are capitalist. A socialist nation is likely to have most trouble with (3) and (4), a capitalist nation with (6). In the balance of this chapter I shall try to explain and to justify these six aims, leaving to later chapters a more detailed discussion of their applicability to policy and decision making.

In stating these six goals I have avoided the use of vague, ill-defined political words such as freedom, equality, and justice. This is not for any lack of enthusiasm for these concepts, but in order to be as precise, as instrumental, as positive as possible in my approach. We Americans have too long paid pious lip service to high-sounding terms without stopping to think about their implications.

To what extent do these six goals conform to the traditional ideas of economics and political economy? The answer is that they are similar. Under mercantilism, for example, much thought was given to economic stability and to the national heritage as a sacred trust. Similarly, the physiocrats, as the name implies, emphasized nature as the center of all physical and human laws and paid much attention to competition and to incentives (this was the beginning of the concept of laissez faire), to balances of power, the concentration of power, innovation, equilibrium, and trusteeship. These ideas were greatly strengthened by Adam Smith and especially by John Stuart Mill, whose ideas about moral philosophy and a philosophy of political economy were more mature than those of anyone who has since written on this subject.

Although much in modern economics continues in the old tradition, most modern thinking has been focused on the first of the six aims listed here: a high standard of living. The dominant emphasis in modern economics has been on production, relative efficiency, the channeling of resources into areas where they can be maximized, and the like. In consequence, although economists such as John R. Commons, Thorstein Veblen, and the institutionalists generally have argued for more attention to the engineering and organic bases of economic life, for the most part questions such as balance and stability and social responsibility were largely neglected until the influence of John Maynard Keynes began to be felt.

Thus, modern economics does not emphasize all six of the suggested aims equally; and some of them, especially the last, are hardly mentioned at all, on the ground that they lie outside the realm of economics proper and belong rather to political philosophy, ethics, or religion.

The economist, says Kenneth Boulding, abstracts a system from the complex social and physical world about him. He sees the world as commodities, not as men and institutions, and it is precisely in this abstraction (insularity) that the economist's special skill resides.[3] The center of the modern economist's attention is the market, which is largely concerned with prices, commodities, production, exchange, and consumption, and growing out of this, the marginal utility of various transactions involving value and money.

Paul Samuelson makes clear the difference between modern economics and traditional political economy when he says that economics

tries to answer three questions: *What* commodities shall be produced
and in what quantities? *How* shall commodities be produced—that
is, by whom and with what resources and technologies? And finally,
for whom shall commodities be produced; how shall the total national
product be distributed among the various claimants to it? On the other
hand, when a community mobilizes its *means* to achieve certain *ends*
and learns to appraise and improve both ends and means and to make
the achievement of ends more efficient, then, says Samuelson, it follows the tenets of political economy and not merely those of
economics.[4]

With this explanation of what is to be gained from modern economics and from the older political economy, respectively, I turn to a
brief discussion of each of the six objectives of a viable economy, expressing my own ideas primarily and leaving for later chapters the
more complete application of these choices.

A High Standard of Living

Political economy is interested in a high standard of living because this
objective answers the question, "What should be primarily stressed,
national production or the consumer?" Once the emphasis is on
standard of living the answer is that consumption and production are
equally important, and so also are distribution and exchange. The
institutional outlook makes every step from production to consumption a continuum, part of an organic process, which it is.

Socialist writers have denounced classical economists for stressing
production to the neglect of consumption, claiming that socialism
has reversed the emphasis.[5] But in the USSR the consumer is neglected, and until now the whole concentration has been on heavy production. At the same time, we in the United States are accused even
by our own leaders of going in too heavily for consumer frills and
fancies. A task of political economy is to secure balances and adjustments, in such matters, between production and consumption.

An emphasis on a proper standard of living for everyone is the
acid test of production, not volume of production itself. There must
also be attention to the values involved, especially in production,
which should be for civilized individuals with taste, character, and

integrity. There is no conflict here with the economist's insistence on consumer sovereignty, since the way to improve the individual's taste is through education and opportunity for choice, not compulsion.

The reasoning concerning consumer sovereignty is that prices, if left alone, will seek their own levels, and that an unmet demand will attract resources to its fulfillment, whereas an overmet demand will cause businessmen to turn to a more lucrative field. This process of adding here and taking away there, without central direction and simply because competition demands it, in theory at least is the most humane and enlightened system that has ever been invented, because it gives the consumer what he wants and not what somebody thinks he ought to want. Theoretically, too, the system avoids redundancy in labor and management and the uneconomical use of scarce capital. It also promotes the maximization of effective demand: people can get all they want instead of being restricted by someone else's decision. And finally, it provides for the greatest mobility in allocating and reallocating scarce resources, including trained labor and management as well as capital.

All of which is perfect so long as the natural process does not get clogged up. But it always does, because businessmen, working through their trade associations, in league with trade unions, assisted by Madison Avenue, and relying on restrictive practices sanctioned by government as a matter of public policy, seem everlastingly to be chipping away at the natural market and substituting one that is man-made. The remedy? Education and a better understanding of public policy. Laissez faire alone will never do the whole job, because it has never achieved perfect equilibrium in the past, and the outlook for the future is even less reassuring. What we need, therefore, is a *positive* laissez faire, with economic and political statesmen assuming a greater responsibility for guaranteeing results.

Encourage Ambition, Discourage Indolence

The main problem with regard to ambition and indolence is psychological as well as institutional. The chief difficulty is in providing incentives. Ambition for what? What is the meaning of freedom? Of civil rights? Of the welfare state? What is as important as money? What kinds of skills and values are needed if society is to improve? How can we prevent social security and other welfare programs, such as unemployment insurance, from dulling people's ambitions? How can we remain inventive when the individual tends to be submerged in conformity?

The goal should be to make people as fiercely independent as ever they were in American history and, at the same time, skilled in cooperation. The issue is basic because incentives—what men live by—are an essential element in efficiency and happiness.

For understandable reasons, classical economics has contributed to an attitude toward work which tends to undermine American character and the vitality of the nation. Economists seek to eliminate work because they hold that the more that can be produced with the least work, or no work at all, the more efficient is the system. As a mathematical proposition this may be so, but in terms of survival, it is false.

If, because of automation and socialism, we Americans were ever able to get along without working at all, we should deliberately set out to make work for ourselves because people are healthier and happier when they work than when they are idle. Thorstein Veblen taught that the source of all efficiency and progress is creative workmanship, which is an individual matter. Hence, public policy should encourage the "full discretionary control and disposal of the work" of the creative person's hands, should restore power to the creative individual, and take it away from the manipulator. The technicians whom Veblen would have run industry belong to the creative group; the absentee owners, to the manipulators.[6]

C. Wright Mills, the sociologist, has the right idea, I think, when he suggests that a social science course should answer the following three questions: What is the structure of this particular society as a whole? What does this society stand for in human history? And what varieties of men and women, with varying motivations and values, prevail in this society and in this period?[7]

I would suggest a particular stress on the last of these without neglecting the other two. "Freedom," says Mills, "is not merely the chance to do as you please," (he might have added, without work) nor is it merely the opportunity to choose between set alternatives. Freedom is the opportunity to formulate the available choices, to argue over them, and then to choose. "That is why freedom cannot exist without an enlarged role of human reason in human affairs."[8]

Agreed. But freedom has little chance of permanence if people characteristically become drones, surfeited in an affluent society. The strength of a nation is its workers, its men and women who stay close to the soil, its workmen who remain close to human aspiration.

Indolence could destroy our society. False conceptions of the welfare state cause some people to think they are entitled to a living at public expense. Public assistance, once considered a last resort, tends to become a "right," fully as much as social insurance. This is false thinking. Political economy must face up to this issue, but in a larger context, where the emphasis is on positive incentives and values and improved institutional arrangements.

The term "welfare state" has become a permanent part of the American vocabulary. In a way, this is unfortunate, because it evokes more emotion than careful analysis. If the welfare state is one in which government judges all of its decisions by their effect on the welfare of all of its citizens, then it is hard to find fault with the concept. But if the welfare state is one in which an elite of decision makers monopolizes the power of government, then it is clearly objectionable. And if the welfare state is one in which many people work to provide a living for others who do not work at all, then the vitality of the nation's institutions is sapped. This last interpretation connotes getting something for nothing, being taken care of by someone else simply because society is affluent. Rather, all who work should be rewarded in proportion to their contribution to the total effort.

In the final analysis, therefore, we should make the production of wealth the test of public policy and recognize that any deviation from this rule is debilitating. Such being the case, we must make clear what we mean by that loose expression, welfare state. The proper meaning is that which economists have almost consistently emphasized since the time of the physiocrats and Adam Smith: the welfare state is one in which government judges all of its decisions by their effect on the welfare of all of its citizens.

Avoid Overconcentrated Power and Maintain Balance

Economics stresses natural law; political science focuses on power. The two should be brought together in a working accord.

The first step is to differentiate between the various meanings of power. Power as energy is said to be the secret of modern industrial society's high standard of living, and so it is. At the other extreme, power as monopoly is an invitation to social tensions and even to revolution. One of the greatest challenges to the new political economy, therefore, is to differentiate these and other meanings of power and to come up with the kind of balances that are essential to community goals. It should be noted, however, that balance is never at dead center, nor is it rigid, for such static positions lead only to stagnation and lack of progress.

It is doubtful if we can improve much on what physiocrats, like Pierre Quesnay, who were contemporaries of Adam Smith and who influenced Thomas Jefferson, thought about the secret of balance.[9] The source of all wisdom and happiness, said Quesnay, is in understanding and living in conformity with the laws of nature. These laws make the processes of nature "as favorable as possible" to the happiness of all living things, including human beings. Men have the rational capacity to understand and apply these laws; they should work with nature, not against it. Since ecology deals with the balance between environment and life, in many ways this science comes close to being a basic one, and the new political economy could well draw from it in re-interpreting natural law for our times.

Fortunately, professional economists have been increasingly concerned with the relation between power and balance, beginning with John R. Commons and other institutionalists and coming down through Walton Hamilton and Gardiner Means in the 1930's. More recently, another economist, Donald S. Watson, has observed that "in the broadest and most general sense, power is the ability to control the *minds* and actions of others, to affect or influence them so as to bring about or approach a desired result."[10] If so, then self-determination itself is at stake.

It is difficult to disagree with Adolf Berle and Walter Lippmann, therefore, who contend (in their books *The 20th Century Revolution* and *The Public Philosophy,* respectively) that power is the greatest unsolved problem in American society and that to solve it, both economics and political science will probably have to be reformulated and combined.

Innovation and Entrepreneurship

Do market forces alone assure a nation an adequate supply of enterprise and innovation? Not necessarily, for the determinants are institutional, broadly social, and psychological as well. Traditional economists, therefore, have not succeeded in developing an adequate theory of entrepreneurship; and Clair Wilcox criticizes them for it.[11] As John Jewkes has clearly shown in *The Sources of Invention,* and as I have tried to show in *Administrative Vitality: The Conflict with Bureaucracy,* there can hardly be any doubt that invention and initiative are threatened in our modern urban and conformist society.

"Great and rational organizations—in brief, bureaucracies—have indeed increased," says C. Wright Mills, "but the substantive reason of the individual at large has not."[12] Thus, in their normally limited daily lives, men are unable "to reason about the great structures—rational and irrational—" to which their daily lives are subordinated. To overcome this difficulty we must find the means of protecting and encouraging human imagination and intellectual curiosity within the framework of large, standardizing, rule-ridden organizations.

If we could develop more wisdom in this area and make it fully operational we would have gone far toward assuring the continuance of our free way of life. So long as our system remains reasonably competitive, it has an immense advantage over most forms of socialism, and especially communism; for in their case bureaucracy is built-in, while with us it is easier to prevent and control. Unless, of course, we allow private power to grow to the point where it is socialist in everything but name.

One of the most promising positive measures would be to encourage decentralization, for freedom and decentralization are inextricably connected. It is disturbing, therefore, that a growing number of American economists has been finding rationalizations for the concentration of economic power by simply making plausible adjustments in their theory, as in their concept of monopolistic competition. To be sure, in theory there can be "competition" so long as there remain two rivals in the same field, but what does this kind of competition do to our way of life? What is its effect on entrepreneurship, on the urge to individual enterprise on the part of young people about to enter on their careers? Political economy asks these questions. I am not sure that modern economics does, especially if its chief interest becomes merely "models."

Stability at Home and Peace Abroad

Stability at home and peace abroad may appear as separate problems, but they are of course connected.

Traditionally, the four areas of economics have been production, exchange, consumption, and distribution. To these, owing to the influence of Keynes and other modern economists, such as Alvin Hansen, a fifth area, economic stabilization, has been added. The problem was recognized some time ago by the institutionalists—for example, by Wesley Mitchell in his theory of the business cycle. But it has been only since the United States realized that another great depression such as that of the 1930's might give communists the advantage, that the area of economic stability has moved to the center of the stage in community importance. If one were to analyze the reasons why economists and political scientists have recently begun to stress public policy and political economy it would be found that a concern for economic stability is a chief motivating factor.

The plain truth is that institutional arrangements and structural balances must be right or we lose our values, and the individual becomes stifled and distorted. Hence, a new school of thought has appeared, influenced by sociology, which contends that structural changes are the key to most matters of transcendent importance in the social sciences.

When in a city of 100,000, says Mills, a single man is unemployed, that is his personal problem. The employment counsellor merely considers his skills, his mobility, his family responsibilities, and the like. But when in a labor force of 50 million, 15 million are unemployed, the problem has a different magnitude. There is an issue, and issues require policies and structures if they are to be solved.[13] Or take the problem of war: the personal range of choice is to enlist or not to enlist, to die with honor or try to avoid involvement entirely, to make money out of war or to make great personal sacrifices. For the country as a whole, however, the problems are structural: the type of men who are placed in command, the organization of production behind the military effort, the reduction of civilian supplies, the establishment of priorities.[14]

Behind all these structual and policy matters is the larger issue, with which the United Nations and foreign offices all over the world are trying to deal: the causes of war itself, which are variously economic, political, and religious; which have to do with differences in leadership, production, and governing patterns; and which also, in large measure, result from the "unorganized irresponsibility of a world of nation-states."[15]

If, as I suppose, the foreign and domestic aspects of public policy are inexorably related and if political economy makes the dual approach work better than separate disciplines now do, then the political economy approach is surely imperative. For it seems unlikely that either capitalism or democracy could survive another war, in their present form, even if they won it.

National Heritage as a Sacred Trust

A virtue of mercantilism was that the ruling elite was highly motivated to foster the interests of the nation for which it had assumed responsibility. This feeling is also strong in many socialist regimes, in part, perhaps, because of the intensity of their ideological beliefs.

In the democracies, on the other hand, there is an assumption that one's main interest is oneself, one's family, one's immediate circle. Thus, the total interests of the nation are ancillary. Not in wartime, of course, nor in periods of great depression, but in ordinary times, when conditions are more or less "normal."

A virtue of mercantilism was that the ruling elite was highly moti-"normal" again, or at least not for a long time. The world is in ferment; colonial peoples have thrown off their shackles; the world is divided into two great blocs, with neutralists holding the balance of power; technology is developing more rapidly than man's reason or his managerial capacities can deal with them; the world is apparently destined to a long period of trial-and-error; and there will be many clashes of interest threatening an outbreak of violence. If there ever were a time when Americans need to acquire a more mature outlook and to adopt a more sober view of their natural resources—both material and human—this is it.

The most promising orientation is one that has been mentioned earlier—the husbanding approach, a feeling of pride in what nature has given us, a belief in our own people and their aspirations, a deep sense that as we improve our own values and the life by which they are governed, our example will have a lasting effect on peoples whose support we need. Nothing is so persuasive as example and nothing so obvious as psychological warfare, or any other artificial attempt to create an impression.

We need the long view that Jacob Viner discusses;[16] we should heed the advice of Peter Drucker to businessmen, that "practically every basic management decision is a long-range decision—with ten years a rather short time-span in these days."[17] Most of all, however, we need at the forefront of our minds a clear and compelling idea of what our objectives are and what constitutes the public interest, for in the last analysis this is our secret weapon in our competition with authoritarian regimes; this is the moral equivalent of compulsion.

In summary, then, the new political economy is new only insofar as it emphasizes elements that for two generations have been insufficiently stressed. It is managerial in outlook, organic in nature, stresses ends as well as means, combines freedom of choice with so-called automatic forces, and seeks balance and the good life. The ends of the economy are political and social as well as economic, for they include a rising standard of living, the encouragement of ambition and entrepreneurship, the strengthening of competitive balance, the fostering of initiative and inventiveness, the encouragement of stability at home and peace abroad, and the development of attitudes that regard the national heritage as a sacred trust.

All of the factors in this compound are linked to the past. If we could devise an operational synthesis in terms of policy and administration, the effect would be revolutionary. For freedom would then mean duty as well as right, morality instead of license.

FOUR

THE PUBLIC INTEREST

In the new political economy, the concept of the public interest is
the touchstone of every policy and every decision in the private as
in the public realm. "Public interest," however, is a broad and
ambiguous term that has been varyingly interpreted by different
people at different times. The purpose of this chapter is to help
clarify the issue of what the public interest is, to discover whether
there are any universal principles that may be applied to it, and to
show what an American consensus of its meaning might be in the
present period of testing.

A MAIN CONCERN OF POLITICAL ECONOMY

Every school of economic thought since the time of the mercantilists
has been concerned with proving that its theories are superior to
those of others because they serve the public interest best. The issue
has long been a major concern of economists, as shown in the
observations of Francis Bowen, more than a century ago, that "statesmen have been obliged to make the study of politics second to that
of political economy. . . . Economy has demonstrated . . . that
all classes of society are inseparably bound together by a community
of interest; that the prosperity of each depends on the welfare of
all . . ."[1]

Nevertheless, thinking about the public interest has been vague
and incomplete because each school of thought has invariably emphasized a particular combination of factors to the exclusion of

others, so that rarely if ever has attention been given to *all* of the factors of which the public interest is compounded.

The mercantilists, for example, staked everything on national power, production, money, skillful administration, and pressure groups. The physiocrats stressed nature and natural law, balance, agriculture, and the interaction and interdependence of many other factors. Adam Smith, whose thinking was more complete than most, stressed division of labor, efficiency, competition, morality, equilibrium, free trade, capital, equality of freedoms, the "invisible hand," mobility, prices, value, production, and distribution. John Stuart Mill, being more politically minded than Smith, found the public interest in liberty, utility, happiness, competition, distribution, education, and government. Two socialist writers, Sismondi and Saint Simon, stressed distribution, economic organization, industrialization, and personnel. Werner Sombart, the German, looked to spirit and technocracy. With Alfred Marshall it was competition, managerial economics, efficiency, diminishing returns, and marginal utility. Karl Marx contended for labor value, the withering of the state, and the emergence of "administration" (somehow thought to be different from "government"). And Veblen emphasized power, workmanship, technocracy, and the evils of absentee ownership.

Modern economics, also, is much concerned with the public interest, but the concept is usually left to be implied because the term is not admitted as a "scientific" one.

The economist traditionally says, in effect, to the legislator-statesman responsible for public policy: if you will allow the market to establish prices, wages, salaries, quantities, and styles in response to the free choice of the sovereign consumer; if you will allow efficient enterprises to grow and the inefficient to die or to restore themselves if they can; if you will allow people to generate their own incentives and to develop their own demands, thus encouraging their acquisitiveness, you will find that *in the long run the ambitions of men and of society will coincide.*

Then if you will take pains to study and apply the laws of nature that maintain balance; if you will make competition the rule and not merely the doctrine, so that thousands of competitive units are encouraged and not merely a few oligopolies, then you will find that men of superior ambition will achieve a higher degree of efficiency than is possible under regimentation, whether public or private.

The physiocrats had highly developed ideas of the public interest, which later, through Jefferson, were to find their way into the Declaration of Independence. For the physiocrats, the public interest consisted first in learning and then in applying the principles of natural law. The freedom of every individual must be equal, but not without limits, for it must be consistent with the same freedom of others. There must also be a reciprocity of rights and duties because right without duty is privilege. There must be the highest regard for private property and for the sanctity of contracts, and there must be freedom of economic enterprise, unrestricted competition, and a bar on restraints and on the granting of special privileges—all of these, beliefs that liberals were later to espouse.

Equilibrium theory also was an important aspect of the public interest concept. There is, said Quesnay, a "circular flow" in the body economic, somewhat resembling the circulatory system of the human body. There is a known number of variables, each with its own particular function, and good health depends on maintaining an equilibrium among them. Then, anticipating Auguste Comte, Quesnay held that every political economy is so interdependent within itself that when any important variable changes, every other one is bound also to change in more or less predictable ways.

It is possible that this concept of interdependence and predictability is the first law of political economy. Although we cannot always discover *causes,* we should be able to discover *cause-and-effect relationships,* thus joining philosophy and science and making prediction and control possible.

Adam Smith also saw that equal freedom for all is necessary for all the freedoms: freedom of consumer choice, freedom of competition and of entry to markets, freedom of choice of employment, freedom to invest and to allocate resources, and freedom to adjust to change in technology. For, said Smith, when the capitalist is led by the "invisible hand" to invest where it will contribute most to the wealth of the nation, the people profit indirectly. Necessary however, are the right liberal institutions, the right public policies, and conformity to the "natural" moral law. All artificial privileges and restraints, all methods of monopolizing opportunities for some and denying them to others, are uneconomic and unjust.

The greatest classical contributor to the doctrine of the public interest was, of course, John Stuart Mill, the most notable exponent of utilitarian philosophy and author of brilliant essays on *Liberty, Representative Government, Utilitarianism,* and *Principles of Political Economy.* The value of individual liberty is great, said Mill, and liberty is an end in itself. But it is not an absolute end because of a reciprocal relationship: the freedom of the individual must be compatible with an equal degree of freedom for everyone else. Hence, some social group (usually government) must lay down the rules and enforce them.

The main goal of society, observed Mill, is happiness for everyone; utility is a calculation between pleasure and pain, reward and punishment. Incentives must be positive. Public affairs should further the general happiness of the people, thus constituting a challenge to legislators and officials of all kinds. Moreover, this view of happiness was not merely hedonistic, as is sometimes claimed. It was highly ethical: so to live as to contribute to the happiness of others and to find happiness for oneself not by consciously seeking it but by allowing it to come as a by-product of dedication to values.[2]

FREEDOM AND THE PUBLIC INTEREST

It has been widely held in the United States for the last hundred years or so that the public interest is whatever each individual thinks it is. This flat statement generally ends the matter, on the ground that any qualification might restrict the equal freedom of all people to think as they please. Since freedom is the highest end or ethic in the whole range of choice, nothing less than complete freedom for everyone is considered acceptable.[3]

I find some difficulty with this flat assertion. Is there not more to the public interest than individual freedom? Are there not also group freedoms with which individual freedom must be reconciled? Beyond the essentially negative idea of free will, is there not a dimension that emphasizes positive values? And is it not possible that a failure to think more consciously about what these values are constitutes one of the weaknesses from which we are suffering in the United States? Presumably, even the asking of these questions indicates that I think so. My difficulty is in accepting freedom as a single end instead of one among many. As a political economist my approach is not either/or but both/and. Perhaps, therefore, I should explain my stand at the outset.

The most determinative factor in political economy is the concept of the public interest. On examination, this concept is found to encompass not merely one factor but many, and in combination, not in isolation. Here, as elsewhere, there is a need for a balance of all the factors involved.

It is often argued that two main polarities are freedom and order; instead, I contend for freedom and values. From one point of view, freedom is itself a value—there is none greater. Nevertheless, *standing alone,* the freedom theory of the public interest ends in rationalizations that put group and individual selfishness on a pedestal. This has happened in the United States, and it should be a serious cause for concern. If a nation emphasizes an extreme theory of freedom and fails to combine it with other positive values—such as a rising standard of living and equality of opportunity—which together constitute the public interest, it may unwittingly undermine its own institutions, since it ignores the laws of interaction and balance which are the bases of political economy.

There is no question, of course, about the indispensability of freedom as a principal ingredient of the public interest. The reasons are many, an important one being the need for the equal respect for the personality of every individual. However, the three factors deserving special mention as being directly related to political economy are these: (1) freedom encourages people to be creative and self-reliant; (2) it makes them receptive to innovation and change; and (3) it makes them tolerant of the opinions of others. Dictatorships cannot validly claim to foster these goals. It is freedom that produces the spirit of initiative, enterprise, and risk-taking that are essential to a healthy and durable economy.

POWER OF THE DEMOCRATIC IDEA

The Rockefeller Brothers report entitled *The Power of the Democratic Idea* contains the best recent discussion of the public interest, and its salient points may be usefully summarized here.

The main business of every society, says this report, is to decide which freedoms people especially prize. There is no such thing as freedom in the abstract because freedom always relates to a particular situation. Thus, every decision in public policy must be related to the problem at hand, to the values involved, and to the range of choice presented. In a free and open society a clear line must be drawn between what is private and what is public, the responsibility of voluntarism and that of government. Moreover, since government is servant and not ruler, where its action is to be relied on there must be assurances that those who receive the delegated authority will be held fully accountable. The problem is to lead people to understand that in a modern society "governing" is a universal requirement, that the more governing there is by voluntary and pluralistic groups and the more widespread power becomes, the more self-determination will the people enjoy.

As pluralists, we must realize that government is not the only rule-making and decision-making instrumentality of society—only dictatorships hold that view. In a free and mobile society the aim is to emancipate the minds and spirits of all the people, so that they work voluntarily for the things that are best for themselves and for society as well.

Thus, the public interest, continues the Rockefeller report, is those *common* interests which stand above, and are not necessarily protected by, the governing power of groups. These are the common concerns which might otherwise be "smothered in the conflict of special interest," which, in a free society, vie with each other in striving for their own advantage. Something above this area of peaceful conflict must be "focused, expressed, and brought to bear on the contending parties," so that decisions in matters of public policy are in the common interest. The criteria consist of morality, plus the other social values, such as justice, compromise, honor, belief in the perfectibility of man, and so on. As umpire, government is entrusted with the enforcement of these values.

Government does not have a higher type of intelligence than other groups nor are its officials in any way superior. Hence, it is not particular individuals to whom we attach importance but a *process,* a governing system that lays down the rules of the game in such a way that everyone is assured open and fair contention (access to competition), equal justice, and impartiality on the part of deciding officials. Although these are all important concepts, in some ways the most essential is compromise because "in the best of worlds men have different interests, and since resources are scarce, *no individual, no matter how admirable his purposes, can do everything he pleases.*"[4]

Law, which attempts to express the public interest and to establish rules of fair procedure, must be respected. When people lose confidence in the impartiality of the umpire and in the rules which society has established as its idea of the common interest, then society itself falls apart, and anarchy or tyranny takes over.

It is not enough, however, that the members of society respect the law and the rules of the game, and to assume that that is the whole of the matter. Taking the political economy view, the Rockefeller report argues that people have needs and aspirations and that the degree to which they are assisted to these ends by society also is a vital part of the public interest concept. Thus one test of a good society is whether the individual is helped to grow "in knowledge, sensitivity, and the mastery of himself and his destiny."[5] A society will be judged by the character of the men and women who comprise it and by the "quality" of the lives they live. To build these qualities in our thinking, rights and duties must be combined. Society cannot be content merely to give the individual the right to live his own life without interference of any kind—"it must also place restrictions upon him."

People's needs and aspirations are of two kinds—material and non-material—and both are needed. Examples of the material kind are certain common necessities, such as roads, schools, police protection, sanitation, communication, a sound currency, and personal needs, such as food and clothing. The non-material needs are of a higher order, and we have already mentioned some of them: the preservation of the rights of the individual, the guarantee of fairness, freedom to dissent and to be different, freedom of conscience and religion, and the right to privacy. In every free society a line must be drawn between the things that are public and those that are private. Under no circumstances does the political state have the right to regulate people's thoughts, their beliefs, or their spiritual, political, or economic views. The public interest here says "private," not "public."

If this compound concept of the public interest is to be furthered, *the individual must impose a degree of self-discipline on himself.* Otherwise, the necessary assumptions are invalidated, and the concept fails. Hence, there is needed a widespread dedication to the values of a free society: (1) equality of self-evident and inherent individual rights—no hierarchy and no favoritism; (2) the right to be different—we care about individuals one by one, not en masse; (3) the right to privacy, to do as one pleases so long as the equal and corresponding rights of others are not invaded; (4) an open society in which people are free to make their own mistakes and have the right to correct them; (5) a mobile society, in which people rise or fail to rise according to their own efforts; (6) an outspoken society, in which people are encouraged to bring their conflicts into the open and, hence, are not tempted to conspire; (7) a responsible government, in which the rules of the game are guaranteed by institutions instead of by individuals, no matter how benevolent; (8) an educational society, in which the press and other media of communication are fair and reliable; (9) a spirited society, in which people react spontaneously and have a high morale, instead of being dull and stolid because of oppression; and finally (10) a society devoted to truth, for "the truth shall make us free."[6]

To a considerable extent Americans have lived up to these ideals in the past. The question now is whether we shall be able to respond to new challenges that may prove tougher than any we have met before. The question, says the Rockefeller report, is whether "a comfortable people can respond to an emergency that is chronic and to problems that require a long effort and a sustained exercise of will and imagination."[7] Can we keep the peace, maintain stability at home, adjust to technological revolution, retain our humanity in a world of large organizations, and satisfy "the revolution of rising expectations"?

Sometimes rising above these policy issues, however, are certain doubts about government that will be taken up in detail in the latter part of this book. The Rockefeller report asks us: Can our governmental system respond effectively to the dangerous issues of the times or is government too loose, too slow, and too inefficient to move with the speed, concentration, and daring these problems demand? Can we in America, through voluntary methods, successfully "set definite goals, follow long-range plans," and arouse our citizens to follow these clearly formulated objectives?[8] Such questions themselves are in the public interest, for what good would be our high ideals if the means to their attainment, which are also of our own free making, were so inadequate as to cause us to lose everything?

THE WHOLE INTEREST ABOVE SELFISH INTEREST

Through the foregoing analysis runs the issue of government protection of the general, unprotected interest against selfish interests whose activities weaken the fabric of society and put in jeopardy the good life that people seek. It is in this area that we may find the clues to a new and revitalized political economy.

If people and interest groups came to believe strongly in and to act affirmatively toward the values the Rockefeller report espouses; if government were a better umpire and more skillful in anticipating the onset of tensions; and if there were a more general awareness of and agreement on the area in which government must act with assurance and vigor, we should have acquired something that is greatly lacking in our public life today. The Rockefeller group is apparently not always consistent on this score, however, for it seems to veer between the idea that "the politics of democracy . . . is primarily the politics of what are known as pressure groups"[9] and what seems to me a much stronger position—the idea that democracy is the politics of the public interest.

Be this as it may, we are beginning to make some progress toward defining this crucial area of the public interest as something that someone must protect. We have been a long time reaching this conclusion, because academically, at least, in both economics and political science the main current has been off the course since John Stuart Mill's influence began to wane some seventy-five years ago. In the intervening period some economists have taken a warped and prejudicial attitude toward government, encouraging businessmen to be more hostile than otherwise they might have been. Even political scientists, who supposedly are the special protectors of government and its works, have often taken the narrow and cynical view that government may legitimately be captured by interest groups; that the governmental process is a matter of access and manipulation; and that because of this jungle situation there is a constant circulation of elites, with wealth, business, labor, the military, and bureaucrats all jockeying for position. Such an attitude is partly explained, I suppose, by the fact that government once did too much and that it would no doubt do so again if men were to lose their self-reliance and their dedication to the values behind the public interest that cause them to act responsibly.

Commerce and industry, said Adam Smith, can scarcely flourish in any state in which there is not a certain degree of confidence in the justice of government.[10] Instead of supporting the old chestnut that government is, at best, a necessary evil, we should put the emphasis where it belongs. "The more individuals are thrown on their own resources," observed the Scotsman, J. R. McCulloch, in 1825, "and the less they are taught to rely on extrinsic and adventitious assistance, the more industrious and economical will they become, and the greater, consequently, will be the amount of public wealth."[11] More than any other groups of writers, the Scots have long maintained a sane attitude toward government.

One of the best illustrations of this point is in the writing of Lord Haldane. Haldane was born in Edinburgh in 1856, held several high posts in the British government—especially in education and the war office—wrote a number of books,[12] and died in 1928. The more one's experience is spiritual, said Haldane, the more real it becomes. No systematic knowledge is sufficient unless it leads up to and points to first principles. The strength of a nation springs from a people following common rules. Those who habitually act in harmony with group morality enjoy the greatest freedom of thought and action. A community is not an entity apart from those who belong to it. It is not anything external that binds men together.

High national morale, thought Haldane, is based on three main requirements: First, men must lose themselves in a larger entity, such as the state, and yet keep their independence. Secondly, the general will (public interest) is based not on faction but on general welfare; hence, the government official is a servant and not a ruler. And thirdly, government must be able to rely on a higher civil service, having continuity and agreement on ideals.

The problem of philosophy, according to Haldane, is to account for the actual world of plain man. From various outlooks we seek a single consistent picture. The spiritual view is necessary in order to see what is "real" and what is in right relation. There are principles in practical fields as well as in philosophy. An ability to grasp principles comes from wide experience and training, a broadening of the mind. The problem of today is to weld the educational system (and, he might have added, political economy) into one complete whole because knowledge is an entirety; there is no phase of knowledge that does not bear on another.

The job of the top men in any organization, private or public, is to infuse administration with such a sense of the whole that even routine activity becomes energizing to the individual. Those who work for government must have their objectives set by the public, but their duty lies in using to the fullest their individual initiative. Hence, in a real sense, the public interest is compounded of devotion and initiative. The highest example of statesmanship, concluded Haldane, is to develop and concentrate thought, evolve policy, translate policy into practice, choose the best professional men, and set them to work.[13]

In more recent times, as already noted, a number of promising publications have appeared that favor bringing economics and political science closer together, so as to restore the idea of political economy to its former effectiveness. Since it would extend beyond the limits of this book to mention all of them, I shall discuss only two, one by a political scientist, the other by an economist.

In *The Great Issues of Politics*,[14] Leslie Lipson, who was trained at Balliol College, Oxford, and at the University of Chicago, adopts what I have called the political economy view of the public interest. Politics, says Lipson, is a sphere of purposeful behavior and study, from which we hope to learn to live better than we now do. The concern of politics is to achieve the citizen's welfare by means of the most worthwhile of the policies that are possible. Politics is the pursuit of human betterment by organized public means, a search for "public ethics," the process of directing "active controversy" toward the public interest. Government comes into being because people want what government is able to provide; it is the only institution capable of taking the interests of everyone into account. The same basic issues are present in all governments and in all periods; the challenge to students of politics is to discover what these issues are and how to solve the problems they pose.[15]

The ends of the state toward which people aspire, continues Lipson, are protection, order, and justice. Government's essential role is that of impartial umpire. Individuals and interest groups need "an orderly process for composing their differences, and a recognized tribunal to give decisions whose binding character they accept." Order is not merely a system or a method; it is also justice. Hence, justice is both a method, which is fair dealing, and a certain kind of result, which is the recognition of the interests of all individuals and groups and the promotion of a harmony between them.[16] This is the public interest. On the basis of this ethical concern, the ends and the means must be interrelated, because unjust means may degrade or even demolish desirable ends.

Lipson devotes several chapters to issues that are directly economic or that have economic implications, but more important for our present purpose is to discover what he considers the basic or abiding issues, since we may assume that these describe what is meant by the public interest. There are five great issues, says Lipson, all "mutually connected and interacting" (our first principle of political economy); and although various ancient and modern states alike have dealt with them differently and have formed various combinations of factors and solutions, the issues themselves are constantly recurring. They are:[17]

1. Equality or inequality: is the coverage of citizenship exclusive or all-inclusive?
2. Pluralism or monism: are the functions of the state limited or unlimited?
3. Freedom or dictatorship: is the source of authority in the people or in the government?
4. Dispersion or unification: is power concentrated or dispersed, and how is it organized?
5. Many units or one: are there a multitude of states or a universal state; is power geographically concentrated or is it dispersed?

We have met all of these issues before in the history of economic doctrines. For the term "state" or "government," simply substitute "economy" or "corporation," and what do we have? Questions such as these: Should there be freedom of entry and equality of opportunity in trade and commerce? Should competition be enforced or is monopoly the better policy? Should there be consumer sovereignty or administered prices? Should the market be allowed to control or should prices and values be artificially determined? Should there be free trade or autarchy? The issues are not wholly parallel but they are analogous. In both cases concern is with structure, power, and public interest in just about that sequence.

It would be superfluous to labor the point that Lipson's book is a healthy and refreshing approach to political science, for obviously it helps to restore the balance. Government is both power to beat the other fellow down and power to build everybody up. It is repressive and progressive, negative and positive. And somewhere in the play of these forces is found the balance which constitutes the public interest.

The results are safest when these judgments are made on the basis of particular issues, policies, and decisions. In this area the skills of the economist are indispensable, for it is he who understands the principles that help society to arrive at the right judgments. Only in matters of structure and institution and in the managerial approach is he presently weak, but it is a deficiency that is easily remedied. He and the political scientist should help each other.

The economist who favors restoring the balance between economics and political science is Donald S. Watson. In his *Economic Policy*,[18] Watson identifies five goals of economic policy: (1) economic growth and development, (2) stability, (3) the efficient allocation of resources, (4) the maintenance of economic freedom, and (5) an improved distribution of income. There is an immediate resemblance among these five areas, the five that Lipson urges, and the main principles enunciated in the Rockefeller report on democracy and the public interest. Another striking fact is that Watson gives much attention to efficiency and balance, especially in his emphasis on stability.

Watson has worked out his analysis of public policy in much detail. Thus, he speaks of primary, secondary, and tertiary areas of public policy,[19] all of which are interrelated. Maintenance of competition is a secondary end of economic policy, for example, but it relates to the primary ends of economic growth, the efficient use of resources, and the maintenance of economic freedom. Other secondary goals of economic policy relate to monetary, fiscal, farm, foreign, natural resource, social insurance, transportation, and patent policy. Each is related to a primary goal and has its appropriate means of achievement.

The principal areas in which broad public policies must be developed, according to Watson, are national security (including national defense and foreign policy) and the maintenance of order, freedom, progress, development, and equality (social justice, social policy).[20] Lipson mentions protection (security), order, and justice as the three ends of the state, so here again is a parallelism.

For the ethical values that relate to economic concepts, Watson offers a six-fold classification: happiness, freedom, equality, justice, humanitarianism, and progress[21]—all of them broad and difficult concepts; but classification is a start. Watson notes that in the past, economists have tried to identifiy the "general" or public interest in a number of ways: by relating it to a certain interest group, such as business or labor; by calling it the consumer interest; by contriving the concept of "economic welfare"; or by stressing economic growth.

These are broad concepts. Others, such as high levels of production, full employment, price stability, and the like are more narrow, and Watson believes they might be related to one or another of his primary or secondary goals of economic policy.[22]

Authors such as Watson are in the process of developing the sequence of analysis from problem to structure, to principle, to policy, to institutional means.[23] Further, they trace (again sequentially) the impact of decision in one area to all other areas, this being the test of statesmanship. When it is said, for example, that the maintenance of competition contributes to the primary economic policies of efficient allocation, maintenance of economic freedom, and economic growth; and that further, competition contributes to the public policies of maintaining freedom, progress, and development, we are beginning to trace cause-and-effect relationships to their economic and political consequences.

AN AMERICAN CONSENSUS

In later chapters some of the principal areas of public policy will be dealt with in more detail, after which it will be easier to decide how effective the subject of political economy is capable of becoming. At this point it is possible to suggest, in summary form, certain guidelines of principle relating to the public interest as Americans might conceive of it.

The concept of the public interest may be defined in several ways: (1) The public interest is universal and consists in identifying the laws of nature that produce wealth, balance, and individual growth. (2) The public interest is the sum of individual interests, a composite at once representative and democratic. (3) The public interest is everything that is not inconsistent with law, but law must be "just" as well as "legal" in order to command respect. (4) The public interest is the higher law that conscience and government must protect because politically effective pressure groups cannot be relied upon to do so. (5) The public interest is an evolving wisdom that comes from experience; it is the principles of political economy as applied to new problems and needed adjustments.

The roots of the public interest run deep into the soil of common attitudes and native wisdom learned from generations of struggle. A basic law of nature concerns balance: for every act there is a corresponding reaction. When the law of balance is ignored, men and groups veer crazily from one extreme to the other, but at a certain point the pendulum starts swinging toward the center, and there is the possibility that balance can be restored.

Justice is more likely to endure if society respects work. Work generates a fellow feeling for other people, a sense of self-confidence, and a respect for the property and the rights of others. Self-development through struggle and work is a challenge that unifies all aspects of the life of the individual. It is also through struggle that one learns the satisfactions resulting from initiative, the assumption of responsibility, and the taking of risks on a calculated basis.

Men enjoy honors and recognition and the feeling of success secured through their own efforts. Therefore, they must be loyal to group ideals but free to serve their own individualities as well. There is no conflict between individual and public interest so long as values are consistent, and in both cases the emphasis is on the development of character and a better way of life. So far as there is any conflict it is at a lower level, where selfish interests detract from the interest of the whole, as in organized crime or corruption in the awarding of contracts. In such cases there is an added offense against workmanship and its common accompaniments of honesty and respect for the integrity of the craftsman.

As a basis of respect, work is superior to property, or status, or power; for this reason political philosophies that emphasize status and elitism are not only distorted but are also destructive of public morals. A respect for work must be based on fair treatment and justice. Hence, men insist that governments shall be of law and not of men, that property shall be protected, labor contracts enforced, and monopoly controlled. To the extent that such safeguards fail, men gradually lose confidence in the fairness of their institutions and become receptive to whatever radical measure promises an improvement. Such rebels are called lawless or revolutionary. This is true only in a superficial sense because their animus is more simple and basic: they want to protect the results of their own efforts from those who live by the efforts of others.

Men as individuals do not usually become dangerous to the public interest so long as they are still growing in emotional maturity and living by their own abilities. If they begin to slip, however—because either their ambition has waned or they have become dissipated, or for some other reason—then they may decide to live by their wits, to become manipulators of others, to live off society instead of themselves.

A test of the public interest, therefore, is the degree to which people are sensitized to its meaning to the point where they will accept institutionalized means of discouraging would-be exploiters from living artificially as the manipulators of others. This problem has nothing to do with political ideologies; it seems to be a universal aspect of every society, and probably always will be.

Being close to the laws of nature, the public interest is a rugged concept. It rewards work and discourages indolence. It whets the ambitions of the able by every fair means, and penalizes the idle. It encourages a love of the beautiful and all that appeals to the senses, and punishes excesses. It requires men to reconcile their own selfish interests with the interest of all.

As a political ideal for America, these many private and public factors inhering in the concept of the public interest may be expressed somewhat as follows: In order that the necessary balances in society may be protected and natural forces may be allowed to play their proper roles, governing institutions must have the managerial technology necessary to effective functioning; these institutions must also have an integrated, consciously directed policy centering reliably on the public interest.

FIVE

THE ELEMENTS OF STATECRAFT

The word "political" in political economy is statecraft, which is the means to influence and survival among institutions. Statecraft is the skills determining attitudes, insights, and a sense of fitness among the holders of authority, guiding their choices in matters that promote the life and vitality of institutions.

Survival is not merely the difference between life and death; it is the whole range of matters affecting the health of an organism, from a clear appreciation of the values that prolong life, to the balances on which organic functioning depends. The first law of statecraft is that the more closely values and methods are related, the greater is the chance that health and vitality will be maintained in the political economy.

I propose in what follows, therefore, to use the term statecraft in a generic sense and apply it to the economic order as well as the political state, to consider the need for adjustments between the natural and the artificial man, to discuss how we may assure necessary structural balances, to consider how we may promote cohesiveness and a sense of belonging, and to deal with the underlying elements in the concept of power.

My thesis is that in the modern world of industry and finance, leaders in business need a knowledge of statecraft more than they need a knowledge of business technology; that what business and political leaders must know is much the same; and that unless these two groups of administrator-statesmen rapidly acquire a basic knowledge of statecraft, America's survival as a great nation may be in doubt.

GOVERNING IS GENERIC

Statecraft is a much neglected subject. Although there is much study of government, for the most part it is segmented, emphasizing structure, legalism, and pressure groups—in short, power and manipulation. Thus, the governing function is not seen as a whole, as a distinct skill. In addition, emphasis is usually on operational processes to the neglect of economic principles and social values. Such an academic orientation, with its attention to taxonomy and "schools," contributes to splintering and hair-splitting. In consequence, it is possible to pile course on course, to deal with constitutions, laws, executives, bureaucracies, legislatures, federalism, legal powers, and protection of the individual, and still not communicate an understanding of the interconnections and interstices with which the modern statesman—economic and political alike—must deal.

The statesman of today must know what men want, what the principles are that govern public policy and decision making, and how to weld the elements together so as to promote human ends. Instead of giving our students these understandings, we divide into different "schools," each one playing on the theme of the essence of government, one calling it power, another finding it in authority, another in access, and so on.[1]

The mercantilists, who, like ourselves, emphasized efficient public service and skillful government, were wiser. The mercantilist businessman, says Philip Buck, was always aware of both economic and political considerations; he realized that a balanced and ordered national economy and harmonious relations between social classes depended on a continuous exercise of statesmanship in both the economic and governmental areas. Thus, "the merchant and the manufacturer were the directors and managers of the active business of the nation. Upon their energy and ingenuity depended the employment of the people and the treasure of the kingdom."[2] One can still find this active rapport between business and government in certain countries today—in Canada, Sweden, Britain, and Switzerland, for example—but in the United States we seem to have forgotten this secret of successful public policy.

One of the reasons may be that many of our leaders are some distance removed from the natural forces they should understand, and hence they tend to become artificial and power-oriented. A first test of governing leadership is the ability to do the "proper" thing, to focus on the basic needs and attitudes of the people, and avoid a will-o'-the-wisp pursuit of artificial values such as power and national prestige.

In the United States we seem not to have progressed very far in giving both businessmen and government officials the sense of mission they should have. Consequently, Auguste Comte's observations still have a modern ring. He speaks, for example, of an "organic period that has passed away," during which all the elements of society, including business and government, were bound together by common values. The strengthening of society, he said, awaits the reorganization of our social ideas, our polity, so that *our business leaders will understand the "real value" of our political institutions.* This new polity must also convince them of the superiority of moral over political solutions. Finally, we must outgrow "political maxims" and develop a sense of society based on the deeply held wants of the common people.[3]

Comte was convinced that the central area of a science of society is where politics and economics meet to become political economy. If properly conceived, this social engineering approach could solve most of society's problems that cause men to be frustrated and angry instead of exhilarated and content. The proper field of statecraft is this kind of social engineering, not how to outsmart the other fellow and hold him down, as Niccolò Machiavelli, Thomas Hobbes, and some other deprecators of the common man have argued.

Instead of assuming statecraft to be merely the knowledge of how to organize and deploy material and human resources within the confines of as large a power structure as can be accumulated, therefore, we should consider other more basic matters. One of these is the growing gulf between natural and artificial man.

ADJUSTMENT BETWEEN NATURAL AND ARTIFICIAL MAN

Like political economy, of which it is the operational phase, statecraft is a matter of combining seemingly opposing principles in such a way as to serve human values.

The first reconciliation to be made is between simplicity and sophistication. Sophistication is the result of new vistas and new opportunities, a widening of horizons. But Rousseau's natural man is by no means a fiction of the imagination. People who are close to nature learn the value of work, of honesty, of unaffectedness, of other simple virtues. My experience in foreign lands is that when you meet a worker of the soil on a village street he will look you squarely in the eye and greet you in the manner customary in that area. Unaffected people seem also instinctively to understand the principle of balance, which is a basic principle of political economy.

As society becomes more complex, however, these natural attitudes tend to be replaced by artificiality and sophistication, until, at last, in the "well-bred" individual they reappear again as unaffectedness. Unfortunately, most of our manager-statesmen come from the middle group, where artificial standards, symbolized by the gray flannel suit, are most likely to prevail.

The first problem of statecraft, therefore, is to foster policies that will strengthen and preserve the values of simplicity while blending them with the socially valuable advantages of specialization and community living. Maintaining the family farm and small-scale agriculture as a way of life is one means to this end, and it is not too high a price to pay. Maintaining the family business firm and other small-sized enterprises is another way of effecting the needed reconciliation, instead of allowing the economy to be dominated by monopoly.

What the statesman should seek, therefore, is not economic power, which feeds on and eventually destroys itself, but a way of life that is balanced and satisfying. Man is not wholly nor even principally motivated by narrow economic considerations; he is also a home-maker, a citizen, a churchgoer, and all the rest. In other words, he has as many identifications and loyalties as he has interests, and tries to tie them all together by the values that these institutions support. Karl Marx was clearly wrong in his assumption that whoever owns property determines public policy. To own property is a nearly universal urge, especially among natural people, and he who achieves this ambition will more easily find balance and contentment in his own life than he who fails. In the USSR today, for example, there is wide evidence of a fundamental struggle between the cultural traditions and tastes of the people and the iron ideology that has been imposed on them by their governing elite. The greater the distance from Moscow, the greater is the resistance to conformity and the more obvious is the reliance on the good life based on a natural balance. In the matter of housing, for example, the regime prescribes massive tenements, on the assumption that communal living predisposes children to act like collectivists. But the further one gets from Moscow the greater is the resistance to this invasion of privacy. It seems to me, at any rate, that in the long run the human and cultural factors will prevail over the political ones, as Comte said they should.

We in the United States also have a split personality, as William H. Whyte so clearly showed in *The Organization Man*. One side of us is materialistic, power-actuated, and negative toward anything but self-interest. The other side is warm, generous, and oriented toward good citizenship in a good society and toward the active pursuit of the public interest. The quick response of many Americans to the Peace Corps is clear evidence. Our problem is in bringing these two opposing sides together. The means is to focus on the kind of society we want America to become.

The objective of statecraft therefore is not, as modern economists so widely assert, an act of maximization of mere quantities. Rather, as Rostow puts it, statecraft is "balancing alternative and often conflicting human objectives in the face of the range of choices men perceive to be open to them."[4] Thus, whether one calls it politics or statecraft, the connection to ethics is close. According to Bismarck, politics is the art of the possible, choosing the most worthwhile policies from among the feasible. By extension, the essence of statecraft is choice based on structure, a deliberate choice of a particular set of values over another in order to keep man human.

This striving for values injects into statecraft a purpose and a rationale. Decisions involve choices between rival means and ends. It is true that reality may never quite conform to the ideal, since the laws of logic do not precisely equate with the laws of politics or of ethics except in an evolutionary sort of way. Moreover, one ideal may be in conflict with another, as in the case of liberty and order; if either is driven to an extreme the other vanishes. Accordingly, statesmanship, as Franklin D. Roosevelt was fond of saying, is a blend, but not a promiscuous one.[5]

MAINTAINING STRUCTURAL BALANCES

A test of statecraft, therefore, is the ability to combine ideals and practicality. Whether in business or in government, he who possesses this skill is political in the best sense of that abused term. He is sufficiently idealistic to want what will contribute to the health and durability of his community-serving program, and he is sufficiently practical to know how to get it. The late Elton Mayo of the Harvard Business School—perhaps because of his British background— understood this relationship, and some modern business leaders are learning it to their advantage. As observed in an earlier chapter, it is beginning to be realized that some of the key concepts basic to statesmanship are values, organization, cooperation, decision making, and power; and that worthy goals for the economy are a high standard of living and long-range objectives such as economic stability and peace.

Statecraft as a process must include what to do and how to do it. Under the first heading comes the determination of objectives, the formulation of policy, the institution of planning, including financial planning, and the fixing of targets on a time schedule. Involved also are the principles by which the public interest is judged, the gauging of public opinion, an analysis of alternatives and a choice among them, and the development of long-range strategy and short-term tactics. In other words, in the real world of affairs, politics and administration, which in university teaching are usually considered separate fields because one deals with ends and the other with means, become a closely knit unity. In actual practice, therefore, it is hardly possible to differentiate between the relative importance of policy and structural factors, much less categorize them.

Under the heading of the "how" of statecraft, first, there is the engineering of consent, which, to be successful, must be honest and direct and not manipulative. Then, there must be leadership; the delegation of authority to secure motivation and verve; supervision and coordination to secure teamwork; adaptation to change; the development of initiative; and finally, the welding of the whole enterprise together by means of a control function that emphasizes progress primarily, and compliance only when necessary.

Here, too, the political and the administrative areas in practice form a blend, and if the categories exist separately it is only in the mind. Indeed, the better the blend, the better the results, in large corporations as in government.

Equal considerations also apply to both institutions when it comes to growth and decay. An organization goes through various stages of growth, and there is a different emphasis in each. In the entrepreneurial stage, for example, it is on personality and daring; in the consolidation period it is on order and system; and during the bureaucratic period that follows, when the mechanism tends to run down, to become set in its ways, even to show signs of hardening of the arteries (social statis), emphasis is on the *status quo* and changelessness.[6]

At this final stage the statesman must either recognize what is wrong and correct it or resign himself to the further decline of his institution. Clues to remedial action will be found in the balancing act: the rationality of bureaucracy combined with the verve of initiative and risk-taking; an emphasis on standardization and conformity in some areas matched by large draughts of independence for those men who are put on their own to accomplish stated objectives. In the realm of government, a standardized state will become a slave state, and a wholly unorganized state will become a shambles.

The issue on which liberals divide more than any other is whether ends and means must under all circumstances be consistent. The conservative wing believes that if free enterprise is the goal, then government should not under any circumstances interfere with the economy, because they assume that once it is started, interference continues inexorably of its own momentum and would create permanent restraints on freedom.

The opposing view, and the one advanced in this book, is that since the political economy is organic and constantly changing, it is regulated by forces that must be kept in balance if human needs and institutional stability are to be served. It follows, therefore, that equilibrium can be maintained without governmental interference only so long as non-governmental decision makers are sufficiently intelligent and self-controlled to act consistently in support of natural balances. Once they fail in this, the longer the delay in supplying correctives, the more drastic the remedy which government must impose and the greater the danger that the restraint, once imposed, will not be readily removed.

Hence, the conclusion is that under today's conditions, planning —which may be for the ends of freedom as well as for those of restraint—is usually preferable to the traditional remedy for excesses, namely, creating yet another governmental regulatory body in order to keep balances in repair. In other words, an objective of statecraft should be to use forethought in creating conditions that will assure the maintenance of necessary balances, for failure to act in time may mean detailed regulations and controls that interfere with progressive management.

From this line of reasoning we conclude that ends and means *ought* to be consistent, but that when decision makers—private and public alike—fail to do the right thing at the right time, remedial action becomes imperative even if it involves methods that are not wholly consistent with the objective. If long delayed, a failure to correct imbalances must destroy the system that liberals of both persuasions are trying to protect.

The problem is how to secure balance *within* the institution as well as in its relations with *outside* forces. Here again, the situation as it affects political and business organizations, especially when they have attained large size, shows a remarkable similarity.

The first rule is to prevent the same set of officials from wholly monopolizing the making and execution of policy, as now still happens in some corporations. Paid management should be a part of the policy-making body (board of directors, legislature), but there should also be outsiders who, in the case of boards of directors, at any rate, have no connection with the institution except as they serve in a policy capacity. This is not to say that the same person should never wear two hats, one as policy formulator and another as the administrative head of a program. This happens in large corporations as well as in the cabinet form of government as found in Great Britain, and there is nothing wrong with it. Indeed, it is probably about as efficient a system as can be found. The only vice is in giving the same persons a monopoly of both policy and administration to the exclusion of the outside viewpoint in matters of policy.

The advantages of unified power at the top are that it saves time, makes quick action possible, magnifies the abilities of exceptional individuals, and preserves secrecy, thus keeping the opposition guessing. But these strengths may become weaknesses: too much secrecy diminishes accountability (even able men may make costly mistakes of judgment), and sometimes a broader deliberation results in a wiser choice. There are additional factors, however, that make outside representation worth the price. First, it brings a fresh viewpoint to counteract the myopia that afflicts even the most able man who stays too close to his work. Throughout history, some of the greatest discoveries have been by men whose competence was not in the same but in a related field, and whose viewpoint, therefore, was fresh. On the boards of business corporations and in legislative bodies, the job of a member is to feel like an insider but to retain the independence of the outsider. Here again is an illustration of how statecraft is invariably a fusion of opposite factors.

A second advantage of the outside policy maker is to promote favorable public relations. The public has more confidence in an institution where there are checks and balances than in one which, from the outside, looks like a closed conspiracy. Since the modern corporation is as dependent as any government on the good will of the public, this factor must not be overlooked.

A system that permits too great a separation of powers is as objectionable as one in which there is no separation at all. Our American government is perhaps the outstanding example of a good thing carried too far. Congress tries to do too much and, hence, does not do its main job well, which is legislation and general oversight of the executive branch. Congress spends too much time interfering with the proper role of the executive branch. It sets up administrative boards and commissions and keeps them under its own control instead of that of the executive branch, giving them so vague a status that their work is ineffectual and they are not held to a proper accountability. Congress also interferes in civil service matters and in personnel administration generally; it deprives the executive branch of a free hand in appointments and in the conduct of internal financial administration.

A requirement of statecraft therefore is that policy and administration be clearly distinguished in areas where the main job is the discussion and determination of policy; but where policy is translated into action, and responsibility and dispatch are necessary, the executive should enjoy a unified authority. The most effective system therefore is one where professional managers (the executive branch) and outsiders (elected legislators) together make corporation (government) policy. This is the procedure in the cabinet form of government, and it is increasingly the procedure in the American business corporation.

The advantages of democracy and popular control are plain. Democracy sometimes appears to be slow and inefficient, but the appearance is deceptive. It is merely that some of the functions of democracy, by their nature, cannot be fast. Thus, democracy must educate the people to make them better able to rule themselves; it must also widen the base of discussion so as more faithfully to reflect what all the people want instead of what only a segment wants. A deliberate pace is the best assurance of continued progress toward goals that are liberating rather than confining. A person who is treated like a child all his life never becomes a man; similarly, to distrust the ability of all the people to discuss and decide issues of public policy (including voting) is to cause them to become second-class citizens and dependents of the state.

As irritating as democratic procedures sometimes are, therefore, with crackpots who speak too long and too often, with mental laggards who enjoy the benefits of freedom but never seem to contribute anything to it, we nevertheless realize that in the long run democracy is not only right but superior to any form of minority rule. Following the principle of balance, democracy assures discussion in its time and place and unified administrative action when necessary.

Another element of statecraft, if democracy is to work well, is the need for what may be called public persons, individuals serving both the legislative and the executive branches in business and government whose sole loyalty is to the common interest. In this, the United States is fortunate in already having many such people, who compare favorably with the best to be found anywhere. But we need more. Those who think in terms of an elite contend that because management is now the dominant factor in institutional life, we must develop a new elite, this time an executive elite. Although I dislike the connotations of the term, I agree as to the need.

Most people recognize, I think, that we should have a civil service that is above partisanship and special interest, dedicated instead to the common interest of all. What is perhaps not so widely appreciated is a similar need in the legislative branch, which determines major public policy in the first place. A legislator must not only represent the special interests of his constituency, he must also be sufficiently principled and courageous to decide issues on the basis of what is best for the general interest, even if this causes criticism from some of his supporters at home. The personal problem of the legislator, therefore, is to decide according to his integrity without at the same time neglecting the legitimate interests of his constituents and destroying his chances of re-election. A man who takes his supporters into his confidence and explains to them the reasons for his decisions—in the manner of George Norris, George Aiken, Paul Douglas, and Estes Kefauver, for example—can usually solve this problem without violating his integrity and self-respect.

A balanced institutional system, therefore, is one in which roles are clearly defined. One branch discusses general policy and determines the final choice; a second executes policy, settling matters of subpolicy as it proceeds; a third branch, the judiciary, checks the other two as to legality, and protects the individual rights of citizens. These are all necessary and complementary roles, each checking and balancing the others so as to avoid an abuse of power. In addition, in the relations between legislature and executive there must be co-operation and a degree of harmony. Respective roles must be so defined that neither branch encroaches on the job of the other. These conditions are lacking in the United States today.

COHESIVENESS AND A SENSE OF BELONGING

Standing alongside the elements of statecraft that have been mentioned so far—natural man in a sophisticated setting and the maintenance of structural balances—is the need for cohesiveness, for individual loyalties, for a sense of belonging. This factor has already been alluded to in connection with the discussion of pride in America's heritage and its importance as a goal of political economy.

America is held together by common values. If we could strengthen them and make them increasingly operational, no national crisis would be too great. Such a development is not likely to occur, however, so long as we pay lip service to the traditional values of the nation but follow the philosophy of selfishness, the principle of every man for himself.

To strengthen our values, we should have more public persons who are individualists in their private lives yet broadly loyal to the common interest plus a greater dedication to our tradition on the part of all the people. Adam Smith was right, it seems to me, in stressing empathy. It is not merely pain and sorrow that bring forth our fellow feeling, said this Scotsman; more broadly, "Whatever is the passion which arises from any object in the person principally concerned, *an analogous emotion springs up,* at the thought of his situation, in the breast of every attentive spectator."[7]

More recently, Martin Hillebrand has enunciated the principle of cohesiveness in these words: "Underlying any state which is not based on sheer tyranny there must be a foundation of common consent which unites those opposed to a specific policy or party in power. . . . It is the will for the continuance of the associational framework which constitutes a specific state . . . [it] is the fundamental law of the state itself which is greater than any narrow or transient majority."[8]

For my part I would go further: we also need a *pride* in country. Nowhere have I found this better stated than by a Canadian economist, V. W. Bladen: "If some sort of state is necessary for the functioning of even a free economy . . . it must not be assumed that the state is only a means to an economic end. . . . One must not forget that there is a value for the individual in feeling himself a member of a greater society, of a state. Individual happiness depends on belonging to groups. . . . Their value is, in part, in providing some satisfactory group life."[9]

How we regard our country depends not only on our civic attitudes but also in large measure on the spirit of the state itself, that is, whether it is mainly repressive or mainly beneficent. If repressive, it will emphasize police and armies; if beneficent, it will stress services such as education and welfare. All of these functions are necessary, of course, but it is possible to make the positive predominate over the negative; it is also possible to make police agencies more civil and democratic in their outlook and behavior. This can sometimes be done by adding non-police functions to offset the weight of the others, as when an educational program in American citizenship was created in the Immigration and Naturalization Service to balance its police functions. In this instance, the addition of the new program influenced the behavior of the older function, with benefit to the whole service.

The fact is that government takes on the spirit of the predominant functions it administers. If the functions emphasize force, government will be feared and hated; but if its programs help people to help themselves, it will be loved and respected. As our servant, government can be prevented from doing too much. If it is hated, it will almost certainly get out of hand. Lacking support, it may become inefficient and negligent, so that eventually it must do more than would otherwise be necessary, and freedom is restricted. Or, again for lack of popular support, it may become so feeble as to fall under minority control. Hence, paradoxical as it may sound, a weak government generally ends up doing too much, whereas one that is loved and respected is easier to keep in check. Such is the case in Sweden, for example, where there is a mutual respect and confidence between the people and their government.

On the assumption that government exists to serve the needs of society, that government and the citizen alike belong to a cohesive whole, then each citizen has a right to say, "If government is my friend and if it values as I do the qualities of independence, self-reliance, and trusteeship, then it should not interfere with my freedom *so long as I am true to my trust.*" These last words deserve underscoring, because any weakening of individual or group responsibility inevitably results in an increase of responsibility on the part of government.

THE CONTENT OF POWER

Economists and political scientists alike sometimes argue that when the new political economy is written it will revolve largely around the concept of power. They point out that concentration and centralization are main currents of our times, that small businesses and small governments equally are at the mercy of the large, and that big corporations increasingly resemble political governments in their policy and administrative problems. From this it is concluded, as Gardiner C. Means did as early as 1935, that economists must turn increasingly to political scientists if they are to secure the basic understandings of power and administration that affect the economic system.[10]

I grant the conclusion but demur when the concept of power—which is a vague and ambiguous term—is made to cover a number of related problems that can be more fruitfully dealt with if the matter is analyzed into its constituent parts. I do not mean to say that power is not a useful concept. It is as useful to study power as it is to study efficiency or some other abstract concept. But in the case of power, at any rate, if the discussion is to have practical applicability it must be clear what the elements of power are and which combination of them is being considered. Without clear understandings in this area there is the danger of unintentional obfuscation and even propagandism.

Power is a persistent theme in the writing of Marx, who argued that the basic control in society is control of property and production. He believed that when men lose control over the products of their labor they lose all real participation in society, all self-determination. His proposed solution was essentially anarchistic: once the proletariat has appropriated all property, he said, the state will disappear, and there will remain only "administration." Being a poor political scientist, he overlooked a number of factors in the theory he was considering. Thus, large-scale enterprise tends to be impersonal; the average worker is unable to see the relation of his own work to the whole effort; he has little or no responsibility for the results of the enterprise; and therefore he feels himself a mere cog in the mechanism.[11] In other words, here is a universal or generic problem that is only further confused by the attempt to solve it simply by the application of a new set of labels. To substitute a "new class" for an old one is no solution so long as power and control continue to be concentrated, no matter who directs it at the top.

Perhaps now it will be understood why I distrust the indiscriminate use of the catch-phrase, power. It is wiser, it seems to me, to say clearly what one has in mind. Concentration? Yes. Centralization? Surely. Control? To be sure. Participation? By all means. And so likewise with the concepts of self-determination, pride of craftsmanship, and freedom of the individual to govern himself. These are the elements that are involved in the concept of power.

In statecraft, there are good reasons for objecting to an overconcentration of power: it stifles competition, encourages conformity, stimulates size beyond the optimum for efficiency, denies opportunity to the many, creates privileges, results in bureaucratic inefficiency, frustrates innovation and experimentation, thwarts initiative, becomes overly conservative, and, as in the case of privilege everywhere, often has a corrupting influence on society and government alike. This is not to argue, of course, that the reverse of power is desirable, that institutions should be atomized. On the contrary, power is indispensable to the creation of organization and cooperation.

The problem of statecraft, therefore, in each case where the concentration of power is concerned, is to discover where the law of diminishing returns begins to operate. The criteria are the values of society and a sense of the kind of life it is trying to produce.

Centralization is another facet of the power complex that can be considered in a logical way. The advantages of centralization are that order can be maintained over a large area; large units sometimes coincide with a particular problem better than smaller ones do; over-all planning is facilitated; unit costs may sometimes be reduced (but only to a certain point); and the strategy of the chief executive may be facilitated because of the greater resources at his command. But against these favorable factors are equally powerful disadvantages: opportunities for individual self-determination are lessened; opportunities for experiment and to be different are fewer; conformity is likely to be imposed; initiative is dulled; people look to authority for guidance instead of to their own responsibility and resourcefulness; all of which has a deadening effect on morale and on enterprise.

Concentration and centralization threaten competition; the reverse encourages competition. If competition is necessary to freedom and progress, as I believe they are, then too much centralization and concentration of power must be regarded with suspicion. If life is better when men and women are delightfully different instead of standardized in a common pattern, then there are additional reasons for fearing these power-concentrating developments. And finally, if the most efficient undertaking is the one in which people have a wide scope for initiative, the balance must be in favor of competition and medium-scale enterprises instead of big ones.

Another key term in the power complex is control, which is what writers seem mostly to be talking about when they use the word "power." To clarify our thinking on this issue, Paul R. Harbrecht, in *Pension Funds and Economic Power,*[12] offers the following analysis: Power does not follow property but attaches rather to him who controls the *use* of property. Such an individual employs others, creates wealth, and to a degree, influences the functioning of the economic system. In other words, property rights are a source of power only if they are joined with the right to control the *use* of property.

On this basis, which seems to me convincing, Harbrecht suggests five principles relating to control: (1) Power follows the control of property. (2) Control of property gravitates to those able to perform a valuable function. (3) Where control is dispersed, there is less interference from government. (4) Where control is concentrated, compensatory (i.e. interfering) reactions appear. And (5), resulting restrictions on power originate from the same source that authorized its concentration in the first place. For example, most stockholders today are without any function in the corporations of which they are part owners, and the paid management is dominant. Hence, the way for stockholders to secure more control is to find the means of recapturing some of their former authority.[13] Or, if government sanctions liberal incorporation laws with almost no restrictions, the requirements can be revised and tightened up.

A moment's reflection on these five principles will indicate to the student of statecraft that the considerations affecting large economic empires and large governments are the same. As Gardiner Means, Walton Hamilton, Adolf Berle, and other far-sighted writers have long recognized, governing is now a political-economic function, not a political one alone. In political economy, studies of structure look for repetitions and regularities in both fields.

Another reason for my dislike of the power concept as the center of speculation is that the inevitable connotations of power are subservience, subordination, coercion, and dominance, all of which are antithetical to American traditions and standards and to the kind of life that men everywhere aspire to. In other words, the term power too often denotes power *over* instead of influence *with,* and there is a world of difference. The first describes a class society or at worst a dictatorship; the second, a democratic society ruled by free discussion and value judgments. C. Wright Mills drives this point home in differentiating three connotations of power: (1) The final form of power is coercion. (2) Power justified by the beliefs of the voluntarily obedient is authority. (3) Power wielded unbeknown to the powerless is manipulation. These three connotations describe the gradients of power, and they are all interrelated.[14]

THE POVERTY OF MANIPULATION

When manipulation is used in a neutral sense and refers to techniques, it is a valuable concept; but when it means taking liberties with the rights of individuals, it is harmful. For my part, I believe that a rule of statecraft is that the more a holder of power relies on manipulation, the greater is the chance that he will eventually be found out and his credit fall so low that he may be destroyed. A long history tends to confirm this moral faith: the rebellion of subject peoples, the struggles of labor to improve its condition, the slavery issue, and many others. The best rule would seem to be to behave in a way that is morally right and in the long-range interest of the common people; though there may be periodic setbacks, one's influence will steadily increase. Thus, I am skeptical of much that is called Madison Avenue and psychological warfare.

Equally, I disagree with political scientists who argue that elites are the natural order of society and that the history of politics is subsumed under the concept of the circulation of elites. To me this is unrealistic. In American history, the early impulse was toward classlessness, equality of opportunity, and finding the public interest in attitudes of social cohesiveness, not in the Marxist doctrine of domination and exploitation. If we were ever to abandon the idea of a classless society and the Marxists were to practice what they preach, I should expect them to win the issue. François Guizot was right in his judgment that men desire immensely, but will feebly.

No theory that reduces human motivation to sheer personal or group selfishness, says Hillebrand, "can create any obligation to observe unselfish ideals," and modern nations cannot be held together without such ideals. I must also agree with his conclusion that no modern attempt to establish criteria for the control of power has succeeded, the reason being that none has been established on a valid ethical basis.[15]

A task of statecraft is to encourage knowledge and attitudes that will cause the holders of power to know when, and when not, to grasp additional areas of control and authority that could be theirs if they reached for them. In other words, somewhere along the line there must be a self-denying ordinance; economic and political statesmen alike must know when to grasp and when to hold their hand. The so-called realist, whose claim to the title is that he simply has a selfish philosophy, contends that this preachment will not work; that the only way to deter men from certain behavior is to coerce them, control them, restrain them, apply sanctions; and further, that these sanctions must be power sanctions, not moral ones. This is the main criticism leveled by self-styled realists against the books of Berle and of Walter Lippmann, in which they contend that power must eventually be self-controlled by civility or by the enlightened morals of the holders of power themselves.[16]

These skeptics of enlightened morals underestimate the force of ideas and of acceptable codes of conduct. I have heard more than one corporation executive say something like this: "We control X percent of the business; beyond that we will not go; if we did we would be 'socialized.'" One might dispose of this by ascribing it to fear, or a psychologist might suspect a guilt complex. Be this as it may, the plain *behavioral* truth seems to be that some holders of power do in fact set limits for themselves and that those who assume that a drive for power can never be checked except by outside compulsion overstate their case.

We should rely more on this force, call it what you will—moral force, self-restraint, the concept of the public interest—the term does not especially matter. But without these understandings we cannot develop statecraft to a high level; and without statecraft, modern man, who now moves at rocket speed, will lose his sense of direction.

As much as I admire his contributions to an understanding of economic power, therefore, I cannot help but take mild exception to one of the themes running through Berle's book, *The 20th Century Capitalist Revolution.* "Not often in history does the holder of potential power decline to use it . . ." says Berle. "Power has laws of its own. One of them is that when one group having power declines or abdicates it, some other directing group immediately picks it up; and this appears constant throughout history."[17]

The first part of this statement is doubtless true, although there are so many exceptions, especially in a politically wise nation like Great Britain, that I would hesitate to make the flat assertion. It is the last part of the principle that seems dubious. The major difficulty, I think, is the use of that ambiguous term "power." If for power were substituted the idea of human need, then I think it would be correct to say that if one group does not respond, another will. The proposition would be equally correct if C. Wright Mills' idea of structure were used: when one group abdicates or fails, another is likely to come forward to restore the balance.

To suggest that any relaxation of power or refusal to assume additional increments of it inevitably results in its being seized by someone else, overlooks two points. First, if power is given up it may then be widely dispersed; and secondly, self-abnegation at the top may cause people to become more self-reliant, and the need for that particular segment of power thus disappears.

On balance, therefore, I think we should profit by the British example and talk about what we mean instead of employing as widely as we do this glittering generality called power. The terms "power" and "forces" are appropriately central in the physical sciences; in the social sciences where ethics is a factor, the more correct terms are "needs" and "growth." The final test of statecraft is knowing the fitting thing to do, which involves both ethics and taste.

In conclusion, then, statecraft is knowing the deep desires of the common people, keeping the human spirit alive within the artificial framework, translating ends into means while keeping the two consistent, maintaining the balance between the making of policy and its successful execution, developing a cohesive society that depends on sentiment instead of coercion or bribes, using power to fulfill the highest ambitions of the community while avoiding the dangers inherent in concentration, and looking upon one's proper role as that of servant and not as manipulator.

In the latter part of the eighteenth century Adam Smith said that higgling and piggling over prices is the essence of the role of the businessman. In the middle of the twentieth century the essence of the role of all rulers—both business and governmental—is wise policy, democratically administered, with a view to making the whole people grow in dignity and contentment. This is the new statesmanship.

PART II

THE APPLICATION OF POLICY

SIX

REVITALIZING THE DOMESTIC ECONOMY

Of the six objectives of political economy mentioned in an earlier chapter, those that would strengthen the American economy are discussed in this one. Briefly, there is needed a bold and imaginative viewpoint, combined with decentralization, to encourage the natural forces that promote initiative, widespread ownership, and on-going vitality.

THE NEW FRONTIER

If America is to go on to greatness it is imperative that we take a broad view of the ideas and the structural changes that are needed. Instead of continuing uncritically to accept the old narrow line that there is some innate virtue in great size, be it of a corporation, a trade union, or a corporate-owned farm; instead of assuming that maximization in every endeavor will make it possible to outdistance the communist bloc; instead of these obsolete notions, we need to realize that great size and maximization belong to the way of life of our authoritarian competitors and that our own traditional assumptions are better than these.

For some time now our top business leadership has acted as though drunk on the heady brew of power politics. It has been assumed that power is the force that governs the world, that manipulation is the indispensable tool of power, and that power may be indefinitely concentrated so long as people are led to believe as one wants them to. These hazardous beliefs are held and practiced in virtual ignorance of what political philosophy and the history of power show. If business leadership were more sophisticated it would probably be scared to death of the collectivist fate that may overtake it unless it returns to earlier assumptions more in line with American traditions.

From the time that an animal is born, says an English biologist, it must make decisions. Thus, "it has to decide which of the things around it are for eating, and which are to be avoided; when to attack and when to run away. The animal is, in effect, playing a complicated and potentially very dangerous game with its environment, a game in which the reward is survival and the penality for a mistake discomfort or obliteration."[1]

Whether consciously or not, American business leadership also is playing the survival game, making decisions that are equally fraught with dangers, temptations, and the possibility of extinction.

America today resembles an unimaginative person, the ways of whose father are good enough for him. We have been doing the same things for so long on the same set of assumptions that we have lost some of the ability we once had, as a younger nation, to chart new objectives, to find the means of reaching them, and then quickly to move toward them. Our thinking is cast in a bureaucratic mold.

The behavior of the automobile industry in recent years illustrates our basic difficulty. Acting on the half-truth that Americans love speed, size, and display, each manufacturer tried to outdo his rivals in turning out automobiles as big and befinned as possible, so that in the end a Ford and a Cadillac looked much the same. Foreign manufacturers, meanwhile, were proceeding on a different set of assumptions. Cars, they thought, should be small and durable. Design should not change radically from year to year because with each alteration in basic pattern the purchaser loses part of his investment. It was also realized that in congested areas where traffic is normally heavy, automobiles should be short and manageable instead of being built on the lines of a hearse.

The simplest explanation of the behavior of American motor car manufacturers is that they misjudged consumer demand. But why, with one notable exception, did they *all* misjudge it? Why did they persist in their error in the face of the heavy buying of small foreign cars? Why did they continue for so long to offer substantially the same product when similar models of the preceding year had failed to move fast enough to clear inventories? The short answer would seem to be that the manufacturers were the victims of their own propaganda. In line with the persuasions generated by their own advertising campaigns, they continued to insist with stubborn determination that people want big, showy, expendable vehicles.

With an assist from Madison Avenue, American business leadership has created an image of America and has nearly convinced us that it is the real thing—an America of bigness, showiness, and status. There has even been an attempt to make other nations think of us in these terms, and they have made it clear that they prefer the older image, the vision of Americans as hard-working, modest, competent, and realistic. The result of our brashness has been to paralyze our progress toward more worthy and more humane goals in the United States and to lower our prestige abroad.

The crisis is not, of course, solely in the area of the motor car industry. It is in values on a national basis.

ELEMENTS OF A PLAN

America is continental in area, with a low density of population over much of it. There are vast areas that await development or that have been so improvidently treated as to need redevelopment if they are to be restored to their original potential. Instead of regarding our economy as mature because it is already creating surpluses, therefore, we should consider our birthright as a challenge to provide a decent living for many millions more, at a higher standard than we now have.

To this end, the first requisite is to decentralize in earnest. The frontier is still open in the realm of values and public policy as well as in land. Instead of accepting the allegation that the big will get bigger and the independent will eventually drop out, we should realize that with proper policies we can greatly increase the number of property owners, of self-owners, of independent farms and entrepreneurs. If these objectives were achieved, they would constitute our secret weapon against totalitarian rivals. A society composed of independent men and women does not know fear. A nation that is variegated, resourceful, and full of initiative, and where happiness is natural because people have opportunities of their own making, has more power in reserve than any monopolist has ever been able to command.

How are these objectives attained? By decentralization into regions, and then the determination in each region of that which is ripe for further development. The basic approach here is ecological. By analyzing the potential of a particular region and discovering the kind of life that should be fostered in it, the first step is taken to that end. If a region has natural advantages due to soil, location, topography, natural resources, and the like, these should be utilized to the full. There should also be an effort to encourage variegated industries and agriculture as the ingredients of a balanced economy. Resources that are lacking would be the responsibility of planning commissions similar to those now operating in New England, the Pacific Northwest, and some other areas.[2] Land ownership and the family-sized farm would be increased. Better transportation would probably have to become a public responsibility in the charge of a limited public corporation. No region should necessarily strive for self-sufficiency, and there would be no trade barriers.

In such a scheme, a duty of the federal government, already armed with ample constitutional powers, would be to prevent sectional discriminations. As regional sentiments and self-government increased, however, federal responsibilities for domestic affairs would gradually diminish. Hence, federal administration might become more manageable; and greater attention could be given to international affairs, where it is most needed.

Additional aspects of such a plan would be decentralization of both industry and labor. The largest corporations, such as American Telephone and Telegraph and General Motors, would have to deconcentrate. So far as possible, industrial plants would be located in rural instead of urban areas. At the same time, we would take Veblen's advice to heart, give foremost place to the manager and the craftsman (who are producers in the economy) and minimize the influence of lawyers and investment bankers, who are frequently manipulators and, more than any group, encourage monopoloy and the concentration of economic power.

A present tendency toward employee participation in ownership should also be continued but on the part of the individual worker and not the union. Once industry is decentralized, unions should be required to bargain on a basis that is commonly local and never wider than regional. One of the heaviest responsibilities of government would be to supply vast amounts of water, probably by the use of solar rays and atomic energy. Government would also have to engage in tree planting and resource development, with work groups made up of young people doing most of the job. (This would also help to make them good citizens.)

With this kind of decentralization, the future of capitalism would be safe. Many small units are more efficient than a few very large ones, as the Soviets are now discovering.[3] Property ownership and owner-management give a motivation and result in a sense of contentment that no other system can offer.

As part of a program to increase incentives and morale, we should take a fresh look at our income tax laws, which now frustrate ambition and entrepreneurship—all the creative impulses. To correct this error it must be recognized that it is socially desirable for people to earn substantial fortunes in their own lifetimes. To push the analysis a step further, when creative men leave their money to those who have not earned it, they encourage an indolence which society cannot afford to tolerate. In addition, it is wrong in principle for the inheritors of wealth to exercise power accumulated by the work and talents of someone else. Hence, with a liberalization of the income tax laws there should also be found the means of making inheritance laws more effective.

With determined leadership, such a plan of regionalism and decentralization is far from Utopian. We could have the equivalent of our former urge to Manifest Destiny. We could make cities habitable for decent people. We could stop the wastage of our resources. As a people, we have the wealth, and we have the necessary planning and administrative skills to do all these things. But first we must have the vision and the incentive.

A decentralized, property-owning system is in harmony with the principles of nature and of balance, which are the heart of political economy. Concentration of control is opposed to this natural wisdom, for it stifles the individual, stimulates monopoly and bureaucracy, and prepares the way for some form of authoritarian rule.

On the basis of these broad outlines of a public policy, let us take a closer look at its main components.

PROBLEMS OF DECENTRALIZATION

Regionalism is the all-inclusive development of the economy—its agriculture, industry, water, energy, and the rest—of a particular area.[4] Plans revolve about a natural geographical unit such as a river and its watershed. Since the area is determinate and every important factor is considered in relation to all others, a planned type of development makes it possible to trace the interaction of every part of the program and to evaluate and guide it. Central emphasis is on plans, the execution of which is left to the agencies of local governments. Hence, regionalism is both decentralized and democratic.

Although the exact boundaries of various possible regions may be arguable, certain definite cultural, economic, and political regions already exist in upper New England, lower New England, the Middle Atlantic states, the Southwest, the area of the Tennessee Valley Authority (TVA), the lower Middle West, the North Central area, the Pacific Northwest, and the Pacific coast. An amendment to the federal Constitution could provide for a subcapital in each region and make administrative decentralization a reality. The federal government would then be relieved of its present overload of responsibility for planning, financing, decision making, and trying to operate an overgrown bureaucracy. What remained in Washington would constitute a reasonable administrative load.

The difficulties are, first, the need for a constitutional amendment; second, the fact that the states might feel themselves threatened; third, the fear that a new level of government might increase the total cost of government (although, for my part, I doubt this, because in the long run regionalization would make it possible to rationalize patterns of government that are now duplicating and wasteful); and finally, the fact that at present the forces of apathy probably outweigh those that might recognize the value of regional governments.

If regionalism is not immediately feasible, it should nevertheless immediately become a goal toward which to work. In the meantime there are two steps that might be taken at once to help reduce the overload in Washington. The first is to create regions not by constitutional amendment but by act of Congress. We already have a TVA. A Pacific Northwest planning and administrative authority is in the making through the consolidation of existing agencies in that area. Similar plans are well advanced in New England, the Middle Atlantic states, the Missouri basin, and the Pacific coast area. Such regions could be used as TVA now is, to further a rational pattern of government in all its aspects.

The second possibility is to give state governments more to do by turning over to them everything that can be as well administered by them as by the federal government. This is not a substitute for regionalism but a complementary aspect of it.

The decentralization of governmental operations involves a number of problems, of course. Fortunately, a careful recent study offers a guide. Three major principles are these:[5]

1. The way to avoid unnecessary concentrations of governmental responsibility in Washington in the first place is to prevent in advance the need for "crash" programs. The failure of state and local governments to anticipate needs creates a vacuum which, experience shows, the federal government must almost irresistibly occupy. Prevention through *prévoyance,* which is anticipating and planning for problems before they appear, is easier than cure.

2. Many federal programs or parts of programs could be shifted to the states without in any way disturbing the social effectiveness of the project. Experience here, however, shows that once a program has been vested in the federal government, the real obstacle to change is apathy and pressure-group resistance. Unless this resistance is countered by the determined efforts of a responsible leadership, not much of consequence can be done in the way of decentralization.

3. If certain sources of federal revenue could be turned over to the states to finance functions that were once administered at the state level, or that might with mutual advantage be administered there in the future, the problem would be half-solved. Power follows the flow of tax revenues. The states and localities are deficient in this respect, while the federal government has almost limitless possibilities. If

certain sources of taxation were transferred to the states exclusively, there might follow a marked reduction in federal aid to them and a corresponding increase in decentralized administration.

There has been some progress in recent years in turning programs back to the states.[6] Among others, the regulation of safety in pleasure boating and the control of radiation hazards in atomic energy have been transferred to the states, although both lie clearly within the constitutional authority of Congress. Again, a Northeastern Resources Commission to handle water and other resources and using the interstate compact device is nearing final form, although this area also is traditionally a federal one.

Because there are likely to be additional moves of this kind, Congress has created a permanent Advisory Commission on Intergovernmental Relations. When the predecessor to this body, the Joint Federal-State Action Committee, offered a sizable list of functions and funds that could be turned back to the states, however, pressure groups began to make their power felt and action was stalled.

Vocational training, for example, was once a small program; it is now a large one, but could just as well be administered by the states as from Washington. Old-age and other forms of public assistance could be administered almost wholly by the states if sources of tax revenue also could be transferred. The school lunch program could be locally administered except in some states that prohibit grants to private schools.

In many other areas—such as health, land-use payments in agriculture, responsibility for highways and airport construction, employment security, civil defense, and housing in these areas—the real problem is not the feasibility or social desirability of the states replacing the federal government as banker, but rather the difficulty of transferring tax revenues from the federal to lower levels of government. It should be recognized, however, that the difficulty is not insuperable.

When the issue of transfer is brought up, most liberals respond with the belief that federal control is the only effective control, that there will be more rather than less of it, and that for most practical purposes the states might just as well disappear. What those who dispose of the issue in this manner overlook is a factor as crucial as "inevitable trends." There is an optimal size beyond which additions to federal institutional and administrative responsibilities are likely to cause, at the very least, an inferior level of performance for all programs and perhaps even the collapse of some of the vital ones.

Two practical steps toward federal decentralization are, first, to determine which functions of government *must* remain federalized and then assume that everything else can be devolved to the states; and second, to list functions in terms of their priority.

Some of the functions that will doubtless always be exclusively federally administered are foreign affairs, defense, currency, economic stabilization, and interstate commerce. These also are priority areas, and if Washington's overload is not soon eased they will inevitably receive less attention than they require for effective administration.

As to the tax difficulty, there are several approaches. One is to make consolidated or block grants to the states, which would then be allowed a greater discretion in the matter of policy and administration than under present federal-aid formulas. This assumes that most of the money will continue to come from the federal government. The only change is in the degree of discretion. Such a plan apparently works well in Great Britain, and most students of decentralization seem to favor it. Under consolidated grants for welfare purposes, for example, states that wished to spend more on vocational training than on food for the poor would be free to do so. Or in the case of agriculture, states that wished to spend more on soil conservation than formerly might do so, possibly by eliminating subsidy payments in other parts of the program.

The second alternative is variable grants, under which a state would not be required to accept as much for one purpose as the formula provides, while in another area it might get more. Or it might decide to take nothing at all. In other words, the strength of federal control, which is uniformity, is also its weakness; for the states and their problems differ greatly, and conformity is sometimes irrelevant. Hence, like the consolidated grant, the variable grant also is a means of securing flexibility as against inflexibility, which is often wasteful.

A third alternative is called "return of tax revenue," which is what the term implies. Under federal law, all states are forced to contribute to federal programs because taxes fall on individuals and not on state entities. Once the tax is collected, however, a state might decline federal funds for an approved program and its pro rata share would be returned to it to use on programs more urgently needed elsewhere within its jurisdiction.

In some countries the revenue system has been successfully decentralized by other means, the object being to assure the required revenues to governments that are closest to the people and their needs. In Switzerland, for example, the local collector receives taxes not only for the local commune and the canton but also for the Confederation. Funds move up, not down. Similarly, in the USSR, monolithic as the government is, the local tax collector takes in local, republic, and federal taxes in a single payment. After the local share is deducted, the rest is sent on to the republic, the proper deduction is made there, and what remains is passed on to Moscow.

The Swiss system is superior to that of the USSR in at least two respects. First, the whole cultural pattern of Switzerland favors local control; in addition, there is no rigid central planning system, as in the USSR, imposed from the central government down to the lowest levels. Something like the Swiss procedure could well be adapted to our needs in the United States and would help to make decentralization a reality. Thus, local governments would be freed from financial starvation and from an unseemly reliance on hand-outs from Washington.

In the United States, the turning point in federal-state relations occurred around 1920–1923 when the Supreme Court decided the federal-aid cases of *Massachusetts* v. *Mellon* and *Frothingham* v. *Mellon*. These decisions upheld the right of the federal government to tax in order to assist the states to administer programs that the Constitution clearly vests in them and the right of Congress to demand uniformity and conformity. The result is that by means of the federal-aid device, Washington is, in effect, the administrator of state programs in areas of important policy, including the determination of what to do, how much to do, the amount of individual benefits, personnel qualifications in the administration of the programs, the methods of holding officials accountable, and even, in some cases, the form of organization and administration to be used.

Hence, to a considerable extent, the overload of the federal government in recent years is due to a sharp increase in the variety and number of its holding-company functions. The point has now been reached where responsibility for almost all state functions has been added to those that are exclusively federal. And on top of this, of course, many new federal functions are constantly being created in response to the demands of pressure groups and the needs of the changing times.

Summarizing the analysis to this point, there are three main gradients in the area of governmental decentralization: (1) Both power and execution may be centered in the national government, as is generally the case in the United States today. (2) At the other extreme, power and execution may both be highly decentralized, as has traditionally been the case in Switzerland. (3) There may be centralized power in many areas and decentralized execution, which is probably the best solution under modern conditions, for it allows execution to be guided by ecology, makes variations possible, and permits of *horizontal* relations among federal, state, and local governments in particular regional areas. Such a scheme would promote the rounded development of America's major regions according to their basic needs and would help to reduce the overload in Washington by encouraging local initiative.

ECONOMIC DECENTRALIZATION

If government is to be decentralized, then industry and labor also should follow the same pattern. To this end the antitrust laws and their administration should have a good overhauling. They have long needed it, and to do it now would greatly improve national morale. As explained in the following chapter, I believe that the antitrust laws should state clearly the objectives sought, the practices that are illegal, and the machinery for effective enforcement. In addition, there should be certain positive prohibitions relative to corporate powers, corporate size, market-to-consumer monopoly, and concentration in banking and finance.

It will take a determined mood on the part of Congress and the nation to accomplish such a revision, but I see little hope of continuing the capitalist system unless we are willing to face up to the issues of property and control. I would even favor an affirmation of the control of property as an inalienable right of the individual, to be included in the law itself when antitrust legislation is undertaken.

Since industry and labor are interdependent, when concentration of control in industry is considered, the same issue in organized labor must be dealt with. I have never been able to accept Galbraith's view that the more power becomes concentrated in one quarter, the more is it offset by a countervailing power in another.[7] Under such circumstances, government also would have to become more powerful, as a giant referee among other giants, and this is no solution to the problem of concentration. The more useful course would seem to be preventive measures taken in time, because once power is consolidated it is hard to break up. If industry were deconcentrated, then I believe labor would realize the logic of the situation and would willingly agree to deconcentration for itself. In both areas, the policy should proceed simultaneously.

Along with an overhaul of the antitrust laws, there should also be an overhaul of the income tax laws. These are radical in that they empower government to redistribute and to level differences in wealth. The income tax is a tax against the rich; it is aimed against corporations as well as against those individuals who are the biggest earners. Most people seem to think that "to soak the rich" is evidence of democratic vitality.

In contrast to this American policy, in the USSR, which calls itself a proletarian regime, the biggest earners are treated with careful tenderness. In 1959, for example, I was told of physicists who received tax-exempt prizes amounting to the equivalent of from $25,000 to $50,000. I also learned that when doctors take on private patients (a practice tolerated under certain conditions), their fees also are tax-exempt. The reason for such policies may be partly that in the USSR the most talented individuals are assumed to constitute an elite, and partly that the Soviets are becoming past-masters of incentive psychology.

Perhaps Americans could learn more about incentives. Why not deliberately lower taxes or remove them altogether when entrepreneurship (that rare, delicate plant) is the object? Why not reward all forms of creative effort, as in literature, music, and the arts, by either lowering or abolishing the normal incidence of the income tax? The answer, I suppose, is that the present policy is easier. One simply creates a progressive tax rate and imposes it uniformly, irrespective of the sources of income or the amount of creative effort that produced it. In Washington, such a policy is called administrative convenience: the best way is always the easiest way. The trouble with this bureaucratic thinking is that from an economic and social standpoint, the easiest way is often the worst way, and the hardest way is the most effective. Of such discriminations is statecraft compounded.

A final problem in an over-all program of decentralization concerns transportation. Almost everyone admits that the state of national transportation is depressing, and no one seems to know what to do about it. The railroads, once too powerful for the public good, are now facing bankruptcy in many cases, blaming too tight a control by the Interstate Commerce Commission. Critics of the railroads, on the other hand, contend that the difficulty is due to bureaucratization and unprogressiveness on the part of the railroads themselves and to the demands of the railway labor unions; that if large draughts of competition were permitted, the railroads could be revitalized.

To this the railroads reply that unfair competition from trucking and from water and air transportation is a chief cause of their plight and that if the ICC would allow them to integrate with their competitors to the point even of owning a stake in them, the financial problem would soon be solved. To which the critics retort that such a course would reduce competition still more. Rather than allow the railroads to price themselves out of their market a variety of panaceas has been suggested, including artificial tax reductions, financial subsidies, and loans.

The basic difficulty is that the government's approach to the transportation problem has long been inadequate, being solely regulatory and restrictive and, hence, lacking in the positive features of planning, coordinating, and promoting the interests of transportation as a whole. In other words, although there has been a political economy approach to transportation in many other countries, including our next-door neighbor Canada, in the United States such an approach has never been attempted.

A positive remedial course would be to create a federal department of transportation and attach the regulatory functions of the ICC to it in a subordinate position. The positive emphasis would be on the encouragement of greater competition and the coordination of the various railway systems into units optimal for greatest efficiency. There would be fewer units, but they would be of greater territorial advantage. Then, instead of subsidizing weak lines in order to maintain the fiction of private ownership, we should wherever necessary create public corporations in order to secure progressive business management.

The fact is, of course, that public corporations are not a bad solution at all for the transportation problem. In some cases there could be both public and private funds, in others wholly public funds. As it is found in Canada, Great Britain, and many other countries, the public corporation has most of the advantages of its private counterpart, combined with the financial strength of government. A public corporation should be allowed to operate as much like a private venture as possible, and this can be done. I foresee that we shall have to use such instrumentalities many times in the next hundred years, for they will be indispensable to any process of decentralization that may be undertaken.

When one considers the antitrust laws, income tax policy, and transportation, the generic problem is always to be solved by the political economy approach. Such an approach emphasizes the kind of life America wants, stresses economic and social factors, and recognizes the interrelations among the parts. Instead of this, for too long our approach has been narrow, legalistic, and segmented; we would have outgrown it long since had we had responsible political parties and a cabinet system of government able to coordinate public policies on a broad base of principle.

One difficulty has been that pressure groups have come to exercise an inordinate influence on government. No narrow, selfish interest is capable of finding the public interest without help from a responsible political party and a coordinative cabinet. In addition, our pressure-group system encourages the dominance of the lawyer who, *qua* statesman, suffers from several inherent disabilities. First, he is trained as an antagonist and special pleader, not as a statesman capable of finding the public interest among competing separate interests.

Secondly, corporation lawyers especially have proved extremely adroit in finding ways of getting around every antimonopoly law that Congress has ever put on the books, for the methods of the restrictionist are limitless where there is the will to find them. Any company willing to pay the fee can get the manipulative technique it wants, as the record of antitrust prosecutions all too clearly shows.

Hence, the legal profession urgently needs to do what Adolf Berle and others have long recommended: return to a view of itself as the champion of the public interest. In time, such a view might discourage some members of the profession who, through shortsightedness, are now helping to undermine our institutions.

In addition to more responsible behavior on the part of pressure groups, we also need a new type of person as legislator and government official. Not lawyers, for we have tried them and failed. Here the exceptions are people who early in life stopped thinking like lawyers and became statesmen, men such as Henry L. Stimson and Franklin D. Roosevelt. Instead of lawyers, in both the legislative and executive branches we need more men and women who have been trained in philosophy, history, the concept of the public interest, and the principles of political economy.

Because government is presently dominated by pressure groups and lawyers and has acquired a bureaucratic orientation, it has itself contributed to economic concentration and discouraged effective competition. The story is convincingly told by Adams and Gray in *Monopoly in America.*[8] Like Walton Hamilton before them, these writers show clearly how it is that when pressure groups get *inside* government, the policies of government are naturally made to favor an increased concentration of power. Subsidies are multiplied and so are give-aways, as in the case of the industrial plants which, at the end of World War II, were sold to the biggest corporations for a fraction of their value. Depletion and depreciation allowances enrich big companies at the taxpayers' expense. Tax laws are made to fall proportionately heaviest on small businessmen and independent farmers. Regulatory commissions, as in the field of public utilities, come to be dominated by the interests that supposedly are being "independently" regulated.

Faced with this state of affairs, a man who believes in the public interest would try to "get the rascals out," insist that all interests deal with government at arms' length, and then try to find public servants who are above faction and selfishness.

PEOPLE ARE TOO CROWDED

It seems clear that if America is to get off the plateau where the nation is presently resting, Americans must substitute the values and images of the good life for outworn dogmas. Thus, the antitrust laws are not the enemy of business and never have been; rather, they are the protector of business. Decentralization is not a threat to efficiency, it is a guarantee of efficiency. It would not subvert the American way of life to allow government to assume wider responsibility for regional planning, adequate transportation, and new sources of water if by that means we could broaden the control of property and increase the number of homeowners, small farmers, and independent businessmen.

At the risk of seeming bourgeois, let us admit that people are happier when they own and control small properties and businesses of their own than when they are minor parts in a huge machine. With independence there goes self-confidence instead of fear, pride instead of envy, simple pleasures instead of artificial ones. Political economy encourages not concentrated power but the cumulative productive power of thousands of small units, each operating at a higher average level of efficiency than that of the monopolist and none lacking in managerial resiliency that can be drawn on in time of crisis.

Much of the blame for our delusions may be traced to those intellectuals—mainly economists, abetted by businessmen and Madison Avenue—who insist that the goal of the economy is a vast forest of smokestacks, with no agriculture to speak of. What if there is a filth of smoke, what if there are juvenile gangs in our streets, what if people do seem to lose a sense of beauty and an appreciation of nature, these theorists seem to say. Are we not rich and powerful? Can we not build better rockets than our rivals? Do we not have bigger plants for making tin cans than any nation in the world?

Let us ask ourselves if this is our idea of the good life. Do people grow toward human nobility under such conditions? Of course not.

Then how hard are we willing to work for decentralization, cultural balance, and happiness in a fundamental sort of way? That is the real issue between a narrow economics and a humanizing political economy, not whether we want to produce on an ever higher level. Of course we do, but in balance, and for worthy purposes. There is nothing wrong with an affluent society except wrong values.

To reorient our economy toward human values we should stop worrying about our totalitarian rivals and take a good hard look at our traditions and the qualities that once caused us to be widely respected around the world. We would then recognize our nation as one that still has open frontiers, and we would start to build or to rebuild cities as beautiful as those the Mormons dreamed of when they sought their land of promise in an area short of rain and natural cover.

This view of an ideal America is a far cry from the America of smokestacks, filling stations, and crowded, rotting tenements behind a fancy façade. To erase this ugliness, we Americans must acquire a strong and compelling feeling for our national heritage as a sacred trust. We should settle for nothing less than a high standard of living for everyone who works. We should encourage ambition and discourage indolence and manipulation. We should reward innovation, initiative, and entrepreneurship, factors that more than any others differentiate free systems from those that are authoritarian. By such means would we create stability and contentment at home and contribute to a solid peace among nations.

After writing the above I read for the first time W. C. Allee's *The Social Life of Animals*.[9] Survival values, says Allee, are basic to all forms of social cooperation. In addition, certain other data have been learned experimentally about animal colonies, and although Allee expressly states that they are not necessarily transposable to human groups, he seems to indicate that as an individual released from strict scientific ethics, he thinks they are transposable. At the least, they are suggestive.

Thus, animals that are overcrowded grow less rapidly than their uncrowded relatives, and they may not grow at all. Complete isolation, on the other hand, may be as socially harmful as overcrowding because there is no competition, no fellow-feeling, no sense of belonging. Under these conditions even appetite falls off. The ideal ecological situation, therefore, is an optimal population size, neither too many nor too few. Hence, optimal population has a positive survival value and a definitely stimulating influence on the growth of individuals and the improvement of groups. Optimal population size lies somewhere between the largest and the smallest and differs according to species and environment. In addition, although social conformity leads to degeneration, the natural basis for cooperation is a spontaneous drive for social relationships. Groups are woven together by environmental factors and by a mutual attraction between the different members of different communities.[10]

Allee then turns to a subject that bears suggestively on our discussion of regionalism and decentralization and the flexibility and variation that would result. Experiments with the social reactions of animals show that since no species can produce permanent adaptations to change as quickly as they may be needed, there must always be a store of concealed potential variability in order that the species may be persistently successful. Here I am also reminded of large and small business competitors, one rigid and bureaucratic, the other flexible and relying on native cunning and well-tested intuitions. The French businessman compared to the German, for example, has these latter abilities.

Allee also finds that when a given species is divided into separate breeding groups, given sufficient vitality, dissimilar local races are likely to evolve,[11] some having a greater survival value and some less than the average for the species. From this one might derive the social principle that to experiment, one must first decentralize. Allee also reports a finding that to me, at least, bears on the affluent society: too many stimuli (like too much food, for example) produce a "confusion effect," causing individuals to be less effective than they are under more simple conditions. Along the same line, animals with a trained leader respond to tests faster than animals without such a leader. Similarly, in a large, hierarchical organization, animals lowest on the social scale almost invariably show signs of chronic fear and anxiety.[12]

Applying Allee's findings to the field of political economy, it is possible to project certain conclusions. Thus, it is natural for humans to cooperate, and for this we may be thankful. But excessive cooperation leads to crowding, which inhibits growth, and to subordination, which generates fear. Hence, these extremes should be avoided. The middle way is decentralization, which encourages variation, more interesting combinations, more freedom, vigor, and growth.

If it seems that as a nation we have stopped growing, therefore, there is a simple solution. Let us consider every major region of the country as a separate entity and concentrate on making it flower as the small countries of Europe do. Similarly, instead of thinking of a mammoth business as a finished product, let us split it up into several parts, and in time each will be as prosperous as the parent. To redevelop initiative to the point where it stood in the nineteenth century, let us produce more individual owners and managers. Our democratic system is competing with an iron-clad collectivism. Because they are more consistent than we are in their aims and methods, the collectivists may win. Our salvation lies in being true to our own system of decentralized ownership and initiative operating under policy goals democratically arrived at.

Let us be bold. Let us recognize that America is young and vigorous and imaginative and the earth is good. Let us assume that even a firm trend can be changed, that centripetal forces can be reversed to produce decentralization and deconcentration, both in government and in the economy. With a clear perception of what needs to be done, and why, and with the backing of an aroused and intelligent public opinion, the job is not impossible.

SEVEN

COMPETITIVE BALANCE

No area of policy formation is in greater need of clarification than that which has to do with competition. We continue to say that we favor competition, but increasingly we act as though disillusioned with it. We repeat that competition is the main support on which economics and the market system rest, but in late years even economists have tried to explain that forces unknown at the time of Adam Smith—such as machine technologies, the more intense competition of the few, and improvements in communication—make the need for competition much less than was formerly the case.[1]

Thus, we seem to be rationalizing competition out of existence while still maintaining with more fervor than logic that a belief in the sanctity of private ownership and private profits is enough to assure the continued success of the capitalist system. In this, we are clearly wrong, because economics without competition is collectivism no matter which way you add the figures.

This chapter deals with the bearing of competitive balance on two of the six objectives of a viable political economy, as suggested in an earlier chapter. These, it will be recalled, are to avoid an overconcentration of economic power so as to maintain balance, and secondly, to create an environment favorable to invention and entrepreneurship.

THE CASE FOR COMPETITION

The five key words in the case for competition as an essential of a viable economy are choice, chance, rewards, self-determination, and balance.

114

Competition maintains choice, and choice is an aspect of freedom. Freedom, in turn, is the *sine qua non* of innovation and of political and economic self-rule.

Competition gives more people a chance, thus providing the conditions for individual self-growth and social experimentation.

Competition rewards superior effort and, hence, renews incentive, which is a sustained drive to excel. Under competition there is no place for sinecures and special privilege. Even in the USSR, professors are appointed for five-year terms, and the renewal of a contract depends on the record made.

Competition encourages self-determination and personal resourcefulness, which are the bases of self-government and innovation in all areas of life from art to management.

Competition maintains balance, a basic law of political economy. When balance is upset by concentration, the result is monopoly. Under monopoly, the only protection of the public interest is a self-imposed benevolence on the part of the monopolist, which history shows to be a weak reed where outside sanctions by government cannot legitimately be imposed.

Such are the ethical or natural philosophy bases of competition. There are also economic and political bases, which include, in addition to the above, factors such as institutions, and the market, the latter supposedly the play of forces beyond the control of the individual. In the economic and political area the advantages of competition are these:

Competition allows prices to seek their own levels through supply and demand and the influence of marginal utility.

Competition promotes the allocation of scarce resources on the basis of utility, that is, what consumer demand justifies.

Competition minimizes losses due to poor judgment or other human failings. Thus, when a weak link in the economy breaks, the damage is more readily repaired when economic power is widely distributed than when it is highly concentrated. In the latter case, the whole edifice may come crashing down.

If nothing is monopolized, protected, or privileged, said Adam Smith, and if the businessman's *only* motive in competition is to respond to consumer demand, he will put forth his best competitive effort in order to survive and make a profit. Thus, efficiency is served and wealth produced. In addition, the process is consumer-oriented; and hence, people get what they want, when they want it, and by means of a sales approach instead of by having the same old wares unimaginatively offered, as a monopoly or a government enterprise is likely to do.

John Stuart Mill was sometimes half-way sympathetic to socialism, but he was also a stout defender of competition. "They [the socialists] forget that wherever competition is not, monopoly is; and that monopoly in all its forms, is the taxation of the industrious and the support of indolence, if not of plunder."[2] Socialism, he continued, overlooks the natural indolence of mankind, its passivity, and its tendency to stagnate. Competition is a necessary stimulus without which there is no advance.

The ultimate form of society, Mill thought further, depends on one overshadowing consideration: which of the two systems, individualism or socialism, is consistent with the greatest degree of human liberty and spontaneity. For once the "means of subsistence" are assured— and he foresaw that they would be—the next human craving is for liberty.[3]

Veblen believed that in its early stages capitalism emphasized initiative, personal sacrifice, and similar qualities because the system was small and businesses were individually owned. Capitalism encouraged "the instinct of workmanship," which is perhaps man's most valuable incentive. Small-scale business presented few of the problems that large, absentee-owned business now does: power over others and over the market and prices; indirect control through financiers; bureaucracy and class conflict. During the early period natural rights meant something and were sufficient regulators of men's ambitions and lives. Now natural law is not enough. Instead, we must reorganize industry and break up the unholy alliance between predatory interests which control government as much as they control business.[4]

The economists' concern for price as the center of economic calculations is a zeal well invested, of course, for price is the acid test of competition, efficiency, and enterprise. More important than price, however, is how price, institutionally, comes into being and what the side effects of this procedure are. Prices must be flexible, for example, in order adequately to express changed conditions, both favorable and unfavorable, but this always with the manager's constant concern for trend lines. If the effect of lowering prices in a certain area is merely to destroy competition, after which the price is set higher than it was before, any realist must admit that flexibility is being bought at too great a social sacrifice and that society ought to interfere. In other words, although price is the point of departure for other supplementary economic processes, it is not the whole of the matter.

Certain objections to competition may be raised. How, for example, does one square the economic claims of competition with the ethical claims of cooperation, which at first glance appear to be the antithesis of competition? The short answer is that one must cooperate in order to compete. Indeed, without cooperation in business associations, in labor relations, in the conduct of government, and in all other institutional processes, conditions would soon become intolerable.

Another possible objection is that competition is a relative and not an absolute concept and may be found to a significant degree under so-called monolithic regimes as well as under those that are capitalist and democratic. This must be admitted. The Soviets, for example, try to secure the advantages of competition in many ways: by comparing the costs of units doing the same work; by efficiency audits; by using different wage and salary scales; and by emphasizing growth incentives for workers, managers, and the professions. The point is that in the USSR there is lacking some of the main essentials of competition, including freedom of choice, the right to start one's own enterprise, to endure the risks accompanying one's own failure, and the acid test of consumer sovereignty. In an elite government there is the necessary assumption that the elite knows best.

A monopoly may permit a relaxation of control and a degree of competition, but in the last analysis there can be no competition in the basic sense until there has been a dispersion of monopolistic control over property, institutions, and decision making.

It is interesting to note, in passing, that competition is apparently a hardy perennial—despite the care with which it must be nurtured—and that because of some inner necessity it keeps cropping up even in totalitarian regimes. The monopolistic regime of the USSR, for example, needs the benefits of competition as much as any other and endures problems directly traceable to diminished competition on the same scale. The problems of the USSR are these:

How are the beneficial effects of competition to be secured in a managed economy? How can efficiency be encouraged by a pricing system based on true costs? How can flexibility of management be secured and the deadening effects of bureaucracy avoided? How can labor unions play a constructive role without unduly interfering with responsible management? How are distribution and consumers' goods industries to be organized, offering as they do many more difficult problems than straight-out production and manufacturing? How are farmers to be made collectivist-minded when by nature they are individualists? How can effective incentive systems (including capitalist ones) be used so as to increase the zeal of management and labor alike? How are centralization of planning along with a decentralization of unit operation and day-to-day decision making to be secured?

Further, how are syndicalist devices, such as autonomous corporations, to be encouraged without weakening central guidance? How is a class of skillful managers to be produced when it is hard to learn the practicalities of business because there are no independent businessmen? How are traditional governmental and private business services to be operated side-by-side without making special exceptions for the latter in areas of personnel, purchasing, retention of profits, and the like—all of which tend to undermine the "symmetry" of the system? And how is exceeding the optimum in matter of size and managerial supervision to be prevented?[5]

Theoretically, in any regime, it may be argued that a sound intelligence is more likely to produce balance than too great a reliance on the natural factors of competition. The answer must be incomplete because even the sharpest intelligence is faced with practical institutional and human problems: In a complex economy, can all the facts be marshalled? When the returns are in, is the human mind capable of a complete synthesis? If the natural balance is badly upset, can arbitrary factors be eliminated? How are consumer desires to be determined? And towering above all these, of course, is the fatal weakness of monopoly: Who is to guard the guardians and keep them decently honest?

Granted all these factors, replies the skeptic; granted that power is best when widely distributed, worst when narrowly held; granted that men lack pride and the desire to govern themselves unless they are free. Even so, how does one *know* that innovation fares better under competition than under a degree of concentration? Do not our giant corporations have research facilities which smaller, competitive industries lack? Have not the Soviets themselves done well in the field of scientific invention and technology? Maybe we are mistaken in thinking that innovation thrives best under competition.

The best evidence on this issue seems to indicate the following conclusions: Over the entire period of technical advance since the mid-nineteenth century, it has been the individual researcher and the small unit, not the largest, that have been most productive.[6] Discovery seems to be an individual matter, the result of a synthesis based on the previous work of many but flowing through one mind. Moreover, the essential condition of innovation and creativity is maximum freedom. Men work best at tasks set not by others but by themselves. Hence, the free system of economics and politics has a long-term advantage over one characterized by regimentation. Neither individuals nor groups behave like entrepreneurs unless the climate of opinion expects them to.[7]

From this it may be concluded that if the United States were to espouse a competitive philosophy but tolerate a bureaucratic functioning, and if the USSR were to insist in theory on a monolithic framework but were in fact to allow large areas for innovation, they might come off the winner. The clear advantage of capitalism lies in playing the same game it talks. The present divergence between principle and behavior may be one reason that many economists are worried about the decline of entrepreneurship in the United States.

THE CONDITIONS OF SUCCESS

I have argued for competition as the most effective way to secure balance and a viable economy. I realize, however, that an atomistic view of what is involved in competition is not enough. Some economists have contended that if every unit is competitive, the economy as a whole will be competitive. Unfortunately, this conclusion of micro-economics does not follow through to the problems of macro-economics. The whole does not take on the character of the parts for the simple reason that with size, new elements are added to the equation.

There is, for example, the element of so-called maximization. In recent times, American economists have put a good deal of emphasis on this concept, but whether this is a useful thing depends on the assumptions one makes. What is being maximized? Is it the relative advantage of a particular firm? If so, maximization is desirable to the point where concentration appears, production is restricted, or unfair methods of competition are used. Or in speaking of maximization, do we mean the exploitation of a nation's advantage in, say, growing wheat or oranges better than others? If this is meant, then the advantages of maximizing production are immediately offset by the encouragement of a one-crop economy or an imbalance of production, making for a lower over-all standard of living than balance can produce.

Paul Samuelson seems to recognize the dangers in the maximization concept when, in discussing profit, he says that "it is misleading to talk about a 'profit system'; ours is a profit-and-loss system. Losses are the carrots held out as an incentive to efficiency. Losses are the penalities paid for using inefficient methods or for devoting resources to uses not desired by spending consumers."[8] If profits alone represent maximization, then profits and losses together represent balance, which is the desired competitive condition.

Partly to avoid false interpretations of maximization, Samuelson adduces the following corollaries of imperfect competition: (1) The more product a monopolist offers in violation of the concept of perfect competition, the more is the market spoiled. (2) It pays a firm to limit the supply of its product. (3) Part of what is called profit is the return on a contrived scarcity. (4) Every factor of income contains within it an element of surplus and an element of incentive payments.

Thus, although the emphasis of modern economists on maximization may be technically right, when applied to political economy its overtones may be wrong. Its connotations may be objectionable when measured by the need for competitive balance. An indiscriminate application of the concept may cause great mischief, and in the practice of political economy it should be sparingly used. Physical scientists and engineers understand these aspects of maximization, but professional economists seem sometimes to overlook them.

Balance in the economy as a whole results only when human and institutional factors play their necessary parts to assure the desired outcome. This is not unconventional doctrine. Adam Smith was convinced that it is in the nature of businessmen to conspire and to monopolize, and he thought the most important role of government to be not in public works (legitimate as they are), but in preventing the business community from undermining the natural forces which, when understood and respected, assure balance.

The areas in which businessmen conspire are, generally speaking, institutional: pressure groups, the halls of legislatures, the field of propaganda—all of which lie outside the present field of economics. Political scientists have occupied it, but their knowledge of economics and public policy is limited. Hence, when business ideology pays lip service to competition and tolerates monopoly, the reason turns out on examination to be less a matter of moral hypocrisy than a functional weakness of our educational system.

I believe that if, in decision making in American institutions, there were more of the engineering and managerial mentality and less of the lawyer and banker mentality, we would more easily adhere to competition and the free system. Unless lawyers and bankers suffer an eclipse of their legislative influence or become so apprehensive of socialism that they reform in some miraculous way, there is likely to be a steady movement toward rather complete concentration.

When public opinion is indulgent, it is easy to conspire. A trade association fixes prices and leaves no embarrassing records lying around. An innocent price announcement in a newspaper is made by the leader in the field, who is always the biggest producer. An agreement is made to establish the same price for a product no matter what the distance from the purchaser, making it possible for all producers to charge more for sales close to home. Campaign funds are raised to elect legislators who are sympathetic to the trend toward concentration and may even once have been on the payrolls of corporations they are now to serve. A group of corporations decides to "bore from within" by placing key supporters on the public payroll where "they can do the most good." These and countless other artifices are almost impossible to detect and punish unless public opinion is militant in its defense of competition.

Political economy stresses what the economist and the political scientist each know in their separate compartments but seldom bring together: Balance in the economy depends on maintaining a dispersion of power among its units, and the only institution sufficiently comprehensive and neutral for the job is government. The balance we seek is not a balance among all of business speaking through a single national organization. Nor do we seek an oligopoly, where typically two or a few big corporations dominate a particular field. This might stimulate competition among brand names and in advertising outlays, but it is not price competition. The apprehension of the oligopolies, as I have repeatedly been told by executives of big companies, is the threat of socialization. Hence, the oligopolist treats his competitor tenderly for fear of putting him out of business and then having to go beyond the total percentage of the business of the industry that he has set for himself. Usually this is less than 50 per cent, but sometimes it is impossible to hold the limit to that figure.

In other words, as Adolf Berle has so clearly shown,[9] once a corporation becomes big enough to be power-laden, it thinks and behaves in a political way. This is elemental survival behavior. Unfortunately, the present divorcement of economics and political science prevents the future policy maker from seeing this as clearly as he should; consequently, the peril constantly increases. I doubt that once he gets too big, the oligopolist can save himself. I do see some hope that with sufficient human intelligence, a consequent favorable public opinion, and more effective governmental action, we can prevent undue concentration in the first place.

The most frequent criticism of competition is that it may be carried to excess, that it may become cutthroat and destroy the efficient along with the inefficient. This is true. The manifestations of cutthroat competition are familiar: The oligopolist charges prices in areas of remaining competition that are lower than those where he has control.

Discount houses sell on a thin margin and rely on volume for their profit. There is price fixing in production. In some cases, of course, smaller competitors are marginal and, hence, are poor risks anyhow in any competitive field; but under cutthroat competition many good risks fall along with the poor ones.

If cutthroat competition is to be avoided, the question arises of whether society is willing to pay a small *social* price to maintain competition as a way of life. Unless one believes in "pure" competition—and few now do—then this is a legitimate question, *so long as it can be instrumented in the public interest.* For in political economy, as by now must be evident, social cost is as legitimate a yardstick as production cost is in the corporation. If the social cost is a degree of governmental control, it must be forthcoming.

Another main criticism of competitive excess is that it encourages a narrow and essentially destructive selfishness. A voluntary change of emphasis based on an acute awareness of the requirements of the public interest doctrine and support of a balanced type of competition would solve this problem.

Yet another charge is that a preoccupation with narrow competition disqualifies business leaders for the wider kind of economic statesmanship on which our way of life depends. This also is true. But the solution is not to create a deliberately trained elite to run the country, as in certain collectivist nations. The solution lies, rather, in a conscious attempt on the part of businessmen to understand the elements of leadership and statesmanship in economic as in political matters.

In other words, the excesses of competition are by no means fatal, and the advantages of balanced competition far outweigh the disadvantages of the excesses. To avoid excesses, we need better structural balances in the economy and a better control of monopoly; and we must raise the literacy level of institutional leadership by inculcating the principles of the public interest.

The three parts of the essential role of government with regard to economic concentration are: first, to prevent undue concentrations of power within particular fields, such as steel, transportation, or motor cars; secondly, to prevent excessive concentrations among whole segments of the economy, such as banking, pension trusts, manufacturers' associations, and labor unions; and thirdly, to guarantee the continuance of competition.

On this last point, economists support the necessity of competition and are able to describe the facts and methods of concentration, but in the matter of solutions they are generally impotent. They have not studied institutions and the way they operate. Practical businessmen, on the other hand, have studied institutions, have been trained in them, and with the help of the corporation lawyer, can gain almost any end they desire simply by manipulation. The prospect of changing this pattern often seems discouraging to those who prize the values of freedom and competition, for they realize that the former depends upon the vitality of the latter.

A POSITIVE PROGRAM FOR LAISSEZ FAIRE

Agreement on beliefs and institutional roles and balances is far more basic than the details of legislation and administration stemming from them.

Generally speaking, we are proceeding along the right lines when we rely on the antitrust laws and on legislation restricting the antisocial aspects of labor union activity. Nevertheless, the march toward concentration will continue unless public opinion recognizes the necessity of maintaining competition, instead of flirting, as at present, with the notion that monopoly might be better after all.

If public opinion clearly supported the maintenance of competition as a source of freedom and progress, then a chain reaction might be anticipated:

Congress would overhaul the antitrust laws, strengthen the enforcement agencies, and make more money available for policing the competitive system. Next, programs to make small business more efficient and better served in terms of credit and taxation would immediately be advanced. Government would be made to operate responsibly and the doctrine of the public interest would be considered to be as basic to national policy as the federal Constitution. Businessmen would actively support the ideology of competition and the enforcement machinery on which it depends. Businesses that have exceeded optimal size would begin voluntarily and on the basis of sound logic, to deconcentrate. We would recover our faith in the individual and in entrepreneurship. We would regard large size with suspicion, recognizing that the only justification for it is technological factors that make lowered unit costs dependent on large operations.

Along with the deconcentration of industry, labor unions also would be encouraged and even required to deconcentrate. There would no longer be nation-wide or even industry-wide bargaining. Sympathy strikes would be more effectively controlled than at present. The features of unemployment insurance that tend to weaken the moral fiber of people—such as the growing practice of taking a "paid vacation" instead of finding equivalent work—would be given a good going-over. Labor unions would become more democratic because their power would be closer to home.

Some will say that this is Utopian dreaming, that major social movements, once started, must go their appointed path to collectivism, private or public, or to a combination of the two. Others will argue that concentration is a good thing in itself and that if we are to survive we must match fire with fire, which means imitating our communist rivals.

I am not disturbed by either of these objections, because as a student of management I am convinced that business efficiency and individual contentment are found in competition, freedom of choice, and voluntary teamwork, not among the rigid grooves of big institutional machines. I am equally convinced that the USSR also will eventually be forced to deconcentrate in the interests of the survival of its own industrial system. These beliefs are not merely a matter of faith; they are based on years of observation and study of large corporations, labor unions, and governments.

As early as Biblical times it was known that the big will not inherit the earth. In more modern language, the median is more efficient than either extreme. To quote again from Allee, the biologist: In evolution for survival, the desirable unit is neither the largest nor the smallest, but one that lies at some intermediate point.[10] Or, turning to engineering, which is closer to economics: "All through the nineteenth century and down to date, science and invention have been piling up examples of the value of big machines, big factories, and mass production. . . . In some lines of production . . . larger operations turned out more goods for less money, compared with the smaller production units that they displaced. . . . How could the public ever guess that *the big plant is only sometimes more efficient, or that in most industries the middlesized plant works better than either the small or the big.*"[11] The giant only assumes he is superior because, being arrogant and sure of his strength, he thinks only in short-term rather than in long-term sequences. He is interested in power instead of innate efficiency and human motivation.

There is a logical and workable way of encouraging competition and deconcentration in the economy. First, there is needed full and widely disseminated information about the degree of concentration that now exists. This step will largely depend on reports voluntarily compiled. What are the basic facts? Stigler found that as of 1939, one-third of the national income was produced by monopolies, meaning that twice as much was produced in areas that were still comparatively competitive. Generally speaking, these included agriculture, construction, trade, finance, and the service industries. Since 1939, however, there has been a wave of mergers, including some very large banks. Stigler also found concentration to be greatest in the area of public utilities, railroads, motion pictures, medicine, and nearly half of manufacturing.[12] By 1960 it was estimated that 0.5 per cent of all manufacturing corporations in the nation accounted for 57 per cent of total sales, and had a higher rate of profit than smaller companies; that employment was increasing in large companies and declining in the smaller ones, the largest 5 per cent of companies showing an increase of 22 per cent in the four years between 1938 and 1942.[13] The quickest way to concentrate is to merge, and mergers are always more plentiful in prosperous than in bad times.

The next step is to organize pressure-group support in favor of strengthening competitive business and preventing concentration. This would mean supporting organizations such as the National Federation of Independent Business, Inc.; the Small Business Administration in the federal government (whose job it is to improve the management efficiency, credit, and tax features of small, competitive businesses); and the Committee for Economic Development (CED), a nation-wide organization of liberal businessmen dedicated to a competitive economy and favoring sensible relations between business and government. Support for these efforts also would have to be largely voluntary.

Thirdly, there should be a thorough revision of the antitrust laws, codifying the many scattered laws and amendments in a single major statute. In this legislation, emphasis should be on prevention, where it belongs. An agency in the Department of Commerce should study continuously the facts of concentration and competition in all segments of the economy. Before mergers could be legally consummated in certain specified areas, such as banking and among large manufacturing concerns, the government would have to give its permission. Corporations already monopolistic or nearing that point would be dealt with in one of three ways: they could be ordered to deconcentrate (probably requiring court action); or they could be reincorporated under federal instead of state statutes in order to give the federal government greater actual and potential control over the power of these firms; or finally, corporations that seemed hopelessly monopolistic could be converted to some form of public ownership and operation, preferably by using the corporate device. It should be stated as clear national policy that any private enterprise that cannot keep itself decently competitive may expect to be "socialized," that monopoly power is always objectionable, but that if it must exist, only government may safely exercise it.

A fourth step to encourage competition would be legislation to stimulate what George Romney calls industrial births.[14] According to Romney's plan, the antitrust laws should provide that when a particular firm in a basic industry, such as automobiles, exceeds a specific percentage of total industry sales over a specified period of time, it should be required by law to propose to an administrative agency of government a plan of divestiture that would reduce its percentage of sales. Moreover, if the firm is engaged in more than one basic industry, the maximum allowable percentage of total industry sales would be lower than for companies operating in only one basic industry. The reason is that where a company operates in more than one field its competitive position is relatively strengthened, and it can dominate either market with a lower percentage of sales in each case. It can concentrate its resources on a single industry or product at will and expand one market by relying on its earnings in the other. Divestiture under this plan would cause new births in industry. Where there is now one corporation, for example, there might be thirty-four, as happened in the case of Standard Oil following the Supreme Court decision in 1911. Business would be more profitable for investors, and new businesses would have more vitality owing to greater competition and to the absence of the bureaucratic factors that inhere in large size.

Finally, a committee of the cabinet should study the problems of small business, along with the whole problem of keeping the economy in balance.

The success of any such composite plan as I have outlined here would largely depend on keeping the interested public fully informed. Consequently, much publicity and education would have to accompany these measures. In some countries, such as Sweden, public discussion and exposure to publicity has been found to be a workable device in gaining support for public policy.

It will perhaps be objected that if the antitrust laws are opened up to codification and improvement, the net result might be less of a law than at present, that pressure groups might force a weaker law than we now have. This is a possibility. But at least we would then know where we stand. If business pressure groups reject competition and effective antitrust laws, those who favor them would have to find more workable solutions; and, in addition, the area of hypocrisy would have been removed. It seems basic, however, that the antitrust laws can never be made to succeed unless predominant business sentiment is loyally dedicated to the purpose which these laws serve.

Antitrust enforcement also must be more effective than at present, for education and voluntary action cannot do the whole job. There must be unified study and a unified attack on enforcement. The weakness of the present system (and this has been true since 1914) is divided jurisdictions. The Federal Trade Commission deals with one part of the problem and the Antitrust Division of the Department of Justice with another. As in all such cases, there are confusions, delays, and uncertainties. I would therefore abolish both the Federal

Trade Commission and the Antitrust Division, transfer their functions to the Department of Commerce, separate regulatory duties from those relating to policy, prevention, follow-up, and enforcement, and place the two sets of responsibilities in separate bureaus. If divestiture is ordered, for example, the bureau in charge of enforcement would have a clear duty to see that the court order is carried out in accordance with the decree. This has long been the weakest aspect of monopoly control, and the chances of overcoming it would be greatly improved under a unified responsibility such as this plan offers. As the government's legal agency, the Department of Justice would, of course, continue to prosecute cases that go to court.

Along with this plan of organization, there should also be some kind of formal determination of optimal size to which an enterprise may legally attain. Such size might be defined as a percentage of the business of the industry, although some better method can doubtless be found by engineers working in this area. Such a limit might be expressed in the law itself or as a general authorization to the enforcement agency to work out its own solutions in particular cases. There might also be a combination of both procedures: a stated policy plus an indication of a maximum limit on size, with more precise determinations to be made through the administrative process.

At the time that these antimonopoly measures are taken, there should also be a careful review and codification of labor legislation. The antitrust laws themselves should *not* be made to apply to labor unions; the unions should have laws of their own. Conspiracies with employers are already punishable by law. The remaining need, as already suggested, is to assure bargaining at a lower level than nation-wide, once corporations have been deconcentrated.

This whole deconcentration program would take a lot of doing. The codification of the antitrust laws, especially, would require a high-class commission working for the better part of two years. Similarly with the organizational changes that have been recommended. Without dedicated leadership in Congress and an aroused public to support the program, nothing much is likely to happen. There are such men presently in Congress. About public opinion there is more uncertainty. The public is emotionally opposed to monopoly, as studies show, but too few people realize what needs to be done.

THE TAX REMEDY

There is one remedy for the ills of excessive concentration that transcends all others in importance. This is the power to tax. If the earnings of the largest corporations were taxed at a much higher rate than at present, it would make it harder for the giants, who should be discouraged, and easier for the medium-sized companies, who should be encouraged. For the power to tax is not only the power to destroy, but also the power to "foster and promote," that goal so often expressed in federal legislation.

Instead of the present rate of 52 cents on the dollar of corporate earnings, for example, the rate might be increased to as much as 90 cents for companies whose relative earnings go beyond a certain limit. Similarly with individuals who have excessively large incomes not due to their own effort.

A limit on the earnings of a corporation might be set at $5 million a year, for example; then if it earned more, because of size and power, a law such as Romney proposes, or its own common sense, would cause it to deconcentrate. Where there was once a single mammoth corporation, after the tax law went into effect there might be half a dozen or even twenty separate companies. What would this do to corporations such as American Telephone and Telegraph? Would the Bell System be as useful to the nation if it were reduced to a network of twenty operating companies, which is the present number, each with a separate identity? I think it would. Cooperation on long-distance service does not require a holding company for its operation. And as for manufacturing, Western Electric should long ago have been cut off and made independent of the operating companies.

This taxing proposal is not as radical as it sounds. In the USSR we are faced with a formidable competitor whose power comes at present from concentration in planning, finance, operations, and grand strategy. But it is concentration directed from a single source —from government at the top—and already it shows signs of falling of its own weight as evidenced by failures in agriculture and a recent policy toward a degree of decentralization in the industrial area. To assure ourselves that our competitive power will remain equal to or superior to that of communism, we should emphasize what is best in our own system, namely, competition. But not a watered-down version of this concept, in which monopoly is combined with a pale imitation of the real thing. It must be the best model of competition we can provide.

Under our economic system the principal motivation of behavior is profit. When slums occur in cities, for example, it is basically because it is unprofitable for a property owner to maintain the condition of his buildings, more profitable to let them run down and then fill them with as many dwellers as possible. The surest attack on this problem would be to find the means of making slums unprofitable and causing property maintenance to be profitable.

By the same token, if tax laws caused corporations automatically to lose their earnings over a certain percentage or a certain amount (it might be both), they would need little coaxing to split the business into a number of independent, competitive units. As already noted, in 1960 0.5 per cent of all manufacturing companies had 57 per cent of total sales. If a tax law raised the corporate tax from 52 cents on the dollar to from 70 to 90 cents, there would be an immediate movement on a wide front to deconcentrate, because not to do so would be unprofitable.

It bears repeating, therefore, that the power to tax is the power to destroy, and by its use, concentration could be made unprofitable. At least as important, however, the power to tax is also the power to encourage and to promote, and through its use the profit motive may be employed to make people *want* to compete.

The success of this tax remedy would depend in part on a new idea of what is involved in efficiency. Efficiency is not a matter of using the largest possible unit operating at the lowest possible input-output ratio, although there are still some economists who accept this naïve assumption. If efficiency is to be used as a yardstick, which is its proper role, then *all of the factors of enterprise must be taken into account.*

The shallowness of machine efficiency is easily shown if one assumes, for example, that all the fences in Kansas could be eliminated and the whole state operated as a single farm by a single corporation or by the government. Why not? There are tractors and combines big enough for the job, and the organizational problems could easily be solved. In other words, if the objective is to make every business enterprise as big and as mechanized as possible, there is almost no limit to what might be done.

But what would be the result? Millions of workers would go on the unemployment rolls. Private ownership would be virtually abolished. There would be extreme gyrations in the business cycle, with periods of boom followed by intense depression. Some of these evils might be avoided, of course, if government owned and operated these huge businesses itself, in which case it could give everyone a job simply by "making" work.

To carry the idea of limitless size to its logical conclusion, therefore, shows how shortsighted is the narrow view of efficiency. To assume that efficiency is linked to the biggest machines, the biggest farms, the biggest businesses, the biggest banks, the biggest labor unions is to invite government to run the whole economy in order to maintain a decent balance.

If, on the other hand, it were decided to promote *more* competition, *more* private ownership, *more* individual satisfaction from owning and operating a business of one's own, then the role of government would be reduced to discouraging harmful concentrations through penalties on earnings due to size. There is no question that such a law would be found constitutional in the courts. So long as it were made to bear equally on whole categories, there is no essential difference between a tax of 52 per cent and (say) one of 70 or even 90 per cent. Such laws already govern rates on the incomes of individuals.

What we should recognize, therefore, is that competition is something broader than mere efficiency; it is a way of life. Real efficiency is a matter of motivation and contentment, virtues that flourish under widespread ownership and operation. To avoid chronic unemployment and depression, we must reinstate competition in place of the present bastard system that is corporate monopoly or oligopoly operating under a fictitious competition. Furthermore, if people owned and operated businesses of their own, their morale would be so high, their governing capacities so developed, and their achievement of a human kind of efficiency so great that as a nation we could easily compete with any country operating under a monopoly system.

VALUES AND COMPETITION

In a prolonged struggle between a belief system and a behavior pattern that are different, the behavior pattern always wins. One day one hears, "I favor competition and private ownership"; and when this tenet of belief has finally been worn down, one hears instead, "I still favor competition, but it doesn't work." The public is remarkably tolerant. It would like to believe in competition, but when policy has been allowed to drift out of control, the public is practical enough to ask what the alternative might be. Experience shows that the alternative to competition is government ownership.

Watson insists that the maintenance of competition strengthens the primary ends of public policy by contributing to the efficient use of resources and economic growth, and these in turn help to preserve equality of opportunity, to prevent undue concentrations of private economic power, and to promote political freedom.[15]

Thus, even if communism could actually produce more goods than capitalism over given periods of time, a competitive society would still be superior at renewing and revitalizing itself and, hence, would prevail over its rivals in the end. A competitive society stresses freedom and incentive to experiment, to innovate, to excel, and to provide leadership widely. Businessmen become businessmen by developing acumen; they develop acumen by making their own decisions, arising from the course of their own struggles. Under a monopolistic system, few executives can become well-rounded because most of them are never more than a small part in a big institutional machine. One may say that it is differences in efficiency that cause a competitive system to excel over a monopolistic one. But this is true only if the concept of efficiency is sufficiently broadly defined to include the spiritual and motivational factors of morale, the atmosphere that pervades the place.

One may reasonably conclude, therefore, that when the benefits of competition are weighed against its deficiencies, the balance is undeniably in favor of competition as a primary asset of public policy. The faults of competition are due to a neglect of balance, of the public interest, of the need for self-control, and of a sense of higher duty. These faults are readily overcome when approached according to the guidelines of political economy.

We should codify and tighten up our antitrust laws, set limits on permissible size, use the tax weapon to force competitive units to become more numerous and smaller, strengthen the preventive and enforcement machinery of the federal government, and undergird the whole with a program of education that will show people how it is that competition is essential and monopoly harmful to a free economy.

EIGHT

GUIDELINES OF FOREIGN POLICY

If the principles of political economy were consistently applied by foreign offices, what would be the effect on foreign policy? How would that policy differ from the traditional pattern?

None of the objectives of a viable political economy outlined earlier—a high standard of living, the encouragement of ambition and discouragement of indolence, the stimulation of invention and entrepreneurship, of competitive balance and decentralized power, and finally pride in the national heritage—would mean much in the long run if there were not stability at home and peace among nations.

POLITICAL ECONOMY AS THE BASE

The anxieties of modern man, expressed on all sides, concern the possible extinction of civilization as we know it. Despite the many excellent studies of international relations—such as the reports of the Rockefeller Brothers Fund[1]—the plain truth is that a broad and realistic application of the principles of political economy would do more to assure world security than the relatively new field of international relations, important and as necessary as it is, can offer to do alone.

This is not to say that economic factors are solely involved in the cause and cure of war. It *is* to assert that political economy as statecraft, as a body of knowledge enabling peoples to work together toward a decent standard of living and the good society, is the solid base on which international relations must be built; further, that

135

the superstructure of peace is not likely to be durable until national economies have been established on a solid base.

The answer to the initial question here, therefore, is that a political economy approach, judiciously and consistently applied, would make a decided difference in the traditional patterns and procedures of foreign offices. Too often these offices emphasize power politics, take a dim view of the motives of the opposing bloc and, hence, tend to adopt a manipulative view of diplomacy, in which the main idea is how to outsmart the other side. A more fruitful approach is to recognize that people everywhere are much alike, that they all want the same things, and that none are innately less virtuous or more dastardly than the nationals of one's own country. The common problem in every country is how to master institutions, values, and techniques and how to foster cooperation so as to assure a basis of life that will make people behave responsibly in international affairs instead of pursuing a policy that threatens to wind up in national—if not international—suicide.

A typical rebuttal to this argument is that throughout most of its history the United States has had a moral approach to foreign policy; recently, this approach has been shown to be inadequate against the power politics of the communist bloc; hence, the United States must emphasize long-range strategy, power politics, psychological warfare, and deterrent armaments if it is to succeed against the communist nations.

I find this argument unconvincing, and so do many others. In contrast to the view that in the future the world must be run by Machiavellian schemers I would contend that especially in the modern world, the most moral nation is the one most likely to survive and to hold the respect of uncommitted nations. I stress the present world situation because it seems to me that the moral content of international relations has greatly accelerated since World War II. For example, there are now a hundred or so nations in the United Nations instead of half that number, and new nations are being created almost every month. It takes no clairvoyance to foresee that colonialism and imperialism are on the way out and that both will eventually be as extinct as slavery in the United States.

To be sure, many new nations will have troubles. Some will slip

temporarily into dictatorship because at the outset they lacked sufficient discipline and leadership to make democracy work. But they
will never lose the burning, irresistible passion for freedom, self-
determination, political evolution, economic progress, and the good
life which caused them to throw off colonialism in the short span of
fifteen years. The world is in revolt, not so much *against* as *for* something. It is a moral revolution. Consequently, if the powerful nations
would keep the respect of the new, uncommitted nations, foreign
policy must be formulated on the basis of moral law. These are the
principles of political economy.

In fact, of course, the world only *seems* to be run by the big
powers and the force of armaments. In reality, it is run by world
opinion and the minds and attitudes of hundreds of millions of
"little" people the world over. If the prestige of the United States
dropped during the past fifteen years, as clearly it has, the reason is
not that the USSR was first in space or first in anything else. Our loss
of prestige is mainly due—as several contributors to the symposium,
The National Purpose,[2] show so well—to a weakening of dedication to the principles enunciated in the Declaration of Independence,
especially those burning phrases declaring *all* men to be born free
and *all* men to be entitled to the equal pursuit of happiness. These
basic principles of moral law are the guidelines of a proper diplomacy.

Another reason for our loss of national prestige, of course, is that
our deeds have not always measured up to our protestations. We
have sometimes appeared hypocritical, pietistic instead of charitable.
A fatal weakness of a power philosophy is that the common man sees
through it.

I do not mean to push the moral basis of foreign policy to the
point of offering the other cheek to the aggressor. Here as in all
other areas of public policy—labor relations, for example—the experienced negotiator will be sincere and moral in his behavior, but
at the same time he will be a strategist and will be alert for trickery
on the other side. It has never been contended, so far as I know,
that the naïve shall inherit the earth; it is only the meek, whom I
take to mean the virtuous, who will be so blessed. The best foreign
policy therefore adheres to Theodore Roosevelt's dictum, "Speak

softly, but carry a big stick." That is, be forthright and honest, but do not allow yourself to be caught unprepared.

SUGGESTED POLICY LINES

Most nations could do with a revolution in their diplomatic thinking. Too often a foreign office official, no matter what his beliefs, seems to put his professional biases above his human understandings. Being heir to a proud tradition, he acts as though he were still living in the age of Metternich. A nation, he assumes, is a discrete entity, with national interests inherently in conflict with the national interests of nearly every other nation. Every gain to a competitor, he thinks, is a loss to his own country, while every triumph on his part weakens his nation's rivals by that amount. There is a scarcity of the good things of life, and every nation must try to get a corner on as much as possible. War is inevitable, and it is only a matter of time before it appears; indeed, according to this view, war is simply one of the means by which a nation gets its way and weakens its rivals.

I have deliberately overdrawn this characterization of the professional diplomat's set of mind but not, unfortunately, as much as I would were the case. For he is still thinking according to mercantilist theory in its senile stages: foreign policy is a matter of *exclusive* national power and not, as should be the case, of *mutual* national power. This distortion is likely to persist so long as our orientation is toward power as the ultimate criterion, instead of toward service and human welfare for *all,* as the master principle.

There are also some strong residues of scarcity economics in the thinking of professional diplomats. Against this, I would argue that before the revolution in our thinking can catch up with the revolution in our condition, we must recognize that there is the potentiality of creating enough of everything, so that people everywhere can attain to a high standard of living. With atomic energy, modern technology, sensible family planning, and the right institutional arrangements, this condition, for the first time in history, is now widely attainable. Population could, of course, still outdistance resources, and a task of a realistic political economy is to see that this does not occur.

On the basis of the above premises, the principles of a proper foreign policy are these:

1. The strength of a nation is its people and their skills. These are the important elements in national greatness and the attainment of excellence. Armaments and even manufactures are secondary factors, for if they are destroyed they can be replaced, as Western Europe and the USSR demonstrated after World War II. Strength based on armaments may give a false sense of national security, whereas strength based on a nation's own people creates a security that is never false.

2. The basic causes of war are economic factors; or, more broadly, they are political economy factors. As late as the seventeenth and eighteenth centuries, under the influence of mercantilist policies, which stressed colonialism and discriminatory national power, the acquisition of territory was often a cause of war. Today, war is more often due to the behavior of nations that are economically or politically frustrated and unhappy. Pushed far enough, they seem to see a choice between suicide at home or war on their more opulent neighbors. These are the factors behind the façades of communism, of capitalism, and other ideologies that evoke more emotion than they do analysis. Hence, if war is to be prevented, the economic problems of nations must be alleviated before the reign of international law can be universally established.

3. Two-thirds of the potential lawlessness of the world today is avoided before it starts because of a traditional behavior pattern that is virtually world-wide. Robbery and murder have long been outlawed by custom, law, and the imposition of deterrent penalties. We may look for the same considerations eventually to influence international conduct, for the history of law and morals is of a constantly broadening base from the individual to the family, the community, and the nation. It is time now to extend this influence to the international community.

4. Since modern war is generally due to basic domestic disequilibriums, the starting point for world peace is the nation-state. A nation capable of providing a foundation of wealth and stability at home that will cause people to be content is not likely to be an

aggressor. Hence, the political economist, whose main interest is the nation-state in all of its aspects, may be at least as useful in solving tensions and insecurities as those dedicated people whose approach is from the top down, from the international community to the nation-state. As a corollary, those who would secure world peace by de-emphasizing the nation-state are not thinking clearly.

It is equally true, of course, that if the political economist is to be effective he must accomplish a dual task. Just as every aspect of the national economy is interrelated, so is every aspect of the national economy a part of international relations and foreign policy. This was one of Adam Smith's most important contributions to economics. Later, the growing trend to nationalism obscured these relationships. Today, anyone who works in any area of either domestic or foreign policy knows that interdependence is the key factor. Every political economist must take a direct interest in international affairs, viewing every domestic policy from the international as from the domestic standpoint.

5. The basic rule of international economics is that nations should be helped to help themselves. No matter how well intentioned free gifts, subsidies, and economic props may be, they cannot but increase the dependence of the receiving nation and impair its ability to manage its own affairs. (In my own experience, I saw a large gift of surplus powdered milk from the United States, for example, slow the development of an infant dairy industry in Turkey.)

In the area of international economics more than in any other, the cleavage appears between the power and the political economy approaches to diplomacy. Starting with the assumption that military and economic power need urgently to be increased amongst one's allies, it is easy to conclude that any means to quick results, including give-aways to private interests, will serve the desired end. As a result, not only is the receiving nation's dependence increased and its economic health impaired, but in addition, because of disappointment and disillusionment, public opinion in the receiving nation turns against the donor instead of appreciating his act of seeming generosity.

Hence, it would appear, first, that no donor nation should infringe on the managerial or policy functions of receiving nations; and secondly, that steady progress, even if slow, is better than fast progress if the long-term effect is harmful to receiving nations. For the truth of this principle one has only to look at some of the results of the agricultural and public assistance programs in our own domestic economy.

Yet another principle of international economics is that the ends sought should be exclusively welfare and not political. Every receiving nation supports this view, and we have been slow to accept their judgment. Economic assistance may be offered because either it is a good business proposition, or the donor is interested in the welfare and evolution of the people of a particular country. Hence, it is wiser to offer the helping hand through a neutral, nonpolitical agency, such as the United Nations, than through a foreign office, where the motivation, even if it is not selfish, is likely to be misconstrued. Fortunately, after many disillusioning experiences with bilateral aid programs with strings attached, the United States has now realized the wisdom of working through a nonpolitical intermediary and is prepared to channel most of its technical assistance through the United Nations, the International Bank, and similar agencies.[3]

The psychological reason why the international, nonpolitical approach is better than the national approach was strikingly brought home to me in the course of an assignment to the United Nations technical assistance program in Turkey. Each year hearings were conducted within the Turkish government to determine which departments would be allowed to request funds from the United Nations Technical Assistance Board. To my surprise, I was asked to preside over such a hearing in the Turkish Foreign Office, where sixty officials were presenting their case for funds. I demurred on the ground that I was not a member of their government. "Yes, you are," was the reply. "You are an official of the United Nations. Turkey is one of the owners of the United Nations. In effect, you are one of us." Thereafter, there was never any question in my mind as to whether the economic or the political approach was preferable. The psychology of peoples supplies an unmistakable answer.

6. Diplomacy should be forthright, not devious. Harold Nicholson, an experienced diplomat, once observed that effective diplomacy is a disagreeable business, for it involves plain talking. Thus, it is the opposite of the common diplomatic pattern of affability, good manners, even shyness, and a certain diffidence.

Our western nations, as James Reston reminds us,[4] are in danger of affecting a smoothness that is different from the speech of the American frontier. Instead of the "chirpy triviality" that has often characterized the meetings of the heads of states in recent times, we should face up to certain hard facts. Thus, the western nations need a confederation to match the Moscow-Peiping axis, which is spreading into southeast Asia, Africa, even Cuba. Since the last world war the democracies have been disintegrating their empires while the communists have been building theirs. In the last generation, for example, the French have given freedom and independence to some 40 million people and the British to about 600 million, while China and eastern Europe have allied themselves with the USSR.

With more plain talk, there would be less lip service paid to "interdependence" and more emphasis on how to secure a common market that includes both Britain and the United States, and how to form a political union in which mutual consultation would be the routine procedure instead of the exception. In terms of power vacuums, the moral equivalent of imperialism is a freed confederation of free nations that act as though they were a single government.

7. Finally, if peace and security are to be advanced in the world, national governments must be organized in such a way that they can speak responsibly and effectively to the outside world. This is one of the respects in which our own government needs repair. Since we do not have responsible political parties and a cabinet form of government, no foreign office in another nation can be sure that what is said today through diplomatic channels will be confirmed tomorrow in Congress. Such a situation might be tolerable if, as in 1790, we were a small, backwoods nation struggling for recognition. Today, we are still the most powerful nation and the leader of the free world; today, therefore, nothing short of responsible speaking will suffice.

REPAIRING STRUCTURAL WEAKNESSES

Nowadays a nation must always know what it is doing because a single serious error could cause irreparable destruction. Nothing in recent times has brought this truth home to the American public like the unfortunate U-2 incident of 1960, when an American reconnaissance plane was shot down over Soviet territory. This act was followed by confusing and often contradictory statements from highly placed officials in Washington, culminating in President Eisenhower's assertion that he stood behind the policy of sending observation planes over the USSR.

Senator Mike Mansfield of the Senate Foreign Relations Committee, who headed an investigation of the matter, publicly attributed subsequent diplomatic losses to this regrettable incident, which more than anything else seemed to point to faulty coordination within the government. The incident became a factor in the collapse of the summit meeting in Paris and the withdrawal of an invitation to the President to make an official visit to the USSR; the deterioration of relations with Japan; the embarrassment of allies providing military bases on the Soviet periphery; a sudden intensification of the danger of a shooting war; a strengthening of the cold war and of the position of hard-line communists opposed to peaceful accommodation with the West.

"The shocking disarray of departments, agencies and sub-agencies through which this nation tries to conduct the foreign relations and defense of the nation," said Senator Mansfield, "at best, borders on a national disgrace and, at worst, courts national disaster." The incident raised the question, "Who runs this Administration in the vital matters of foreign policy and defense?"[5] The solution, said Senator Jacob K. Javits, a member of President Eisenhower's own political party, is to "give the Secretary of State a power over national security as well as over the diplomatic activities."[6]

In these dangerous times no nation can afford a form of government where every four years time is taken off from vital matters of public policy for the sake of the circus of political conventions, the hoopla of a campaign, and, if the opposition wins, an abrupt change of faces and policies in Washington. During these periods there is a feeling of suspended animation in Washington and in foreign capitals because the old administration is loath to act. Then, after inauguration, the new administration must take time to settle down. This is not only a problem of government; any institution made up of plain mortals takes anywhere from six to twenty-four months to make its shakedown run, and the federal government, being infinitely larger and more complicated than most institutions, naturally takes longer.

As a people, we are sufficiently practical and resourceful to find a satisfactory solution to the problem of changing political administrations without weakening democratic popular control. But in fact, weak popular control is part of the trouble, for as things stand it is largely lacking in the party nominating conventions and in the functioning of the electoral college.

These governmental weaknesses are partly the reason that public opinion is frequently in advance of official public policy. People have not liked the barter of wheat to feed the hungry, for example, with diplomatic concessions extracted as a *quid pro quo* condition. If party leadership were more secure in its own position—as would be the case under a cabinet form of government where the mandate of leadership holds until a vote of lack of confidence or until the next general election—it would be easier to give charity in a charitable manner without fear of the shrill criticism of a minority and untainted by the dubious motivations of power politics. As it is, Congressmen seem to feel that they will be penalized for give-away policies and that to protect themselves politically they must convince the vocal minority that they are extracting the pound of flesh in the bargain.

Despite what may be supposed to the contrary, I believe that the same policies, attitudes, and proprieties that further harmonious relations between individuals apply equally to relations among nations. The reason is the same in both cases: the influence of moral law.

The greatest need for governmental reform in the United States is in the area of foreign policy. This has been true since the time of Woodrow Wilson. It is now urgent and must be put above partisan and personal considerations. In any attempt to strengthen the frame of government and the public service generally, therefore, let an objective be to make our foreign policy as decent and as courageous and responsible as the people instinctively think it should be. In thinking about this issue, let us keep open minds, realizing with

John K. Jessup that "the Constitution was not a universal document in the same sense as the Declaration [of Independence]. It was a *working document* for Americans, not for Laplanders or Chinese."[7]

As a final point, we must have a professional foreign service closely attuned to the values and belief systems of the common man. To produce a foreign service that is highly skilled and at the same time democratically oriented is a universal problem—in Britain, in France, and in the USSR as well as in our own country. Their behavior depending on factors of personality and attitude, officials who are highly placed in a nation's foreign service often hold in balance a decision between peace and war. According to the British view, which is based on principles of moral philosophy, the most important questions to be asked about a decision maker are, "What is his character? His sense of decency? His view of the fitness of things?" We do ourselves a disservice, I think, when we dismiss these factors lightly, as social scientists are inclined to do, lumping everything together and calling it the charismatic personality. We overlook the fact that the important thing is not charm; it is good judgment, survival judgment.

Moreover, our career men must have managerial ability. The Jackson committee, studying the machinery of policy decision making in the federal government, underscored this point in the comment that "too few State Department officials now possess the background and experience needed for executive tasks. Increasingly, the administration of foreign policy is 'big business,' which must be run by skillful administrators."[8]

INTERNATIONAL COMPETITION

The behavior of both free and communist nations indicates that the struggle for the minds and loyalties of the uncommitted nations seems to depend largely on economic measures, such as technical assistance, loans, and the offering of know-how, to get national economies launched toward higher planes of prosperity. How, then, answer the question of what will happen to our own standard of living if we help every nation to become a prospective competitor? Will there not come a time when they will outproduce and outsell us?

Tested principles of political economy provide an answer. First, we should not spend so much of our own substance in helping other nations that we precipitate internal crises at home, including periodic depressions and a heavy outflow of gold to other nations. Just where the cut-off point in expenditures should be is a matter of economic statesmanship and not political expediency.

Secondly, if we are to sustain large foreign investment programs abroad, we must make sure that our own economic system is in order and producing at a progressively higher level, so as to avoid lowering our own standard of living or courting inflation.

Thirdly, we must not neglect to provide adequately for our own social amenities, such as schools and roads and welfare services, which are part of a national standard of living quite as much as earned family income; in this area the problem in America is already serious.

Fourthly, funds for foreign economic development should be channeled as far as possible through the stream of private business and finance. Thus, they would become a productive resource of private enterprise relying on the repayment of capital and interest, instead of a public responsibility relying on the public treasury and ultimately on the taxpayer.

If all of these difficult issues can be properly dealt with, there remains the stubborn question: Do we want more competition from other nations? The first response is to ask what alternative presents itself. If the lesser-developed countries in Asia, Africa, and Latin America are not helped to keep up with the pace of the world, there will be unrest, violence, instability, possibly bloodshed, and radical solutions to problems that might have been peacefully met. Such an international climate is not conducive to the continued existence of our own system of freedom, limited government, and private enterprise.

Is there, finally, any reason why international competition is necessarily to be feared? The answer is a clear, "No." As nations develop to the point where they are themselves able to provide the minimum needed for a higher standard of living—including improved agriculture, transportation, and communication, plus the beginnings of industry and commerce, plus the means of attracting private investment funds from private earnings—an increasingly larger market appears for nations which, like the United States, are relatively more advanced in the fields of technology and of business and capital generally. If a so-called advanced nation is alert, therefore, it will take advantage of a constantly growing international market for commodities produced by technological means.

International competition also sometimes causes readjustments in the advanced nations that are to their benefit. Thus, when Britain lost much of her textile business she diverted her energies to the engineering field, producing capital goods and obtaining a higher margin of profit than the textile industry could offer under modern conditions. Because of the potential demand from countries where economic development is taking place and the relatively slow pace with which engineering and managerial skills proceed, it seems likely that the advanced countries can benefit for several generations. If, that is, they continue to progress in their own over-all skills and technologies, instead of standing still or slipping backward.

If competition is the lifeblood of domestic commerce, as I have tried to show, then it must equally be the lifeblood of international trade. Hence, the challenge is not so much external as it is internal: Can an advanced nation continue to progress fast enough to maintain its margin of competitive advantage? That is the problem, and it exists to some degree in any nation, irrespective of foreign competition. Indeed, such competition is useful as a spur to acumen and efficiency. If we have the wit to capitalize on our opportunities, therefore, the prospects are for a higher prosperity than has ever been dreamed of.

Nevertheless, there are two conditions in this prediction. The first is that as developing nations increasingly use their own natural resources for their own productive purposes, the percentage on which advanced nations may draw will be smaller than in the past, and the latter will have to husband their own resources better than in the past. This is the subject of the chapter that follows. The second condition is that advanced nations must avoid serious political mistakes that might cause developing nations later to exclude or discriminate against them, thus depriving them of a portion of the prosperity that comes from an enlarged international trade. These two conditions seem to stand out above most others in any survey of the future prospects for international peace and security.

Related to these major issues of foreign policy are several subsidiary ones.

When business goes international, for example, does it not tend to undermine a nation's antitrust laws? There is no simple answer. Outside the United States cartels and government trading companies are in common use, and it is hard for American companies to compete with this type of monopoly. Also, antitrust legislation is far less usual in other countries than in the United States.[9] These factors are distinctly adverse. On the other hand, the encouragement of international trade seems to have had surprisingly little effect on monopoly at home, despite an occasional cartel in which American companies have participated and despite an occasional deliberate weakening of the antitrust laws, as in agriculture, to allow American enterprise to compete in world trade on an equal footing with other nations. On the whole, the efficiency of American production has enabled us to hold our own in most fields.

At the same time, through international agencies such as the General Agreement concerning Tariffs and Trade (GATT), we have been able to persuade other nations to agree to conditions that are more equally competitive for all. If we want to retain competition at home there is no recourse but to redouble our efforts along this line. The problem is a striking illustration of the interdependence of foreign and domestic policy, for monopoly in foreign trade would sooner or later result in complete monopoly at home. One must be willing to pay a price for one's convictions.

In another area, when finance goes international, does it not succeed in evading all control? The answer is, "No," although the Nazis contended the opposite when they inveighed against international money-lenders. Like international trade, international finance also must have government in the center of the operation. The foreign office provides facilities, protects property, and even helps with negotiations that may be needed. In a sense, therefore, foreign investment depends on the efficiency of a nation's diplomacy and the protection afforded by its diplomats and armed forces.[10] Although the picture may be overdrawn, something of this sort will probably always be true, and is another reason for the United States to improve its governmental skills. If a degree of international control is needed, it will be forthcoming only if the general level of governmental operations is high.

In line with a policy to substitute international solutions for bilateral ones in international economics, a group of members of the United Nations has been demanding an international development authority to act as banker for the development of whole economies, not merely those parts where property can be mortgaged as security and the program pays for itself out of earned revenues. It is argued that all existing international agencies are of this conventional type, that the proposed corporation would be owned and controlled by its members, each of which would subscribe capital according to its resources and would automatically increase its contribution as its economy became more prosperous.

This is a "hot" issue that should be settled on the basis of economic principles and not political expediency. On principle, any concert of nations ought to be free to form such a development corporation if it wishes, taking its own risks and its own losses. It is equally true, however, that loans based solely on the good faith and credit of a nation involve a high risk of failure. With enough of these failures the whole house of cards could come tumbling down, dealing a severe blow to similar but sounder ventures in the same area. From a political economy viewpoint, caution might be expressed, therefore, on the ground that unsecured loans are usually a doubtful proposition, especially when made to inexperienced and possibly transitory governments.

COEXISTENCE

The remaining problems to be dealt with here are mainly political and governmental, although I defy anyone to draw a sharp line between what is political and what is economic.

Should we deal only with those nations whose political convictions are in harmony with our own? I would say, "No," for a number of reasons. The first grows out of experience with labor relations practice: even in a seemingly hopeless situation, a feasible solution often appears more readily than anyone involved in the controversy thought possible. From my point of view, international conflicts are only more of the same, but at a higher level. In addition, from a philosophical standpoint it is always better to know what your rival is doing and thinking than to imagine these things; we are all given to hallucinations and exaggerations.

The principle reason that formal relations should be universal irrespective of political ideologies, however, is that when right and wrong confront each other across a table, the truth almost always seems eventually to emerge, not so much because of the relative strength of the adversaries as because of their sense of justice. In industrial relations, the more sensible negotiators almost invariably tone down and discipline their more unreasonable colleagues, giving the lie to the Marxist doctrine that divisions are always according to class lines.

Some pietistic people seem to think that when good and bad confront each other, the exposure of the good to evil invariably results in a loss of moral standards. My observation is the reverse: if the cause is just, those who favor it usually have more influence on the outcome than those who are misguided. It is essential, of course —especially in coexistence diplomacy—that nations, like individuals, also should be constantly on guard to avoid an appearance of stiff-necked, holier-than-thou omniscience.

Morality is a matter of principle, not of persons or of nations. Most diplomacy ends in compromise. Such compromise, however, is not a matter of giving up a little of the good for a corresponding amount of what is less sound. Rather, in diplomacy, the proper compromise is mutual accommodation on the basis of sound principle. Since in secular affairs the ultimate test of principle is what is best for people, the parties to a negotiation should never despair of eventual success. Even in nations that are aggressively nationalistic, there is a feeling for human rights and sensibilities which progressively converts the gross manifestations of nationalism into a common humanitarianism.

Finally, refusal to deal formally with ostracized nations invariably causes them to behave in an uncivilized and irresponsible manner, thus further encouraging international outlawry. If the desire is to avoid war and international insecurity, therefore, the most useful policy is to emphasize higher goals instead of merely calling names, to appeal to the decent sensibilities of public opinion instead of making faces. To be sure, such an approach requires a nobility of character on the part of men acting with confidence and sincerity. But an honest search for the truth is what political economy is all about.

WORLD GOVERNMENT

How is the need for a growing decentralization at the national level, which was propounded in an earlier chapter, to be reconciled with the need for stronger international controls, such as a strengthened United Nations or even some kind of world government?

There is no question but that a policy of decentralization causes people to be more responsible and more willing and able to govern themselves; to take more pride in their work; and to be better able to achieve individual distinctiveness, cultural development, and eventual happiness. At the same time, however, there is what Mary Parker Follett called "the law of the situation." In international relations today, the law of the situation holds that as the community becomes larger, so that at last it is international, society must provide the same sort of understandings, laws, and enforcement programs as are necessary in the local community and the nation-state. By this means is peaceful settlement substituted for violence. Not even an extreme isolationist would doubt the need to maintain law and order at the international level.

As in so many areas of political economy, therefore, here also are two opposing principles that must be reconciled, for neither can be disposed of simply because it appears to contradict the other. Nations want freedom, but they also want security. Technological developments in armaments, in transportation, and in communications around the world must be reckoned with. Hence, the law of the situation requires a continued development of international law, an international police force, and the other necessities of international government, to the point where the safety of nations, under law, can be assured.

Faced with this situation, some experts have concluded that the only workable solution is for nations to renounce a portion of their national sovereignty for the sake of a supranational world government. At the opposite extreme, other experts believe that the best protection, for the United States at least, is to withdraw from the world, follow our own way of life, and raise the barriers of defense as high as need be irrespective of cost—in other words, we should create a "garrison state."

The proper course lies somewhere between these two extremes. We should think in terms of plural loyalties, one of which is to international order and a corresponding international citizenship. There is nothing revolutionary about such a course, since modern man already has many loyalties—to his family, his club, his town, his state, and his nation. The question of a possible conflict among so many loyalties seldom arises because an over-all loyalty is to values, to approved moral standards supported by the many institutions that claim the loyalty of the citizen. In this series, loyalty to an international entity created to preserve international law and order is merely one more loyalty that the average individual is capable of cherishing.

Once that intellectual step has been taken, the practical questions are these: How complete shall be the system of international law? How large a police force is required and what relation shall it bear to national police forces? To what degree shall an international agency be allowed to legislate on problems that cut across national boundaries? What happens when the laws of one jurisdiction conflict with those of a lesser one?

Similar problems have already been solved in countless cases in the past, in the United States with its vast territory and local jealousies, in the British Commonwealth of Nations, in the Roman Empire and, if one wants to go back that far, in the Amphictyonic League of Greek city-states before the Christian era. The solutions are not easy, of course, and perfection is unlikely to be attained, but logic and necessity combine to urge the venture.

If the problem of international disorganization could be solved so that all nations, large and small alike, could feel safer, the possibilities of experimentation at the national level are staggering to the imagination. To take just one example, if the vast sums of money now needed for defense in all the great nations of the world, and some that are not so great, were diverted into peacetime activities, they would change the face of life on the face of the globe.

In summary, then, a viable foreign policy for the United States should be based on the principles of political economy. The safest guides are national self-development, the rule of moral law instead of power politics, the use of economic assistance through international agencies instead of as a tool of national power politics, the granting of loans and technical assistance instead of outright gifts and subsidies with strings attached, the employment of plain speech in diplomacy, the strengthening of the governmental process to make national self-development more effective, the recruitment of a professional foreign service attuned to the values and belief systems of the common man, reliance on free international competition, the further development of international credit agencies, the encouragement of coexistence and face-to-face relations among all nations, unification of the free nations of the world in a single economic and political community, and the further development of a world government operating under universal law and backed by adequate enforcement machinery.

NINE

HUSBANDING RESOURCES

There is a striking resemblance between a woman's charms and a nation's resources. In both cases, how long they last and the intensity with which they glow seem to depend in large part on the steadfastness with which they are admired. Admiration evokes response. Neglect seems to cause a fading of the inner light. If we want a good society in America, therefore, we must regard our natural resources—including people—as a good husband does the creature of his admiration and desire.

To compare woman's charms and natural resources is more than poetic fancy; it also draws attention to a basic problem of political economy: "Instead of living with the land, man insists on dominating it, shaping both the land and all his co-heirs . . . to his own selfish, short-sighted ideas."[1] If man works and lives with the land in accordance with the universal principles of ecology, the land prospers, and we enjoy the good life; but when in his attempt to dominate his environment, man defies the laws of natural balance, the land is impoverished, and so is he.

A SACRED TRUST

There is a chain of principles that starts in chemistry and physics and proceeds through zoology and ecology to political economy. Scholars in all of these fields recognize that the conservation of energy, the balance in nature, and the reciprocal nature of stimulus and response constitute basic balances in the universe in a continuous chain of principle binding the inanimate and the living together.

America's new political economy also recognizes these interrelationships; hence, one of its main emphases is on conservation. The use of natural resources is a trust, not merely alienation, as man sometimes recklessly assumes. If man seeks happiness, he cannot think only of himself. Nor, try as he may, can he afford to live for the moment—as we Americans have unashamedly done for a hundred years and more—for once the fleeting moment is over the celebrant wakes up with an aching head. If capitalism were ever to be pushed into limbo, therefore, I believe it would be due more to our reckless waste of resources than to any mistaken attachment to the private enterprise system.

Disagreement as to values and as to the appropriate means of attaining to them is natural, but to defy nature is asking for trouble. Marxist ideology is rejected in democratic nations as arrant nonsense, but if the communists were to treat their natural resources as a social trust while we continued to waste ours, I should expect their system eventually to prevail and ours to fail.

It would not be the qualities of the two systems that would determine the outcome, but a failure on our part to realize that resource husbandry is a universal principle that man defies only at his peril. Indeed, the attitude of a people toward their resources is far more determinative of national survival than their beliefs as to whether profits should be individual or social, or whether management should be predominantly private or public.

Conventional economic theory has generally treated resources as merely one of the factors of production, distribution, and consumption. This view is too narrow, and if pushed far enough, could even lead to the "maximization" of resources, in which case they would be used up or wasted as fast as possible. But resources often cannot be replenished; once wasted, the loss is final. Places of natural beauty also are to be cherished as an aspect of the good life, to be increasingly admired as they grow along with the nation.

Under the influence of an ideology that considers resources as lifeless digits, we have brought ourselves to a dangerous pass with respect to the land and its natural riches, and the beauty of our country deteriorates every year. In the political economy approach, resources are central, and the long view replaces the short one. By this means we could move swiftly to redress the wrongs caused by our callowness, and then effectively organize our energies to make America as beautiful and almost as rich as she once was.

A central question in political economy is, "What does a nation do with its resources?" If there are few natural resources, as in England and Sweden, then the nation must rely on the skills of its people for a high standard of living. Or, if there is an abundance of both physical and human resources, as in the United States and the USSR, then the consideration is two-fold: First, if physical resources are wasted, as they have been in the United States, but the level of economic skills is high, then weakness in the physical area will eventually cause an imbalance that will hamper a rising standard of living. Secondly, if the wastage is due to faults of national character—such as excessive materialism and shortsighted selfishness— then the consequences affect not only the standard of living but also the skill quotient of the people.

We Americans today are vulnerable on both scores. An abundance of physical resources in our early history caused a profligate use of them, and this is now a habit. In addition, major industry has been so slow to develop a social conscience regarding the use of resources that it is doubtful whether a century of neglect can be overcome in the time left to us. Few realize the seriousness of our peril. We are too firmly convinced by our own propaganda that even if we do exhaust our resources, we will find substitutes that are even better.

Nevertheless, the pie-in-the-sky cult is beginning to show signs of worry. Some resources may be replaced, but not soil, water, and minerals. And when we do come up with substitutes, how can we be sure that nature's intricate balances will be respected and that the results of miscalculation may not move in a wide arc, even to the point of no return?

In what follows I propose to discuss four main questions: What physical resources have we left? What should be our conservation objective? What are the elements of a workable conservation program? What about our human resources? Underlying these issues is the problem of how to buttress our values as a people.

TAKING STOCK FOR THE MORROW

If population continues to explode the world over while resources wane, at the very least standards of living will be reduced, and at the worst there will be hardship and even starvation. In the United States the problem is an eventual shortage of resources even if the rate of population growth turns out to be no greater than anticipated. Hence, the immediate need is to face realities and develop a constructive program several times more effective than anything we have had in the past.

The conservation movement in the United States began in 1873, when scientific men protested against the wastage of resources and the Forestry Bureau was created in the federal government. Since then there has been some progress, owing to the valiant efforts of men like Gifford Pinchot, and there are now several federal agencies in conservation. Nevertheless, after almost ninety years, Americans lack an active realization of the need for conservation. David Cushman Coyle, writing in 1936, was startlingly prophetic when he warned that "we have about twenty years, in which the fate of American civilization will be decided. The road forks here—the steep and narrow path into the land of plenty, and the broad and easy highway down which so many splendid empires of the past have marched with flying colors to destruction." Our main problems, he said, are Mud, Dust, Water, Forests, Animals, Bugs, Land, Power, Metals, Disease, and Human Erosion.[2]

Many Americans emotionally recoil before the unpleasant facts of wasting resources. Their reaction is that of a child reminded by a parent that he is getting too close to the limits of his allowance. Nevertheless, we must face up to the facts. Here is the story in a few broad strokes:

The nation's greatest conservation problem is water, the most priceless natural resource. Nowhere else, except possibly in forestry or in soil erosion, is the whole sorry picture of negligent waste laid so bare. What follows is taken from brief newspaper accounts during a relatively short period in 1960, when conservationists were unusually active:

By 1975, with a population of 235 million people, the United States will be using 90 percent of its maximum water supply, assuming there is no further deterioration of the situation between now and then.

Water shortages have already appeared. Even in 1957, 1000 communities in 47 states had been forced to restrict the use of water. To provide adequately for America's water needs over the next 20 years would require an outlay of $54 billion.

The source of most of our difficulty is anti-social behavior. Water pollution is a national disgrace. "It is tragic," notes one expert, "for the world's richest nation to foul its own nest, limit its own growth, and threaten the health of the people."

The Public Health Service reports that sewage pollution control in our rivers, lakes, and salt water is so far out of control that 6000 new municipal sewage treatment plants are needed to catch up; it would require an annual expenditure of $600 million to meet the need by 1965.

The United States Public Health Service estimates further that it would take $10.6 billion just to clean the nation's streams during the next ten years.

The side-effects of technology are part of the problem. Some synthetic chemicals, such as household detergents, apparently cannot be destroyed. Hence, after passing unchanged through waste-treatment plants to water courses, and then unchanged through water-treatment plants to consumers, the effects of contamination may show up 20 or 30 years later in an unsafe condition. The problem is enormously aggravated by the creation of radio-active wastes from atomic installations.

On the brighter side:

Scientists have determined that more than six times as much water flows across the United States in the atmosphere than is carried by all the country's major rivers, and 99 percent of this is thought to be condensable under proper conditions.

Several years ago the Department of the Interior started half a dozen pilot plants to convert sea water into potable water, and although this is an expensive process, the first of these plants started operation on an experimental basis early in 1961.

In 1960, a leading member of the majority party in Congress proposed the expenditure of $17.5 billion on a planned basis over a ten-year period to meet the nation's depletion needs. "In view of what is at stake, such an expenditure for resources and conservation would not be excessive. . . . [our] survival as a first-class nation may be as much dependent upon what we do with our resources as what we do about our military defenses."[3]

There are many *if's* in what obviously needs to be done. A major one is whether public opinion, which is generally regarded as indifferent, can be sufficiently aroused to the point of developing a social conscience in the matter of resources. A second is whether the government can be geared to tackle the planning, organizational, administrative, and especially the financial problems that inhere in any multibillion-dollar program.

Why do so many good Americans continue to dump tin cans and other rubbish into beautiful streams? Why do saw mills and other industrial plants continue to pollute streams, disfiguring their banks and destroying fish life? Why do motorists discard trash along the highways? Why do they seem to lack pride and concern for natural beauty and cleanliness? I suppose such behavior is a combination of greed, a low standard of aesthetic values, and the mistaken notion that freedom is license. This lack of consideration for others is the aspect of American life that disturbs thinking people most.

We are not likely to correct our behavior and our values until we realize that in addition to other factors, economics is a nation's total resources and its way of life. What a paradox that water and air—the very elements that traditional economics considered free and hence of no economic worth—are now the areas in which, because of public apathy and neglect, we must spend huge sums, raised from taxpayers who already are grumbling. It takes no clairvoyance to foresee that the social budget of government for resources, education, and similar programs is going to become much more troublesome than all the budgets of industry combined.

The story of water shows almost the whole picture of resource neglect because the wastage of other resources is much the same and stems from the same distorted social attitudes and governmental ineptitudes.

It was America's trees and forests that originally set her off from other less favored areas of the world. But look at what has happened: The Great Lakes region was cut over long ago, and today, at the end of the cycle, the Douglas firs of the Pacific Northwest are falling before the chain saw. Trees are being felled along streets and highways all over the country to create wider ways for more automobiles and greater speed. The natural beauty of America east of the Mississippi, where major highways abound, remains only in hinterland areas, and even these are dwindling.

"World Shortage of Timber Feared," announced a recent newspaper headline. The story is of how 2,000 foresters, under the sponsorship of the United Nations Food and Agriculture Organization, met in Seattle. The representative of India struck the keynote of the conference when he stated that "a dynamic new approach is needed." Then the head of our own Forest Service warned that the constant diversion of forest lands to other purposes in the United States threatened to wipe out a third of this nation's commercial timber crop by the end of the century. By that time also, the demand for lumber would be double the present requirement.[4]

Reforestation as a remedy is nowhere near adequate. It was started too late to avoid serious shortages in the near future; the end of our prime timber resources is in sight; already, major research is focused on finding substitutes for wood; sawmills cut logs ten inches in diameter and smaller. Relative to population, our timber resources have been dissipated, and even if no additional trees were cut, it would take generations to replace only a portion of the forests we once had. We are poorer than we were, the nation is less beautiful, and much of the wastage need never have occurred at all. One begins to wonder whether even a state monopoly of tree-cutting, as is found in Germany, Switzerland, and other European nations, might not be better than this.

The worst of it is that only recently have we begun to realize that, as in political economy, the basic law of resources is their interrelatedness and their corresponding need to remain in balance. To skin off the trees from the hillsides causes rain and melting snow to flood the valleys, washing the land away from farms and dumping it into the sea. To use rivers to carry away sewage and industrial wastes ruins the food and other wealth that otherwise would be harvested in the ocean, thus damaging another source of sustenance for a growing population. This last factor is underscored in an article reporting that the sea is limited as a source of food, although we have repeatedly been assured that when the soil gives out we need merely farm the oceans for food. The difficulty is that "the ocean alone cannot possibly free us from the haunting specter of diminishing means unless we exploit it with far more forethought and restraint than we have shown in appropriating the produce of the land."[5] The principle is the same.

The vicious circle continues to widen. As population increases, for example, the acreage devoted to municipal parks, national playgrounds, and wilderness preserves should be increased proportionately. Instead, says a newspaper headline, "Loss of Park Land Called Alarming." Because of the seemingly endless encroachments by highways, industry, and housing on parks and open lands in recent years, there was a loss of $9 million in properties devoted to recreation and conservation; most of it was in large cities.[6] As might be expected, the greatest loss is due to the incursions of highways, the preserve of one of our most effective pressure groups.

Our water, timber, and park resources are out of balance. How about soil, sometimes considered a nation's basic resource? We have rich lands, especially in the middle of the country, and they are among the most fertile in the world. But there is the erosion of increasingly frequent floods; and in addition, millions of acres in the West are dry, suitable only for grazing; through general abuse and through misuse of the plow, they have been impoverished by high seasonal winds that carry the dust of farms across the nation.

Out of almost 2 billion acres of land surface in the nation, a little over half, or 1.1 billion acres, is in farms, and something less than half of this, or 409 million acres, is available for crops. Of the total cropland, however, only 84 per cent, or 345 million acres, is considered profitable, and of this, *only 100 million acres are completely safe from soil erosion.* In terms of what the nation started with, soil also is a dwindling resource.

If population continues to increase at the anticipated rate and more is not done to conserve our soil resource, present farm surpluses are likely to be converted into deficiencies. Fortunately, due to a combination of informed public opinion and energetic public programs, such as those of the federal Soil Conservation Service, the prospect for land conservation is more promising than for conservation in other areas.

Like the soil, minerals also are irreplaceable, and here the pinch is likely to be felt most. It has already been suggested that as less developed nations establish their own industries, they will use more of their prime resources themselves instead of selling them, as in the past, to more advanced nations. Hence, to use a homely phrase often heard in farming communities, "I guess we'll just have to make do with what we've got."

The United States has less than 10 per cent of its need for high-grade manganese; has less than 1 per cent and consumes 50 per cent of the world supply of nickel; produces almost no chromium, but uses about a third of the world supply; has exhausted its high-grade bauxite, from which aluminum is derived; is increasingly dependent on foreign imports for copper, lead, and zinc; uses about half of the world supply of tin, all of which is imported; and produces sulphur at increasing cost because it is extracted from low-grade ore. Only with regard to tungsten, molybdenum, vanadium, boron, magnesium, and titanium are we still in a favorable position so far as sources of supply are concerned.[7]

In the past, America was known as a nation where the supply of oil was apparently inexhaustible. The prospect now is that fairly soon we must search for substitutes or rely on increasingly larger imports. The production of petroleum in this country has not met demand since 1947. By 1955, half the oil and gasoline *ever* produced in the United States *had been consumed during the preceding fifteen years*. It is estimated that by 1975, the domestic use of oil and natural gas will be twice what it was in 1950, when roughly 15 per cent of our total need was supplied by imports. Domestic supplies are either running out or are becoming more expensive to produce, despite deeper drilling, the exploitation of offshore sources, and intensified prospecting and research.[8]

Where coal is concerned, our reserves are fortunately large, despite the fact that half of all the coal *ever* used in the United States has been consumed since 1920. Although, like iron and other minerals, most coal deposits are increasingly costly to mine, the supply seems to be adequate for a long time to come, especially if new and more efficient methods of extraction and conversion are discovered.

There remains, of course, atomic fission as a source of energy and power, the genie of a future technology. This is the ace in the hole that causes many Americans who might otherwise be sobered by the prospect of dwindling resources to be optimistic. The future of this source of energy, however, depends not only on technological developments but also on resolving the business-government relations that are involved in the exploitation of this stupendous discovery.

A POSITIVE PROGRAM

In the course of service as a member of a rural state legislature, I learned with something of a shock that efforts to pass conservation legislation are frequently met with the cry of "socialism!" Although this defense is manufactured by powerful pressure groups such as absentee paper and pulp companies, farmer legislators are the first to put their heads in the noose. A typical response to a conservation proposal is that, "If I choose to cut *all* the timber off my farm, that's my business; this is a free country; we don't want socialism."

So staunch an independence is a national asset; the thing that causes heartache to anyone with a social conscience is the short-sightedness of what is sometimes done in consequence. Skinned-off land grows up to brush and berry bushes. An on-going asset of the farm disappears, and the living from it is reduced. The soil no longer holds water; and hence, it erodes and damages surrounding farm lands and springs. The town loses some of its tax revenue. As the farm becomes impoverished, people lose their sense of property and take jobs in the marginal industries that move into decimated farming areas. And America is both physically and spiritually the poorer.

If it is capitalistic to waste resources and socialistic to provide for the future, then socialism must have a higher ethic than capitalism. But this is a shallow interpretation of what is involved. There is needed a grasp of principle based on cause-and-effect relationships, proper values, and a long view of the future. Accordingly, if a free people wishes to remain free they must develop a social conscience that will assure better, not worse, conditions for their heirs. Failing this, government has not only a right but a duty to intervene, because survival and the American dream of a better way of life are inescapably involved. No man is free to destroy his children's opportunities.

A program to raise conservation to a central place in political economy would include the following:

Children in the earliest grades, as future producer-citizens, should be made vividly aware of ecology, the relation between resources and the possibilities of a better life. Students should be taught, by visual and other means, to recognize the web of nature that unites soil, plants, animals, and human beings—the physical bases of wealth. This type of instruction should be continued through the colleges and universities, so that the relation is seen between ecology, geography, economics, philosophy, and the biological sciences. There is no need deliberately to try to give students a deep love for nature; with half a chance, they would discover it for themselves. They would also develop a social conscience by learning with the biologist in his laboratory that the beginning and end of all social adaptation is survival.[9]

An informed citizenry, both intellectually and aesthetically attuned to nature, would then be the means of constructively molding public opinion in favor of conservation. Such a citizenry, working through many institutions—the church, recreation groups, conservationists, outdoor sports clubs, service clubs, youth organizations such as the Boy Scouts and the Camp Fire Girls—would create a broad base of opinion that might quickly remove the cataract of mercenary outlook that produces social myopia in conservation.

The third step is to introduce certain principles into legislation at the local, state, and national levels. Thus, the heedless exploitation of natural resources should be outlawed. Waste should be penalized. For every tree cut, two should be planted. The projected life of a resource should be rationed out for a hundred years or more.

Most important of all, certain incentives should be specified in legislation to cause reckless businessmen to *want* to conserve resources and to use them efficiently, instead of following the more usual urge to "get while the getting's good; the future can take care of itself." Thus, there are real possibilities in enlightened tax laws. At present, most communities seem mainly interested in taxing where the money can be most easily extracted. I know from personal experience, for example, that the more you reforest, the more you are taxed; the more you dissipate your timber resources, the greater are your chances of reducing your tax bill. A policy far more beneficial to the long-term interests of the community would be a tax program that rewards investment in the future, that takes immediate sacrifice and abstinence into account. Like the sponsors of the group called Resources for the Future, Inc., the real patriots in this country are those who subscribe wholeheartedly to our sixth objective of political economy: the national heritage as a sacred trust. Its enemies are those who cynically raise the cry of socialism against any attempt to prevent them from wasting the nation's birthright.

A major problem of a conservation program is where to get the additional tax revenues needed to rectify generations of resource neglect. The USSR simply takes the cost of resource development and even of cultural activities out of the earnings of state-owned industries. We, however, must think twice before we add billions of dollars to our governmental expenditures, desirable and necessary as the objectives may be. This could be the hardest test of capitalism during the next fifty years. Billions of dollars are needed for conservation, for highways, for schools, for recreation, for health. Where is the money coming from?

To rectify errors in resource conservation it might be possible to create something like a working fund, amounting to, say, $50 billion, with a tenth of the total to be appropriated each year. There should then be a ten-year plan, including carefully worked out priorities, and every item on it should be accomplished on schedule. If Congress felt that public opinion was behind it, such a program would be feasible.

From a practical political standpoint, however, the chances of securing $50 billion are small unless we can pare defense expenditures to make up the difference. The need of the USSR to develop its own resources is infinitely greater than ours, and it is unlikely that they are dragging their feet. Their leaders are apparently still convinced that capitalism will break down of its own internal weaknesses. If we could provide the money needed for conservation it might be an additional form of insurance against the weaknesses that the Soviets are counting on.

With a broad base of education and enlightened pressure-group activity, followed by a revised tax policy, the crowning step in a program of resource husbandry would be a governmental organization to coordinate and dramatize the execution of wise conservation policies. "Democrats Urge Resources Unit," announced a headline in 1960. A group of Westerners favored the creation of a Council of Natural Resources Advisers in the Office of the President, as well as a regional agency in the Pacific Northwest to function like the Tennessee Valley Authority.[10] Laudable as these objectives may be, the first proposal is less than adequate. It would be more to the point if the Department of the Interior were to be converted into a full-fledged department of conservation and public works, as Harold Ickes once recommended. We have tinkered with the problem of conservation long enough and now need something more than study and advice.

The immediate objections to a department of conservation, of course, are that the Department of Agriculture would fight it for fear of losing some of its own jurisdiction; the Corps of Engineers and the Reclamation Service could never be made to work together; pressure groups would raise the objection of socialism. I believe there are convincing answers to all of these arguments, and in the final part of this book, which deals with the reform of the federal government, I shall try to say something constructive on these issues of organization.

At the same time that plans, financing, and organization are being developed, there should also be created at all levels of government commissions of citizens having high standards of aesthetic appreciation, whose job would be to approve or disapprove the plans of bulldozing agencies everywhere—especially highway departments. From firsthand, painful experience I sometimes think every highway engineer is equipped with horns, cloven hoofs, and a forked tail, and gets his chief enjoyment from cutting down trees and straightening secondary roads that once were delightfully winding. If the average American's sense of the fitting and the beautiful is as low as that of the average road builder, with his lethal toys, then I despair of the future beauty of this country.

It is time an aroused citizenry spoke up in condemnation of the depredations that are everywhere taking place in the name of progress. As if progress could ever be claimed when the result is to degrade nature and the people's appreciation of what is seeming and beautiful. The shallowness of our mercenary souls is written all too clearly in the trail of the bulldozers and the chain saws as they desecrate this lovely country of ours.

But people will change; perhaps they already have. Why otherwise would the newspapers find newsworthy, articles such as those I have reported, and why would a conference on stream pollution be good headline material for more than a week? Perhaps we are awakening from our mercenary nightmare and are beginning to develop a national conscience. Probably it is not to be wondered that it took so long. Athens, for example, did not reach its intellectual peak until it was faced with decline. Many American business corporations that started as pioneers, only to become somnolent with success, have recently bestirred themselves and entered on a fresh period of vitality. Arnold Toynbee's theories of history and more recently those of Heilbroner would lead us to expect some such apathy until the challenge of survival becomes sufficiently acute to underscore the need for a better public spirit.

It is a naïve psychological assumption from the very start to expect businessmen to husband resources solely from considerations of self-interest. There are too many other motives involved in the nature of man. It seems more reasonable to expect self-interest to be combined with a larger share of public interest, and all reinforced by an aroused public opinion and a government in Washington that means business. Then there is a good chance that the job will be done.

When we have governments willing to enforce zoning codes, city plans, and park and recreation ordinances, as some now do, and when we become sufficiently adult to create effective planning commissions to make our cities and countryside more beautiful, there will be a change in the face of America. One has merely to recall what a difference it makes when highway departments plant trees along rights-of-way where formerly there were billboards and the gravel pits that these same highwaymen had dug.

In our youthful grubbing for money we have tolerated ugliness and degradation in our cities and along our highways. I think we are about ready to revolt. We seem again to have caught sight of the American Dream. Our country will be in business for a long time, and I think we are going to see to it that its beauty is restored.

PUBLIC PERSONS

Of all the resources of America, we have been discussing those that are material and physical. But people also are resources, and public-spirited people—those whom in a previous chapter I have called public persons—are our greatest human resource of all.

A public person is one who cherishes what is best in both individualistic voluntarism and collectivistic altruism. His higher ethic is the public interest. When the number of such persons increases, the nation is secure. When they decline, the nation is threatened with division and self-destruction.

Public persons come from all kinds of environments, from the poorest to the wealthiest, from the least known to that of the philosopher-statesman. What they all have in common is the ability to put the public interest above self-interest; a respect for all men of all conditions everywhere; and a reverence for the good, the true, and the beautiful.

The public person also realizes that to earn the right to govern, one must first learn to govern oneself. This does not simply mean— as was assumed during the Robber Baron era—using one's skills to think up money-making ideas and then carrying them through as successful executives are supposed to do. Such skills are necessary, but taken alone they do not qualify a man for the prime rank of public person.

To govern oneself is to organize oneself, to coalesce personal ambition and social duty toward a single all-embracing goal. Such a man has a balanced personality; he is psychically healthy; he is thoughtful and sensitive as well as outgoing and socially effective.

The first principle of self-government is the need to do as much as possible for oneself, since where one fails, others must take over. Self-government is strongest where people strive toward self-reliance and voluntary cooperation, a combination that produces individual freedom and institutional vitality. Where apathy is widespread, on the other hand, elites will appear to fill the vacuum. This is the clear and present danger in socialism, the corporate state, and advanced capitalism—indeed, in any system that does not continually encourage initiative and self-reliance.

Hence, a test of a public person is the degree to which he stresses voluntarism. Does he work for the public good or does he acquiesce in adding responsibilities to government? Is he strongly motivated by the human values of an enterprise, even if they are less clear than when institutions were smaller and face-to-face relationships more common? If an individual lacks this strong ethic, he falls back into apathy and finally becomes a collectivist, whether he knows it or not.

The public person also recognizes the dangers of a form of public assistance that makes people less able to govern themselves. Many aspects of a welfare-state program run this danger and, hence, are shortsighted and self-defeating. Except in cases of obvious helplessness, public assistance is not a right, and should be offered only as a fillip to the individual's urge to direct his own destiny. Otherwise, there is the danger of malingering, of sponging off the public treasury, so that many people will never know what it is to work. These hazards have already appeared in connection with both the public assistance and the unemployment compensation programs.

If instead of maintaining thousands of people on public assistance and unemployment compensation rolls, we were to organize work programs designed to employ those who are able to work, we could improve the natural beauty of America; and in the long run, the cost to the taxpayer would be less than the present cost of supporting those who abuse the right to public assistance.

The Civilian Conservation Corps (CCC) of the New Deal is a model of what might be done. Young men who are unemployed or who have left school and cannot find work might be given a choice of worthwhile public improvement programs designed to clean our streams, plant trees, provide cover for ugly gravel pits along main highways, maintain public parks, and engage in many other activities that would improve the face of America. For young men not qualified for military service, such work might be a substitute, and it would also take up some of the slack during recessions. This kind of program would be productive even in a strictly economic sense, as evidenced by the thousands of acres of timber that were available in the South during World War II because CCC boys had planted the trees early in the days of the 1929 depression.

A conservation program takes imaginative leadership, and I think America would welcome it. We *want* our face lifted. We do not *like* to see eighteen people in one family on public assistance when most of them are able to work. It is senseless for 6 million people to be idle during a recession when there is so much work to be done in the resource field. How much more useful than having women follow modern mechanical streetsweepers around with whisk broom and dustpan, as I have seen them do in Moscow, so as to be able to boast that there is no unemployment under communism.

If this discussion seems to have strayed from the subject of the public person, this is not wholly unintended. The public person is altruistically motivated toward human beings, but he is also hardheaded and principled with regard to the larger interest, in the matter of policies that affect our public life as a nation. From this point of view, human excellence is a prime national resource. Labor is not a commodity, but the ability of the working man and woman is a national resource. Moreover, every man and woman in the nation is capable of becoming a public person in some degree.

We could use a healthy increase in that tribe called by H. G. Wells the learned-priestly type,[11] a type that includes all men of vision, teachers, and men of the cloth; all professional people, such as doctors; all government officials who are patriotically motivated; and that vast new group in society that we call managers and administrators. In other words, the learned-priestly type includes all who put ideas, knowledge, and service for humanity first in their attention and who find their satisfactions in life in this kind of work. Work based on universal values may even become an end in itself, so gratifying is it in the mind of the inventor, the scientist, the author, the painter, the government official, the professional man. These people work for the love of their work and its benefit to the public good more than for incidental rewards such as money, approval, prestige, and the like.

These dedicated people are the happiest in society and are most to be envied. It is from among them that our public persons are largely drawn. The goal, however, should be to make *every* person a public person to the limit of his capabilities. If this group constitutes an elite, it is one that can do no harm to our democratic values and our American way of life. For it is not an elite based on skill or birth but on values and work; hence, it is universal and includes no vestige of privilege or domination. I believe that a policy of this kind can be realized and that in time it might even come to embrace political faiths, such as communism, that are presently elitist in the objectionable sense.

Success will not come, however, unless we strengthen our values and make them operational. We should *want* to plant trees on barren hillsides, not only because erosion lowers a nation's standard of living, but also because we admire beauty. For a love of beauty also is a national resource, even if it does receive precious little space in a modern treatise on economics. To improve the average American's taste for beauty and the arts would help to make us a well-rounded people; would lead us to regard our national heritage as a sacred trust; to adhere to high personal standards; and to insist on governments that are more ethical than has sometimes been the case in recent years, more just, and more effective in the public interest. The conservation of values such as these, though considered a relatively minor aspect of economic wealth, must nevertheless occupy a central place in the new political economy. Hence, if what we seek is balance and high standards, we must move energetically to repair our areas of neglect.

PART III

THE NEED FOR GOVERNMENTAL REFORM

TEN

THE CHANGED ATTITUDE

Something had to give, and as so often happens, it turned out to be prejudice, the businessman's prejudice toward government. It is impossible to tell the exact time the change occurred. It has been gradual, but there is no doubt now that it is real.

Recently, a group of young business executives, enrolled in one of the nation's largest executive development programs, was asked, "How would you rate the various institutions in the United States according to their power?" The almost unanimous answer was that government occupies the number-one role.

This reply came to the members of the course themselves as a complete surprise because before that, relying on prejudice and ingrained attitudes, they had assumed the most powerful institutions to be business, the economic system, even the company for which they worked. They had been conditioned in business to think that economic activity comes first and that government is their enemy, or is to be disparaged as cumbersome, inefficient, and even corrupt.

Partly by the use of a kind of shock method, the leaders of the course had given its members a different approach to government. As a result, their individual and collective attitudes changed perceptibly. "Why isn't government better?" they asked themselves. "What can we do to improve it?" Then, according to those who watched this process, these young executives began to think deeply—perhaps for the first time—about social responsibilities. They began to think conceptually, seeing society as a whole instead of segmentally as bureaucrats everywhere do if left to their own devices. The new approach enabled these men to "get outside of their own hides," as the leaders of the course expressed it, and to think of society and their place in it as a whole.

When the metamorphosis was complete these men had acquired a wholly new attitude, and if it should become more widespread in business thinking it would be the most encouraging thing that could happen to the United States. "We must find some way," concluded these corporation men, "to work within the framework of government."[1]

It is not to be supposed, however, that the millennium has arrived. Speakers at business conventions still sometimes class government with ladies of ill repute, and receive hearty applause. But there is not the old conviction. Businessmen are wondering. The old order changeth. Business is in politics. Government is in world politics. The boys are playing for keeps. And deep down, those who yesterday made government the laughing stock know that neither they nor government is as skilled as each should be about survival in the nuclear age.

To me, the encouraging thing is that those whose attitude is changing are becoming not only sober and socially attuned—in many cases for the first time—but also they are confident and self-assured and, hence, better able to act constructively than if they were overwhelmed by feelings of guilt. The new attitude is summed up in the questions now being asked: Why isn't government better? What can we do to improve it? Businessmen would not ask such questions were they not confident that they can henceforth give what hitherto they have withheld.

AN ACHILLES HEEL?

This new attitude is not necessarily all gain, however. American businessmen have long been disdainful of government for at least one reason that makes sense: they were so self-assured that they didn't need help from anyone, or thought they didn't. And, of course, it is this feeling of self-confidence that gives that extra zip to business— the new invention, the sales approach, the resourcefulness, the drive, all of which are so missing in bureaucratic situations.

This self-confidence is a positive asset. Unfortunately, we are in danger of losing it, for like the Old World from which we once thought we differed so markedly, we too have become bureaucratic. As our institutions have matured and, hence, become set in their ways, our giant business firms find that increasingly they resemble the government which they once professed to hold in contempt. Big corporations are regarded as wielders of power, and people are fearful of this power. The corporations are fought over by bankers, labor leaders, consumers, stockholders, politicians, and by those queer persons who advocate—with limited success, so far, in the United States—radical proposals of reform in which business would lose some of its independence. On top of this, the big corporations suffer from bureaucratic aches and pains for which the doctors, knowing so little about the causes, have been slow to prescribe remedies.[2]

Little by little, therefore, and recently with dismaying suddenness, big business in America has learned that it has an Achilles heel. It has so much power that it perforce must govern, but in practice finds that it cannot do this and run a business, too. Someone else must do the governing, and that someone else is the government.

Besides, business seems to be slowing down; it shows disturbing signs of becoming objectionably rigid; businessmen themselves compare it to government. They even talk about civil service conditions and the necessity for them, whereas not too long ago they found the reasons for government's inefficiency in what they called the civil service mentality. And they wonder where the new zip is coming from, now that corporations have become so big and bureaucratic that they must promote from within, advancing men who for the most part are narrow specialists instead of economic statesmen with a breadth of experience.

Businessmen are even becoming fearful of power. Having once desired power above all else, they now wonder if they should go on acquiring it so as to feel more secure, or, alternatively, whether to stop growing and expanding so as not to excite so much envy and fear.

These are difficult questions partly because they are political questions, and no one seems to feel sure of the answers.

Instead of continuing to disparage government as they once did, therefore, America's business rulers now regard government in two ways: first, as a bedfellow, because at night they toss and turn and fret over the same problems; and secondly, as a sword and shield against foreign ideologies that threaten to engulf our individualistic system and, also, against forces within that would join the worst in bureaucracy with the worst in planlessness in a combination which, if it should ever fasten itself on our system, would soon strangle it.

In historical perspective, the antipathy of business to government is understandable, even though it stopped being rational about a hundred years ago. The colonies revolted against a government with concentrated power, and the people turned their enmity against government as such, not against a particular form, as the more rational might have done. People called America the land of opportunity, where every man was his own governor and no outside ruler was necessary. They said that government is inevitably either power or privilege, and they wanted none of either.

Then, shortly after the Civil War, when business became nation-wide in scope, people coined the phrase, "America, a businessman's civilization." Thereafter, being king, business could not tolerate the pretender, political government, for there can be only one king. True, businessmen *talked* pluralism and paid lip service to the idea that government, like other groups, must fulfill its appointed role. But in practice they saw in a weak government a free and untrammelled road to getting rich quick.

A strong government might, for example, interfere with the cutting down of the forests or the wasteful tapping of petroleum resources. It might take this business of competition seriously instead of realizing that business, the king, can do no wrong because it acts always in favor of "the system." A strong government might also eventually interfere too much with labor relations and with profits, and such behavior was not to be tolerated under the genius of our economic system.

Hence, a conclusion that seemed entirely convincing at the time: the best government is the one that governs least, the one that is not too efficient. If government becomes too efficient and people trust it too much, there might be the same consequences here as in older European countries: Government might go into business in competition with its own citizens. Voters might give it more to do. Taxes might take the lustre off profits. Wealth might be redistributed. Incompetent men might come to have as much power in the economy, as well as in government, as men who were born to rule.

The crowning rationalization, of course, was freedom. There is no question that businessmen desired freedom—at least for themselves. What they overlooked was, first, that as size and power and bureaucracy increased, there would be less *internal* freedom even for themselves; and secondly, that if the role of political government were indefinitely circumscribed and rendered ineffectual, the forces *external* to business might in time undermine the business system itself. For a weak government cannot indefinitely withstand the competitions of more hardy competitors; a weak government is costly and, hence, drains the vitality out of free enterprise; a weak government causes people to lose faith in the whole system of which business is only a part.

By recognizing an understandable cause-and-effect relationship, businessmen have now worked around to the point where they are beginning to take an organic view of governing institutions. The corporation is one of these; political government is the other. Together they must sink or swim, work together or fail together. Free business and free government are inseparably bound one to the other.

This is the growing new mood in business; on the whole it is a healthy one, since it is more rational than former attitudes, and it is more likely to achieve survival because it is more responsive to the needs of our times.

Hence the conclusion that the needs of business and of government are identical: how to assure enterprise and the development of governing skills; how to reward and encourage those who show special aptitudes; how to convert specialists into statesmen; how to protect property and profits and still keep them the servants of the public interest. These problems are generic and organic and apply to both institutions equally; they are an integral part of our culture. Small wonder, then, that for some time now some of our largest business firms have been creating departments of government and that those who will rule big business tomorrow are asking today, "What can we do to improve government?"

This is not to deny that some big corporations are displaying more zeal than discretion in some of their present behavior. "Big Corporations Mount Soapboxes," says Peter Bart.[3] " 'Political Awareness' Drive Enters the Stage of Espousing Causes." Dozens of firms have set up public affairs departments to advise top executives. The Ford Motor Company, for example, has some fifteen public affairs experts in Detroit plus eight regional public affairs managers in the field, and these men sometimes call on other experts for additional advice. The over-all purpose is to develop a "corporate opinion," official views about the corporation reflected by its own employees.

Taking a stand on issues before the nation and trying to persuade its employees to the company's own way of thinking is a fairly new development and one that may cause an unexpected backfire. In a short space of time before the presidential election of 1960, for example, one company came out against the McNamara Bill for school construction, another assailed "the deep-rooted, documented corruption in our foreign aid program," another urged its employees to oppose the "big union bosses" who sought repeal of a right-to-work law, and another openly urged Congress to reduce taxes and "halt the dangerous growth of powerful government." Other companies, more cautious, contented themselves with analyzing the pros and cons of pending issues, realizing that handouts in pay envelopes have always been bitterly resented by American employees.

Early in 1960 dozens of companies were carrying on such "soapbox" activities. But underlying all such behavior was a nagging doubt as to whether these programs might not backfire. Said one executive, "We don't think our position-taking will inhibit employees from speaking out, but you can't be sure." Would it be wiser in the long run merely to advise top management and Congressmen regarding the company viewpoint, which has long been standard practice, or would it be better for big business firms to try to influence the thinking of their own employees? Skeptics were saying that corporations, as corporations, cannot possibly have official positions based on employee opinion, that such views merely mirror the ideologies of the president and the chairman of the board. Thus, skeptics and statesmen alike continue to ask, "What can we do to improve government?"

PERSONAL SKILLS NEEDED

Tomorrow's business leader, like tomorrow's government leader, will need the skills of the political scientist, if by that is meant one who understands the strengths and weaknesses of power, the factors that promote survival and vitality in institutions, the balances that secure a combination of responsiveness and responsibility, and the human factors that determine sound policies and provide integration for bureaucratic programs that are inherently dispersive.

Neither political science nor economics working in separate compartments has been able to train such leaders. Together, as political economy, they might succeed.

After groping rather frantically for a remedy to an elusive ailment, business is coming to see that this is so. At first the remedy was thought to be simply more growth, greater size. Then it became more competition for the minds of men, a better public relations technique. Then it was millions of dollars for lobbying, especially to thwart the ambitions of labor leaders. Then it was "togetherness," the gray flannel suit, conformity, unswerving allegiance to the corporation. Then it was stepped-up executive development programs, in which the attempt was to find answers to the perplexing problems of bureaucracy and power.

But although all of these emphases have some merit and will doubtless be continued and even intensified, none has proved to be the capstone of the device sought. Togetherness simply diluted responsibility and generated a debilitating uniformity. We seem to have worked out of that morass and are ready now to return to a more tested and reliable alternative. We need outstanding leaders, men with enough integrative power to make complicated decisions, who know enough about policy and governing to guide institutions along paths that assure vitality as well as survival, men who have learned to apply the wisdom of political philosophers since the time of Socrates.

For its part, government also needs men of experience and wisdom, but in addition, it needs the skills peculiar to businessmen: practicality and levelheadedness. The USSR is not likely to produce such skills in large abundance because it lacks the natural habitat where businessmen develop this set of mind. That natural habitat is the school of experience on one's own, the experience of the man who starts his own business and becomes master of the whole, because in the course of his metamorphosis he has handled all aspects of the enterprise. If he is to survive in the face of stiff competition he must learn what it is that works. One serious mistake of judgment on this score and he may be out of business.

When businessmen charge that there are all too few people in government who are practical in this sense, it must be admitted that they are right. But they are right not because business is business and government is government. They are right because experienced businessmen acquire a practical survival skill deriving from their situation, their inner compulsion. Such a skill is not learned when, as so often happens today, men enter business from the top or, as in the manner of government, through some staff service to the top executive.

Government does things that no practical businessman would do. It constantly reorganizes itself; it denies a leadership role to civil servants; it tries hare-brained experiments; it starts competing and sometimes contradictory programs simultaneously and programs having confused objectives; it uses too many people for work that could often be better done with fewer if they had a clear mandate. Why? Woodrow Wilson knew the answer and stated it as long ago as 1887 in his famous essay on "The Study of Administration."[4] Government, said Wilson, needs business skill which is practical enough to think consecutively, hardheaded enough not to waste money, integrated enough to assure survival.

The fact is that competitive business develops a hardheaded, practical intelligence from handling situations that cannot be reproduced in the classroom or in the socialist laboratory. This does not mean, however, that government is incapable of being as businesslike as business, as anyone with government experience knows. But the condition is not likely to become common in the United States until we do something about upgrading government in our total scheme of things.

Another need is to recognize the gifted individual instead of the impersonal group as a prime asset of our civilization. This individual is more likely to come from a simple environment than from one of wealth and privilege, the reason being that governing ability is largely the product of struggle and of the attitudes toward fellow human beings that come from struggle. This type of person needs the same combination of skills whether his immediate identification is with the economic or the political process. Since personality and skills are an intricate web of traits, no single skill or partial combination of them will do. Consequently, we must take a new view of how leaders are produced, a view more compatible with our traditions than the bureaucratic attitude we have been emphasizing since we became enamoured of scientism, a generation ago.

Above all else, the outstanding leader in business and in government will be a humanist. His personality will have a universal appeal, not a parochial or a nationalistic one. He will be a product of all of the cultural factors in society, not merely of the schools, as essential and influential as they must be. His outstanding traits will include wisdom, derived from personal struggle and a deep reflection on the principles of the natural and moral order; compassion for all men and identification with them; an orientation that puts the interests of society above his own and unhesitatingly places universal values above political advantage in the sense of personal or group selfishness.

This new type will have a penetrating intelligence capable of going to the heart of problems. People will say of his personality that his character stands out most clearly. He will be sufficiently hardheaded to see what a particular situation requires and how to meet it, and sufficiently diplomatic to realize that his will is a hollow reed until those who work with him come to desire the same things he does. His influence, as Ordway Tead has said so well and so consistently,[5] will be with people, not over them. And finally, he will know that power is a delusion and a snare, that it is only a mutuality of interest and of values that makes the world a better place for man.

Accordingly, the political economist of the future, who is the new leader, will identify with the humanities as well as with the sciences. If his professional training is in science, engineering, or a profession such as law, he will have to become a humanist before he can aspire to a rounded wisdom or a winning way with men. And if his professional training is in one of the social sciences, he will have to steep himself in the philosophy of science and technology before he can become thoroughly competent.

That the goal set here is not impossible of achievement is shown by the emergence of such men in our own time and culture as Owen D. Young of General Electric and Arthur Page of American Telephone and Telegraph. These were men with strong religious and ethical convictions, men who were full of compassion. Compassion is the doorway to wisdom, and no one seems to acquire it until he has the modesty and altruism in his heart that underlie greatness of character.

If this type of leadership is going to appear commonly among us, therefore, we must see that our whole organic culture pattern is such as to make the type possible. The values of our society must be clearer and stronger, the church and all altruistic ventures must be more widely supported, the humanities must be recognized as more basic to wise leadership than the sciences, because they more nearly reflect the whole man. Social science, which now tries to ape natural science, should realize that it is more closely identified with the humanities, for it is a science of *man* we are dealing with, not a science of *things*.

It is only in this total context, pervaded by an organic humanism, that the new political economy can transform the life of America and change our segmental anxieties and our artificial specialties into something more vital and significant. A by-product might be a spreading influence among other nations and the "subversion" of communist materialism to the point where even in the USSR, values are seen to count more than power, the gifted individual more than the collectivity.

ENERGY FROM CHALLENGE

It is in a human context that I view the need for American government to become more effective, with a high order of leadership sparked by the energy that comes from challenge. A British experience has shown the way.

At the end of World War II, at a time when Britain was faced with the possible loss of her world trade, the Administrative Staff College was established at Henley, near Oxford, to train top leaders in business and government. Four times a year, a new group of sixty men meets for twelve weeks of intensive work. Half of them come from business, the other half from the public service, and all have already been tapped by their employers for positions of top responsibility. The focus of the work is on high-level policy and on the encouragement of superior executive skills.

After the first few weeks of each session it is nearly impossible to tell by their attitudes which men are from industry and which from government, or which are old school and which are not. They have coalesced, the reason being that their several interests converge on one problem: How can Britain stay ahead in the game of promoting foreign markets, improving her standard of living, and surviving in the atomic age? As the members of each session learn for themselves, the answer is: By developing a superior brand of leadership skill and by business and government *each* doing its part.[6] The British are fifty years ahead of us in this adult attitude toward business-government cooperation.

In Britain, leaders may rise to the top without benefit of college education, or on the basis of training in one of the provincial universities, which increasingly challenge Oxford and Cambridge in the type of leadership they produce. The average age of executives in British industry and government is younger than formerly, and men in their forties, as in this country, head important ventures.

As against this dynamic view of the business-government relationship, government in the United States has been disparaged for so long that many able men and women who serve it have virtually lost their courage. Leadership opportunity, even if it were to come to them now, might find many of them unable to respond as they once could have. If the challenge were better understood, the energy flowing from it might produce quite a different situation.

For centuries, political philosophers have argued about the innate nature of government, some holding that it is inherently evil and some, that it is essentially beneficent. Such an argument has meaning only if one assumes that government has an inherent nature to begin with, a possibility ruled out by every logical consideration. Government is simply a social institution like any other, including the business corporation, the labor union, or the university. Accordingly, government can be put to uses that may be either good or evil, depending on its leadership and the view of it held by the people. Government may be used to exploit the people or to break men's chains, to exercise force or to extend a helping hand, to bring the lawbreaker to book or to supply a hospital bed.

Thus, instead of asking whether government is inherently good or evil, the more useful question is: What must government do now to promote the values and objectives that this society prizes? When such a question is asked in the United States, the answer is that government must provide services and positive incentives and must avoid domination and force.

The challenge of government today revolves around the urgent tasks it must perform and the degree to which the American people are willing to cooperate with it to those ends. Government itself must be strengthened. Half-way measures will not do. There has been enough tinkering. We need fewer study commissions and more reform. At the end of World War II, Britain derived the energy she needed to survive from the challenge she faced, to which she responded more successfully than anyone at the time dared hope. Today, we could lose the cold war because our government creaks and groans. Are we ready for reform, even if it means taking a hard look at some of our sacred cows? The signs, taken here and there and ... the business community, seem to indicate that we are.

ELEVEN

A MINIMUM PROGRAM

The way to make the government effective is to tie it to the economy. For any public official, the question with regard to any proposed program should always be: What does this do to the political economy, the good life?

The grand strategy of government is to provide the policies and the institutional arrangements whereby a free people can go as far as they are able in making a good life for themselves, leaving as little as possible for government itself to administer directly.

There are two sound reasons for the rule of statecraft that government should be a catalytic agent and not a department store. The first, which has repeatedly been argued in these pages, is that the more people are able to do for themselves, the more do they grow in self-government. The second is that at best, government in the modern world must inevitably do so much that even the most efficient is overworked. Hence, we must begin to discriminate between what government should try to get others to do, and what essential programs it must administer itself. Then, priorities must be determined and strategies worked out as thoroughly as any in society.

An aspect of strategy must be to persuade pressure groups to have a care for the public interest, for a pressure-dominated government is handicapped in any program for survival. Such a government is driven hither and yon, must say, "Yes," more often than "No," and hence is never on top of the situation. Being at the mercy of every interest that can enlist political support, government tries to do too much and in consequence, does nothing well. Lacking a leadership group to develop policies to promote the good life, progress toward that objective is impeded. Government is confused. In a desire to promote freedom it permits license. In a desire to avoid the concentration of power it winds up doing too much itself. Most of government's present difficulties stem from the fact that it lacks the structural arrangements that keep policy and practice in balance. The proper role of the central government is to concentrate on policy and then delegate responsibility for administration to governments at levels nearer the people and to private groups.

OUTLINE OF A PLAN

The following ten-point program would overcome most of the hazards and confusions from which governments in the United States now suffer. It is not supposed, of course, that to carry through such a program would be easy. Nevertheless, if enough top economic and political leaders were to be convinced that survival requires certain positive steps to be taken now, it would be possible to bring about a considerable improvement.

The ten points are these:

1. Determine priorities.
2. Encourage voluntary agencies to be more active.
3. Add new programs as needed; lop off what is obsolete.
4. Decentralize.
5. Guarantee responsible party leadership.
6. Define legislative-executive responsibilities.
7. Secure continuity of policy and administration.
8. Realize that the President is not a professional manager and needs help.
9. Organize as other large institutions must.
10. Give the civil service a larger leadership role.

So far as I can see there are only two areas among these ten where constitutional amendment might be necessary. First, the needed degree of decentralization would almost certainly require regional governments along the line suggested in an earlier chapter. And secondly, the security of responsible party leadership would clearly require the adoption of a cabinet form of government, in which the legislative and executive branches are effectively tied together.

Even if constitutional amendment is necessary, however, we should not hesitate to act, for if any rule of statecraft is tested and incontrovertible it is that institutional arrangements are only means to ends and, hence, have no permanent sanctity of their own. If values are to be our guide, we should unhesitatingly make any structural adjustments that promise to be more workable than what we have. To paraphrase William Gladstone, we may agree that in 1787 the federal Constitution was the greatest instrument ever struck off by the mind of man, but like any institutional arrangement, it needs strengthening when new conditions make structural adjustments the better part of wisdom. To conclude otherwise would be to place pride of authorship above the need to survive and to go forward, and no sensible man would do that.

These ten recommendations fall conveniently into three groups, and I shall treat them accordingly. The first group includes the first four points and is discussed in this chapter. The discussion of the second and third groups is opened here and continued in succeeding chapters in this part.

DETERMINING PRIORITIES

If governmental performance is to improve, then it must put first things first, which means establishing priorities. Thereafter, it must do what needs to be done at the right time; this is the timing factor, and it depends on stages of growth.

If these two rules of governmental operation are ignored, the task of the public official becomes hopeless. He looks out over a bewildering area of governmental responsibilities and soon becomes confused and frustrated. He tries to do everything at once and winds up doing nothing well. He regards government as something apart from the rest of life, to be dealt with as a separate and distinctive institution. This is his biggest mistake, because government's priorities are not intrinsic to the institution; rather, they are derived from the needs of the political economy.

How are priorities determined?

Every nation goes through stages of growth from relative simplicity to relative complexity,[1] and at each stage, that which must be done depends on the requirements of the situation. A society differs from plants and animals, however, in not having a definite birth, maturity, and death. Depending on a number of factors, a society that is sophisticated and culturally developed at one point, may revert to a former primitivism, and then advance again to a period of sophistication, as a number of nations have in fact done. Examples among others, include Athens, China, parts of Africa, and Turkey. Hence, there is no fixity in stages of institutional growth nor is there any assurance that the curve of sophistication will always be upward; it may just as well be downward. In other words, the movement of national institutions, as Aristotle understood, is typically uneven, with peaks and valleys instead a steady upward or downward gradient.

Since societies are interacting organisms, political and social factors largely determine factors that are economic. In this complex the role of government is to analyze priorities in terms of what is required at a particular time. In what Rostow calls the precondition and take-off stages of growth, the role of government is everywhere much the same: to maintain law and order, provide a stable currency, build institutions such as accountancy and investment markets, and provide the essentials of communications, transportation, and energy resources. The test of public administration during these early periods is greater than at any other time, for if government fails to provide a minimum basis of efficiency, the economic program cannot even begin to move.

By the time Rostow's fifth and final stage of growth has been reached—one that he calls "diffusion on a mass basis of durable consumers' goods and services," or that Galbraith calls the affluent society—the demands on government are somewhat different. Everything needed at the earlier stages is still needed, but the balances are different. The economy may still be structurally divided into the five areas of agriculture, industry, public utilities, welfare services, and education and institutional building; but the main emphasis of government must be on planning, coordination, looking ahead, and trying to make sense out of a bewildering complexity.

From this line of reasoning I conclude that the first priority in government, especially in periods of relative complexity, is what is called economic analysis, planning, high-level program formulation, and decision making. Generally speaking, in the United States this is the job of the Council of Economic Advisers.

This activity is even more important than foreign affairs. Many will take issue with this statement on the ground that foreign affairs is the key to national security and should come first. I disagree. The importance of foreign affairs depends on a number of factors, including the nation's reliance on foreign trade, the degree to which it is likely to be put at a disadvantage in case of war between stronger rivals, the need for protective alliances, and the like. To solve these problems it is necessary first to analyze the total situation and to know what one is doing in the total political economy.

Third place I would accord to the stabilization function: how to bring about steady economic growth; how to keep from overproducing; how to keep supply and demand in balance; how to avoid surpluses and subsidies; how to keep everyone usefully employed; how to avoid recessions and depressions; how to maintain progress toward a higher standard of living. No longer are such questions "automatically" decided. After the natural forces of the market have done what they can, men in strategic positions in government must make sure that these balances are kept right, for nature can no longer do the whole job alone.

Having established these guidelines, other priorities fall naturally into place.

There must, of course, be a Department of Agriculture, but a much smaller and less costly one than at present. The department is no less important to the nation than formerly, but much of its work can be turned back, in line with a proposal made in an earlier chapter, to state and local governments. Most of the research and production-increase programs, for example, could be run as well by regional and state governments as by headquarters in Washington. Further, by concentrating on the planning and stabilization functions of the whole government, it should be possible to liquidate the most costly part of the department's work, that is, its huge subsidy, food-storage, price-stabilization plan that makes it the chief trader in every commodity exchange in the country.

I believe that if regional and state governments took over some of its present activities, the Department of Agriculture could operate with a third of its present appropriation and the over-all job would be better done.

With regional decentralization, the Department of Agriculture would be free to deal almost wholly with questions of high economic policy. I am one who believes that in fifty years this country will be working as hard to put people back on the farms as it is now working to move them to the cities. For one thing, the cities cannot continue indefinitely to absorb these people and to offer them full employment. For another, if the general farming situation can be improved by assuring the producer a larger share of the consumer's dollar, then people transplanted to the cities would be happier and better off back home. The Department of Agriculture should concentrate on policy in areas such as these, leaving research and how-to-do-it pamphlets to be produced by agencies nearer the farmer in his home state.

The considerations that apply to agriculture apply also to the other economic areas of government. Labor relations and social security can be state and regionally run, with the job of the federal government confined largely to research on standards, which takes only a small, high caliber staff. Similarly with the activities of the departments of Commerce and the Interior and of many of the independent agencies as well. Instead of centrally operating huge programs with hundreds of thousands of employees, these departments and agencies could be relatively small and inexpensive, with the bulk of the work turned over to regional, state, and local governments. The remaining central functions would relate primarily to promotion and development —the great need of the transportation industry, for example—and secondly, to major regulation. But this latter function also could be reduced by turning much of it back to the states.

The idea here would be somewhat like the Swiss plan: Let the central government set the standards; let the state governments administer them. Avoid a huge federal bureaucracy, because if government tries to do too much in too many areas and with too many people, everything gets fouled up and nothing is done well.

Some may ask, "Isn't decentralization a backward step? Isn't this a reactionary position? Must we really give up public controls, as reactionaries have long urged?" The answer is that of course public controls must be maintained unless to give them up would promote a better performance in the public interest. A proper formula is one under which the federal government establishes the norm according to which programs are administered at the regional and state levels. These governments should collect their own taxes for these programs, instead of having revenues rebated to them through federal aid. At present the federal government has a strangle hold on the tax dollar, and it should be broken.

I would, of course, be intellectually arrogant if I asserted my ability to list the priorities of government with complete precision. I make no such claim. I argue only that we must do the best we can; that what we decide depends upon evolutionary factors about which we must know more than we do; and that if we emphasize planning, stabilization, and decentralization we can do a better over-all job at much lower cost than at present.

There is an optimal task that any government (or any other institution, for that matter) can do well. Beyond that point the law of diminishing returns sets in, so that every increase beyond the theoretical cut-off point detracts correspondingly from the effectiveness of the whole job.

Along with the determination of priorities and a policy of decentralization, an effort should be made to prevail on voluntary agencies to take over certain functions now run by government. We Americans have been surprisingly lacking here in constructive imagination. The fact is that in almost every domestic area where government operates today, this devolution of functions is possible. Thus, there are many private organizations concerned with recreation and the protection of wildlife and the out-of-doors—such as the National Recreation Association and the Isaak Walton League—that could act as agents of the government in clean-up and conservation programs supported by federal funds. In this way, a worthy private group would become stronger, and government would have less to do.

Similarly in labor relations, government's duties could increasingly be transferred to voluntary organizations such as the American Arbitration Association, where labor and industry jointly hire experts to help solve their disputes. Again, the promotional activities of the Department of Commerce might be delegated to a voluntary group similar to the Scottish Council in Scotland, by whom the work of promotion is done with greater freedom and probably better results. In the welfare field, cities already are paying private agencies for work that would otherwise be done by the city's own employees. This formula could be more widely used, especially by the federal government.

Government does a mass of inspection work, such as that having to do with safety devices on railroads, sanitation in eating establishments and in barber shops, and the administration of wages and hours legislation. In many such cases government could set the standards, award a contract for the work, and confine its administrative responsibilities to checking on the contractor. This is already common practice with regard to atomic energy contracts and the operation of company towns in that connection.

Finally, government must be alert at all times to add new programs as needed, and to lop off those that are obsolete. In earlier chapters, I have mentioned the proposed creation of departments for transportation and for resource management. I have also proposed a department for urban affairs. Assuming that these areas have become important enough to be made part of the federal government structure (and I express no opinion on this), then we should try equally hard to prune off programs that have served their purpose and continue only because of apathy or bureaucratic tenacity. After World War II, for example, the Corporation Audits Division of the General Accounting Office, in concert with the Bureau of the Budget, studied the many federally owned business corporations that had proliferated during the war and recommended reducing them from 101 to 85; and in a few months the reduction was brought about. One of the most urgent needs in government is a continual pruning of this kind.

SECURING BETTER COORDINATION

Once the priorities of government are clearly defined and its over-all job simplified through decentralization and a greater reliance on voluntary effort, then the next three points in the proposed ten-point program tackle the matter of respective roles and responsibilities and their coordination.

Lack of coordination has long been a major structural weakness in Washington. I remember a meeting of the War Manpower Commission during World War II, for example. General Lucius D. Clay had just returned from a trip to Allied capitals and Paul McNutt asked him, "How do we compare with our Allies in governmental efficiency?" General Clay thought for a moment and then replied, "Our personnel compares favorably with theirs, and so does our know-how. But when it comes to coordination, I must admit that most of them are ahead of us."

Coordinating weaknesses show up in many ways. Primarily there is insufficient continuity of policy. In this day and age, sharp gyrations in policy alienate one's allies and cause the communist bloc to develop jitters. Irrespective of what the situation may have been fifty or a hundred years ago, today the stakes for which government is responsible are so large and the situation so sensitive that continuity of policy in Washington is at least as important as it is in the nation's largest industrial corporations and trade unions.

Men with practical experience realize that no tough problem is ever permanently solved by trying first this and then that, with frequent changes of approach and strategy. A tough problem is solved by analyzing it into its parts, laying out a strategy, and then developing a hard-hitting administrative program.

This is especially true in the areas of major policy on which our survival depends. How is the economy to be stabilized, for example, unless government is stable to begin with? How are allies and potential enemies to be reassured unless Congress and the President speak with the same voice? Our record in these respects is so poor it hardly seems possible that Americans pioneered scientific management. As anyone soon learns who travels abroad, our loss of national prestige in recent years has been largely due to the disillusionment of other nations with the irresponsibility and laxness of our government. "How can you Americans, who pride yourselves on your business efficiency, ever put up with an inefficient government such as yours?" is the question one frequently hears. Without in any way sacrificing the voters' right to choose parties and candidates, we should move as quickly as possible to introduce stability and continuity into our governmental mechanism.

The first step toward coordination is to straighten out the chaotic role of national political parties. It does not trouble me that the Democratic and Republican parties are in basic agreement in many matters of public policy. It does trouble me deeply that they are so often unable to secure effective policy and administration. I am familiar with the well-worn contention that democracy may and often does appear to be inefficient but that in a test it is more deadly than authoritarian regimes whose efficiency seems greater. I acknowledge the truth of this argument and think I understand the reason: A free system based on the resourcefulness of the people always has more in reserve than a system that is regimented.

Nevertheless, we cannot continue to invite irresponsibility, planlessness, and weak leadership and expect to hold our own with governments that have a better balance of institutional factors. Britain and Canada are as free as we are, and yet their governments have vastly more responsibility and effective leadership than we do. I do not suggest that we turn our backs on principle; I do urge that we try to secure a better balance of structural factors so as to strengthen principle. A failure to make this distinction is doubtless one reason for our failure to correct our governmental weaknesses long before this.

Some pessimists contend that our party system is typically American and that if it changes at all it will be over many generations of gradual evolution. The record, I think, points to the opposite conclusion. Beneath the surface, the American party system has been changing faster than we realize, and generally in the right direction. Thus, city and state political bosses have greatly declined during the past generation. National leadership has become less dispersed and more closely knit. The American party—at least when in power—has developed a fairly tight presidential wing, and even the "out" party has developed some continuity of policy under a titular head. Popular participation in the nominating process has increased. Public opinion polls seem to have enhanced the influence of the public on politics. And although the direct primary for state-wide office has somewhat weakened party leadership at that level, at the national level top leadership does not seem to have been impaired by a limited use of the device.[2] Even in the Big Powwow of the national political conventions, James McGregor Burns tells us, delegates are now a superior group in education, achievement, and experience.[3]

There is a good deal of hope, therefore, that the lazy man's view —that what has always been, must always be—may be replaced by a resolve to make the American party electoral system an effective instrument of national responsibility.

This difficult question of how to strengthen party and other forms of responsibility is dealt with at some length in the following chapter. The important thing here is to recognize relationships; to see party responsibility as the key to many other forms of responsibility, in legislatures and in administration.

The second step toward better coordination in government is to bring the legislative and executive branches closer together. The present disjunction was deliberately planned on the assumption that if the two branches were at odds, they would be less likely to encroach on the freedom of the citizen. If this assumption were ever right, which is doubtful, it is no longer valid, and in the modern world we are paying too high a price for an illogical tradition. Few will contend that anarchy is the highest form of freedom. On the contrary, to our allies and to our antagonists alike we must speak with a single voice. In these troubled times it is often more to the point that a nation be able to count on the right action at the right time than that it enjoy the freedom to procrastinate and debate. As any experienced executive knows, timing is of the essence, and once that factor is invalidated, the whole executive process may break down.

Every President since Franklin Roosevelt has promoted bipartisanship part of the time. Working relationships between party and presidential leadership are much closer than they were under Calvin Coolidge and Herbert Hoover. And no modern President is likely to forget Woodrow Wilson and the Versailles Treaty. But this is not good enough. Bipartisanship lasts only so long as it is to the advantage of both sides. It is a brittle relationship at best and is most likely to fall apart during national elections and the subsequent periods of transition, when both external and internal policies are under the greatest stress. If improvisation served a principle more important than those it thwarts, it would be worth the price we pay for it, but such is not the case.

The remedy is a cabinet form of government, in which the executive enjoys the wholehearted support of a majority of the legislature, which works with him instead of frequently against him.[4] Anything else is madness. It does not matter especially whether the President is elected by the people or chosen by the victorious party majority, for in either case the will of the people determines the outcome. It does matter terribly that the President be given full support and every encouragement in the difficult, almost inhuman task of trying to be President.

The third step in securing coordination is in the area of administration, when the party in office is voted out at the polls and the opposition takes over. How is continuity to be secured? Largely by two means. The first is by having a higher civil service with enough prestige and influence to carry on during the interim, because it is looked to for leadership at all times. The second is by carrying over from one administration to the next some of the best brains and administrative talent at the policy levels of government—as kings and other rulers, including modern corporations, have always done—and giving them policy and directing powers that are above partisan politics and yet consonant with the new President's decision in case of doubt. We have been heading in this direction for some time, as a matter of fact, ever since Franklin D. Roosevelt picked some men irrespective of party because they had the best qualifications for the job.

World conditions are now so critical that what was once the exception must become the rule. The President should have an inner circle—an executive group or board of some kind—consisting of men of superior skills and knowledge, men like Henry L. Stimson, Lewis Douglas, Douglas Dillon, and others who might be mentioned.

Such a group, representing the best policy and executive skills the country can provide, would help to assure continuity of policy in a time of transition.

HELPING THE PRESIDENT WITH MANAGEMENT

With a clear idea of our public priorities and an assured system of securing responsible party leadership, we might then expect more generally the same type of efficient administration in government that we have learned to expect in business. So favorable a development, however, is not automatic, for the office of the presidency itself also needs attention.

For one thing, the President does not have a clear mandate, despite what the Constitution says. And for another, we are expecting the impossible if we look to the President to be the actual managing head of the federal bureaucracy, unless we give him a new kind of executive assistance in place of a constantly proliferating staff establishment. These issues are discussed more fully in a later chapter, where a concrete plan is presented for organizing the presidency in a workable manner. At this point, let us simply try to relate the organization of the presidency to the other two aspects of coordination discussed above.

As if the failure to provide responsible political parties and responsible government were not enough, we make two additional assumptions that almost guarantee the presence of the difficulties and confusions now found in the executive branch. First, we seem to think that the President must necessarily do every top managerial job himself because under the Constitution he is legally entitled to do so. Secondly, we insist that he be the ceremonial head of the government as well as its efficient head because there is no one to whom the former function can be delegated. Both assumptions are unrealistic and impractical if what is wanted is a first-rate administrative performance.

The first of these assumptions is worthy of a lawyer but not of a practical executive. Every experienced executive knows that in theory —even in business—all power is vested in the chief executive, but that in practice, the more power he delegates down the line the more efficient and progressive will the enterprise become. Even in smaller institutions than the federal government, one-man rule may work for a short time, but eventually it breaks down of its own inner weaknesses. How much more difficult, therefore, to apply such a rule to the federal government. The President would need help even if a major share of his present functions were eliminated by transfer, through decentralization, to regional and state governments. He would need help even if he were responsible for a million employees instead of the 3 million plus now under his command.

In the last generation there have been many attempts to simplify the office of the presidency, but the burden on the man has grown rather than diminished. The office has accumulated a huge, pro-liferating, cumbersome staff organized around the President himself and jeopardizing his free communication with his cabinet and the departments where the work is done and the money spent.

This line of institutional development has caused Clinton Rossiter to remark that we have loaded the President with so much to do that he can do only some of it thoroughly; we have made so many people directly responsible to him that he can control only some of them directly. "Our chief solution to the problem," says Rossiter, "has been to create that amazing collection of agencies and officials known as the Executive Office," but this in turn has created still another problem, "the danger that the President may be made a prisoner in his own house."[5]

The device of the presidential staff has been built up on the basis of the following reasoning: All executive power is vested in the President; the President cannot do everything himself—in fact, it is questionable whether he deserves to be called a manager in the literal sense of the word at all; since he cannot manage, someone must do the job for him; we cannot trust the cabinet because its members are not the President and might not even be loyal to him; therefore, we must subdivide the President himself into hundreds of parts and allow a staff organization to do what the man cannot do personally.

The logic of this reasoning seems simple enough, but in practice the result is weird. No executive in business or in any other large organization would think of trying to operate in this manner. A usual objection at this point is that business is business and government is government, that the Constitution must be respected. To which I reply that if the delegation of authority to staff agencies is constitutional, then it must be equally lawful to delegate to executive officials, such as the members of the cabinet, who in any case act in the President's name.

In a later chapter I shall suggest how the management function in the federal government might be improved according to this brief outline:

Provide the President with an inner executive group, a sort of management team, with each member responsible for a certain bundle of activities having to do with a major segment of political economy.

Make the cabinet the principal coordinating device for over-all, interdepartmental, government-wide policy and give it the necessary resources for the job.

Assign the major presidential staff services, dealing with finance, personnel, planning, and the like, to cabinet officials at the departmental level, thus releasing more of the President's time for his policy, ceremonial, and other high-level duties.

Determine the organization of the Office of the President according to the best model, the best composite, that can be found in analogous governmental and business practice.

Concentrate on grand strategy and on giving priority to the survival functions of long-range planning, stabilization, the strengthening of competition, keeping programs in balance.

Make the higher civil service responsible for providing the knowledge, the morale, and the leadership to give the federal government a first-class management record. See that civil servants work *with* policy officials, not *under* them, in a team operation. The appointed policy official, of course, must always have the last word in agency matters, for it is he who is accountable to the President and the majority party.

The program outlined in this chapter includes ten basic policies that should accomplish what is needed: determine priorities, encourage voluntary agencies, add and subtract programs as needed, decentralize to regional and state governments, assure party leadership and responsibility, improve executive-legislative relationships, secure continuity of policy and administration, strengthen management at the chief-executive level, reorganize policy formation and decision making at the top of the government, and give the civil service a larger leadership role.

I have called this a minimum program, and in terms of what we should be willing to settle for, so it is. But in terms of what these coordinated reforms might accomplish, the effect should be maximal. With responsibility in policy, unity in execution, and teamwork between Congress and the White House, America would soon have one of the most outstanding governments in all history.

TWELVE

SECURING RESPONSIBILITY

The main weakness of American government is its common inability to act in a unified way. In fact, so divided are its councils that one sometimes wonders that it acts at all, except in times of emergency. We have failed to recognize that basically, responsibility is response, and that it has two equal and reciprocal connotations: action and accountability. Because we have misunderstood the practical needs of action, accountability is often a hollow cymbal. Men are humiliated and even disgraced for their inability to respond to the national will, when in fact the failure has been structural and not personal. Action depends on the power to act as well as on the desire to act, and under present procedures in the federal government, the power is inadequate.

"Congress Does Little to Cheer Democrats," reported Cabell Phillips toward the end of the Eisenhower administration. "In spite of its large majorities, they were not able to take the lead."[1] A person unfamiliar with the complexities of American politics would immediately wonder why. One close to Washington, on the other hand, would understand that the President belonged to the minority political party in Congress and that the majority was divided between conservative and liberal wings.

Unfortunately, the situation is sometimes no less frustrating when the President and the majority in Congress are of the same party. Writing soon after the Kennedy victory in 1960, Sidney Hyman reported that insiders were divided in their predictions of the future legislative-executive relationship. Would there be a row after the wedding guests departed and would the New Frontier be stopped by a divided, wrangling Congress? Or, by some magic of personality and fear of voter reprisal if the new administration were to fail, would the recent wedding turn into a happy life together as Congress and the President "walked together toward the ever-rising sun of the New Frontier"?

Unlike the British Parliament, Congress has no unitary form. It is divided between two houses, each on a different basis of representation. It rarely sits in full view of the nation or acts as a body. Instead, it does its work through three hundred or so committees, "so that no one can ever really call the Congress as a whole to a collective account for what it does or fails to do."[2]

After a brief and uncertain honeymoon, would future happiness depend more on personality or on institutional arrangements?

The lawyer characteristically thinks in terms of legal responsibility. The political economist also is interested in legal responsibility, but his main interest is antecedent to that problem: Is government so organized that response is well-considered, unified, and sustained? By this test, American institutions are grievously deficient. How, then, can response in this deeper sense be assured?

THE GAMBLE ON ONE MAN

At present, almost every aspect of government depends on the political accident of who wins the presidential election every fourth year. If he is a strong President, the government, so it is held, will respond to the internal and external challenges it faces. If he is weak, the people must suffer patiently for another four years until a new President can be chosen; if, indeed, he is a new one and not merely the incumbent continued in office for another term.

Even stranger are the reasons usually given for expecting so much influence from one man:

He is the *only* public official elected by *all* the voters. (Actually, the Vice-President also is elected by the same voters.) The reasoning seems to be that the more people a man is elected by, the more representative will he be, and the greater his devotion to the public interest. But how would one compare President Warren Harding and, say, Senator George Norris in their devotion to the public interest?

The President is party and legislative chief as well as head of the administrative services of the federal government. In other words, if he is a big enough man, he should be pretty well able to make policy as well as execute it.

He is ceremonial as well as directing (efficient) head of the government—prime minister and king rolled into one.

He is the only man who rises above sectional and pressure-group factions to protect the public interest of all the people.[3]

There are at least three things wrong with these arguments. First, rarely if ever do voters succeed in electing the kind of presidential paragon who seems to be needed. Woodrow Wilson came close to being everything expected of a President, but even he had his human limitations. Secondly, not even a President with the most ideal qualifications could do all that is expected of him; there simply is not enough time in the working day nor enough energy in the human frame. And thirdly, even if the first two conditions could be met, it is contrary to American ideas of democratic functioning for one person to be both king and prime minister at once.

It is more consistent with the democratic idea of *shared* power that the President be part of a team and that the team should run the government; further, that although the President is first among equals and responsible for those who serve with and under him, he personally should be expected to do only as much as is humanly possible; and finally, that although those who assist him may have enormous powers of action, in the last analysis it is the President as political head of the nation who should be held politically responsible to Congress and to the voters for mistakes or failures to act.

These assumptions are almost universally found in other American institutions, including corporations, labor unions, and universities. Why should the presidency be viewed so differently?

I can think of only two possible explanations, both of which would be hotly rejected by most Americans. Either the President has gradually taken on the kind of father image that in other countries causes people to view their king with reverence, as a mystical symbol of unity and nationality. Or we are generally uneasy about our structural defects and find a sort of irrational escapism in surrounding the office of President with an aura that defies rational scrutiny. As damaging as these explanations are to the traditional American fear of too much executive power, I should not be surprised if both had a considerable validity today.

Such a condition at the top of one of the largest governments of all time is intolerable, especially in the modern world, which typically is one of crises. The implications and the dangers were shown by James Reston, reporting a situation that arose early in 1960.[4] A crisis had developed in Cuba at a time when there were other crises, relating to nuclear testing, disarmament, the Berlin question, and summit policy. But at the confluence of all these issues the President was in Brazil, the Secretary of State was with him, there was a new Secretary of Defense (the sixth in thirteen years) assisted by a new Undersecretary of Defense (the eighth in thirteen years) and by a chairman of the Joint Chiefs of Staff who had been in the hospital twice within recent months. All this with a Congress dominated by members of the opposition political party.

My contention is that in all situations, and especially in times of crisis, it is best to emphasize the rational and to de-emphasize the irrational. A stronger presidency will not result from an appeal to folklore and genetics; but it might come from a study of institutional structure and dynamics.

The guiding principle is already tested and at hand: Responsibility—meaning the power to act in a unified and effective way and to hold the right people accountable—requires certain conditions. First, an undivided mandate on the part of the political party in power; secondly, a sound procedure for putting the party leader at the helm; thirdly, real teamwork between the legislative and the executive branches, with the party serving as the buckle that binds; fourthly, the recognized right of the President to organize and deploy his team as best suits his and the party's wishes; and fifthly, willingness on the part of the President to assume ultimate personal responsibility for every action taken in his name.

Such a plan, I believe, would quickly assure both vigor and accountability; nothing less, unless based on equally compelling principles, is likely to bring action and accountability into balance.

One more condition is necessary. The strengthening of our republic does not depend wholly on making it possible for political parties, Congress, and the executive to do a better job. There must also be better methods of educating public opinion and causing it to be more vocal. To this end, a first-rate system has been developed in Switzerland to the point where it is now a national tradition. Once the Swiss legislature becomes aware of a national problem, it requests the executive Federal Council to study the matter and prepare a draft law. The Federal Council or a committee thereof does its job with the help of all the expert advice it can get from within the bureaucracy and from outside, if desired. The completed draft is then submitted to all the cantons (similar to our states) for discussion and recommendation. The issues are widely discussed in the press and in local communities, and the members of the legislature are asked to vote only after it is known how the people, the cantons, and the executive feel about the matter. If there is disagreement between the two chambers, a conference committee eliminates the differences. Even after the law is passed, a referendum to the people may repeal it if opinion is against it.

The system works well, partly because Switzerland is small, of course, but even more because the press has come to perform an educational role. The Swiss newspapers are not dominated by chains or by advertisers; they as well as the people seem always to be conscious of the public interest. In the United States, a major opportunity for improvement lies just at this point.

In America's new political economy we could use more newspapers like the old *New York World,* like *The St. Louis Post-Dispatch, The Washington Post,* and *The New York Times*—papers that are considered fearless and progressive because they try objectively to educate public opinion instead of showing meanness, vindictiveness, and narrow opinion, as some metropolitan dailies do.

In assessing blame for any institutional weaknesses the United States may have developed, the press must share part of the responsibility. We should have more leaders of the press whose concern for the public interest is as deep as that of Horace Greeley, or in modern times, that of James Reston and Walter Lippmann. Before our institutions of decision and action can do a better job, the public must be better educated and must be enabled to make its opinions better known on public issues.

THE PARTY SYSTEM

The starting place for reform is obviously the political parties. We have two major ones and boast that in important essentials they agree: they agree in supporting capitalism and popular government. The only difference is that one is a little more oriented toward business, the other more sympathetic to labor; one is more conservative about money and spending; the other is inclined to emphasize the distribution of wealth and widespread purchasing power. And one is inclined to look a little more skeptically on the need for government than the other. Compared to political parties in most countries, however, these are minor differences; there is no great debate, for example, about socialism and the role of private property.

Nevertheless, it requires no crystal ball to foresee that party differences in the United States are going to increase. There will be a movement, for example—led by stockholders—to have the government own and operate the railroads. There will be sharp contests over the issues of private versus public control of atomic energy development and of certain kinds of resources, such as electric power and public lands. The burning issue of public ownership is being generated by a number of economic factors: by the plight of certain industries, such as the railroads, combined with the need to keep our industrial strength in first-class order because of the communist challenge; by the demand, partly rational and partly irrational, to step up economic growth from less than 3 per cent to around 5 or 6 per cent, or even more; by the reluctance of the public to invest in areas of the defense economy that clearly require it, for fear of what might happen if the artificial (defense) support were suddenly withdrawn; most important of all, perhaps, by the need to lay hold of billions of dollars for social purposes—social investments, if you please—in areas such as highways, schools, parks, and urban renewal; by the seeming difficulty of securing these funds out of normal tax channels and, hence, the idea, widely followed abroad, that the solution might be to earn them out of economic ventures run by government itself.

I do not advocate such a development. Indeed, I regret any thought in that direction if only because government already has more to do than it can do well. Nevertheless, I predict that a wide expansion of public programs and services is likely to take place during the next fifty years.

The bearing of this issue on the future of the two-party system is obvious. We are less likely than in the past to hear so much about Tweedledee and Tweedledum. One political party is likely to stand for a brand of constructive conservatism, the other to be labor- and socialist-oriented on the pattern of the Labor party in England and the Social Democrats in Western Europe. As in all these countries, the real contest will be only superficially one of ideology; basically, the objective will be more workable government programs and more skill in governing.

In the United States, therefore, the first requirement of responsible government is a reorganized system of political parties, one in which each party stands for a different approach to the same national issues. Today, each party runs the scale from conservatism to radicalism and, hence, denies the voter an opportunity to choose between competing policies. The second requirement is that the party platform become a plan of action, a timetable, something for which voters at the polls will punish the party if it fails to deliver on it.

The old arguments no longer convince. In defense of the lack of real differences between the two major parties, it has been contended that pluralism requires men of different opinion to work together within the same party; that real differences would accentuate cleavages, not promote settlement; that parties ought to justify themselves by electing candidates, not dividing on issues; that if politics in this country were not merely a game, we might eventually be led to decide issues forcibly.

What if all this makes for aimlessness, lack of real choice, irresponsibility, and a weakened governing ability? The answer has been that we must rely on the fortunate accident of the strong President and on the energies and resourcefulness of the whole American people when put to the test. This last is a good answer, but alone it is not enough to justify gambling on a weak government, when most of the nations in our league have governments that are infinitely better structured. Grim as it sounds and as much as many people will regret the passing of the old parade, elephants and all, it seems clear that conditions are quickly going to force us to take an adult view of politics and political parties.

Do we need a full-fledged cabinet form of government in the United States? I think we do. In cabinet government the party is fully responsible, the executive is drawn from the legislature and assured of majority support, legislative and executive leadership work together or go down together, and the "in's" can be replaced by the "loyal opposition" if the country turns against what the government of the day is doing. Such a system is the only one that makes sense in the atomic age, because it is the only one that is wholly rational and, hence, responsible.

There are, to be sure, many practical problems in such a course, in addition to the main stumbling block of amending the Constitution in a rather major way. This last difficulty has caused many clear thinkers—such as Woodrow Wilson, for example—to despair of going the whole way, with the result that most proposals are in terms of half-measures.

The number of schemes to tighten up our government that have been offered is almost legion. For example, the Pendleton bill, introduced in 1879, would have provided that members of the cabinet occupy seats on the floor of the Senate and the House and enjoy the right to participate in debates concerning their responsibilities, and that they be required to attend Senate sessions twice a week to answer questions. In 1884 Henry C. Lockwood would have allowed Congress to appoint the President and his cabinet officers, this body to become an executive council. Its chairman would be the Secretary of State and its members would have seats in Congress and be responsible to it for executive behavior. (There are features of this proposal that resemble the Swiss plan of an executive federal council, the president of which is also President of the Confederation, on an annual rotating basis.)

More recently, an authority on the American presidency, Rexford G. Tugwell, has advocated that in order to get away from the importunings of interest groups, we should elect representatives-at-large to Congress instead of representatives from districts, in the hope of making it easier for the President and Congress to agree on policy.

It has also been suggested that the President be popularly elected. (Under cabinet government, of course, he would become head of the government if his party won a majority of the seats in Congress.) Another proposal, by W. Y. Elliott, has been that members of the lower house be elected for four- instead of two-year terms; then if the President and the House failed to work together there could be a dissolution and re-election, but not more often than once in a six-year period; in addition, the financial powers of the upper chamber might be restricted, since, according to Elliott, the Senate is the entrenched stronghold of lobbyists and pressure groups.[5]

Thinking along such lines is a step in the right direction, but if a full-fledged cabinet system would be better, would it be so much harder—since constitutional amendment would be necessary in any case—to go the whole way and secure real responsibility? A constitutional convention would be a good thing for our national morale, would reassure our best friends, and might give pause to those who rely on our internal weaknesses to make their ultimate triumph easier.

In short, instead of electing the President as we now do, we would elect only the members of Congress, after which the head of the majority party in Congress would automatically become President. This means that of necessity he would have had political experience; that the public would already know much about his strengths and weaknesses; that he would have had legislative experience and, therefore, presumably would know how to get along with other legislators, once he moved to the other end of Pennsylvania Avenue.

The President would pick his cabinet either from his own party or, if he chose, from outside of his party among people having special qualifications, but who had not previously been identified with politics. As the recognized head of the winning party, he would have a free hand in organizing the executive branch of the government, whereas now—so great is the institutional jealousy of Congress—limitations in this area are one of the major disabilities under which the President works.

Moreover, as party chief, the President would be sure of loyalty and teamwork from the heads of departments and agencies, for if they failed to cooperate he could merely remove them. As things stand, the President is hedged about by so many restrictions in the matter of appointments that he cannot remove certain officials at all. Included in this category are the commissioners of independent agencies, even though many of these operate in some of the most decisive areas of political economy, including commerce, railroads, power, communications, and the like.

Finally, as discussed more fully in the following chapter, the President should operate through a kind of inner executive council.[6] This group of principal ministers and department heads should divide among them the executive responsibilities of the President, much as senior vice-presidents do in business corporations, their duties assigned to them according to the main segments of the economy. Since a chief cause of institutional jealousy between Congress and the executive branch is failure of communication and especially of face-to-face relationships, these key men would appear before joint congressional committees for briefing sessions once every two weeks or so, and anything said or done by them should be understood as the voice and action of the President.

In other words, it is time now to abandon the idea of politics as a game and the sport of demagogues. Illogical as it may sound, modern governing should somewhat resemble that of more primitive times, when the chief, who was usually the strongest man of the tribe, picked his strongest and brainiest lieutenants and carried on the government with their help. Applied on a large scale, this simple formula would help to secure the results we need. Government then would be run by the best policy executives to be found anywhere, their single duty being to serve the public interest. They would speak and act for the President, making his office for the first time in modern history really capable of operation from a practical, administrative standpoint.

THAT WHICH WORKS

I sympathize with the plight of the conservative businessman confronted with the issue of radical governmental reform. If he should decide to muster the whole force of his kind, he could clearly bring about a change to responsible cabinet government very quickly. But he is faced with a dilemma. If he supports a form of government that operates as rationally and as efficiently as his own corporation, he would reduce his taxes, but run the risk that voters might increasingly rely on government and give it more to do. But if he acquiesces in the *status quo,* he knows that there is a serious question whether our free way of life can survive the competition of centralized regimes that know what they want, control every move and are appropriately organized to secure efficiency of movement and strategy.

The instinct of the conservative businessman, however, is to choose that which works as against that which lacks organizational principle, and it is possible that the tide of business opinion is moving in this direction. Furthermore, most business leaders would rather face reform than lose freedom and the other attributes of democracy. They also know that if government had been reformed some time ago, many of today's problems, owing in part to weaknesses of policy or failures of administration—such as the plight of the railroads or the ravaging of the public resources—would never have reached their present proportions, and the danger that America might drift toward collectivism would be less.

But the clinching argument in favor of what works is that if government is not responsibly run by an inner party circle that decides top policy, that knows how to say "No" as well as "Yes," the public treasury and the statute books alike are defenseless against any organized raid that pressure groups can mount. Then the costs of government become an intolerable burden; the public debt keeps increasing; the national credit is impaired; the wealth of the nation is wasted.

In the field of public assistance, for example, we were assured at the outset that once social insurance became operative against unemployment and the hazards of old age, there would be a gradual diminishing of relief payments, except for the crippled, the sick, and those who for other reasons could not support themselves. Instead, non-insurance welfare expenditures have increased so rapidly that among the civilian expenditures of government they are now next only to subsidies to agriculture—something like $2 billion a year. Instead of something to be avoided, public assistance is now considered a "right" and, hence, a large part of a whole generation is willingly living on relief payments and is losing the ambition to work. Individual politicians, no matter how principled, consider it political suicide to hold out against such pressure.

With a built-in machinery of responsible party rule and responsible party government, however, decision makers as a group could stand up against the pressures that undermine the soundness of the dollar and the health of the economy. In Britain, Prime Minister Harold Macmillan is doing this; in New York State, Governor Nelson Rockefeller finds that he cannot. Is one man less principled and less courageous than the other? Of course not. The difference is in the system. Hence, if businessmen want sound policies in fiscal and other matters, they must choose that which works. Nothing less than responsible government will do the job.

In the case of public assistance expenditures, the obvious solution is to attack the problem of dependency by seeing that jobs are made available, by conducting apprenticeship and vocational rehabilitation programs, by doing something constructive to make work more attractive than relief payments. To be sure, there are many programs already in this area, and they could be made to work better. But it is doubtful whether the grand strategy, the close planning and coordination, the day-to-day working together that are needed if the problem of dependency is to be licked, can take place without a full-fledged cabinet system, in which those who administer are also responsible for recommending legislative and financial policy.

Peter Drucker is right, I think, when he contends that we need a leadership "that demands much of us"; that the President is essentially a political chief and not an efficient executive; that a wise President does not try to do everything himself—he gets others to do it; that the cabinet needs idea men as well as executives; and that in facing up to our problems and getting everyone to do his part toward solving them, it is more important that the President's analysis be "relevant" than that it be "right" all the time.[7]

Moreover, when a single scientific journal reviews four major books on the presidency in a single issue, as *Science* did in 1960,[8] one can see the beginning of a great debate on the structure and functions of government. It is clear, said the reviewer, that none of government's branches "is satisfactorily organized for proper functioning"; that no more than six or seven of the thirty-three former occupants of the White House are now rated as "really competent for the duties of the office";[9] and that any assumption that one man can accomplish all that the President is supposed to accomplish is "altogether beyond reason."

We are looking in the wrong direction, continued this reviewer; we are trying the wrong remedies. We need a bold new approach, like that of the Philadelphia Convention of 1787. There is no longer ground for complacency, as a dozen books on the presidency made clear in 1960. And when we do take a hard look at that office, we shall find that for twentieth-century America, "the institutions of a small emerging seacoast power" are not altogether adequate for a continental nation.

INSTITUTIONALIZING THE PRESIDENCY

No one can justly deprecate the importance of the role the President must play nor minimize the need for outstanding personal traits in the individual. The best leadership comes from individuals, not collectivities. There remains, however, the matter of how outstanding people can be organized together in a team to achieve the best results.

In order not to overlook some points that might be useful in the solutions we are seeking, therefore, it might be well to examine more fully present assumptions and methods as they concern the presidency.

"It is because in their hours of timidity the Congress becomes subservient to the importunities of organized minorities that the President comes more and more to stand as the champion of the rights of the whole country," said the taciturn but eloquent Calvin Coolidge. The function of the President is somehow to promote and protect the public interest amidst the "mosaic of conflicting interests represented in Congress."[10] Agreed. But how?

An old and experienced Washington hand, Louis Brownlow, presents his answer in a word picture that reflects some of the mythology noted above. Thus, the President is a symbol, says Brownlow. In him the people see the expression of their purposes, plans, and aspirations. The President holds his executive power by a direct mandate of the people, and it is therefore toward the people as a whole —not to the other two branches of government—that his lines of responsibility run.

Brownlow then explains this symbol more fully in these words:

We expect the President to symbolize the nation in his office and in his person. It follows, then, that each of us identifies the President with his own private and particular notion of what this nation is and what Americans are. *Each person expects the President to mirror that image,* and as no two of us have precisely the same idea of our national being and destiny, we are inevitably disturbed when the man who symbolizes them does not conform to our ideals.[11]

But although Brownlow is rather mystical in his view of the office, he has high expectations of the man when it comes to general management. Thus, the three presidential functions are to be a competent manager of the *entire* machinery of government, a skilled engineer of the economy of the nation, and a faithful representative of the opinion of the people. The order of this listing represents the ideal if the President "is to fulfill to the maximum what the citizens expect of him," but it should be reversed if it is to conform to what public opinion now thinks the President actually does. It is interesting that Brownlow should list the political economy function as second in either case; this is unusual amongst professional public administrators.[12]

According to the Brownlow analysis, some of the President's functions that occupy more of his time and attention than actual management are only incidental to that job. Thus, he will sometimes assert himself and become chief legislator; he will report to Congress on the State of the Union; and on occasion he will use or threaten to use his veto power. He will also need to move into the no-man's-land of the independent commissions and agencies: "Not only do we expect him to do more than administer the departments and win the assent of the Congress," says Brownlow, we also expect him "to manage *in one way or another* those great independent commissions which regulate certain aspects of our economic life . . ." Brownlow admits that these agencies were deliberately set up by Congress in this way in order to keep the President from supervising them, but as general manager his duty is inescapable. Moreover, each step of the way he must appraise the political expediency and the political implications of all his actions as general manager, "not only in terms of party politics but also in terms of popular and Congressional politics."[13]

It is a rather sorry picture, this "symbol" who "one way or another" must maneuver politically to rationalize the administrative structure of the government and give effect to his ideas of political economy, as Wilson did so brilliantly in his first term of office. Nevertheless, the Brownlow analysis rightly calls attention to the political character of everything the President does. "We have created a position of great power," comments Herring, "but have made the full realization of that power dependent upon *influence* rather than *legal* authority. Hence if our President is to be effective, he must be a politician as well as a statesman."[14]

Among the President's half-dozen or so roles are those of chief politician, chief legislator, chief executive, commander-in-chief of the armed forces, head of foreign affairs, political symbol, and titular head of state. In all of these roles the voters and Congress support him some of the time, but never in all of these roles all of the time. We may admire him as a man, but we are no less likely to withhold support from his most cherished measures. The President is the most powerful person in the nation, but the one who needs most to rely on his wits and his charm if he is to lead.

Brownlow holds that the managerial function *should* be first in importance, not that it is. The reason is partly the jealousy of Congress, which leads it to withhold powers that the President needs and to interfere with duties which the Constitution vests in him. Another reason, as we have been emphasizing, is that not even the ablest President has the time or the organization to become a general manager in the usual meaning of the term.

Consequently, for a long time now, we have been improvising on the theme of the presidential office. We have not called it improvisation. As a matter of fact, we have even tried to justify what we are doing on the ground of principle. The fault with the principle was that a good thing was carried too far and was not sufficiently balanced by other requisite factors.

The principle was to supply staff agencies around the President. The rationalization was that the President could not be general manager himself; and, hence, someone else should perform this function for him. It was also assumed that a staff assistant is a divisible part of the President because he is exclusively the President's, whereas a cabinet officer could not qualify because he has a legal and administrative personality of his own.

As a result of this line of reasoning we got ourselves into an impossible box. With every realization of the President's inability to be general manager, to lead and to coordinate, there was created yet another staff unit in the White House office. One need not be familiar with Parkinson's Law to understand that soon there were special assistants to assistants to executive assistants, coordinators of coordinators, and staff men for staff men. Amid this confusion the President *had* to confine himself to a Sherman Adams, or he would have become so busy he could have seen no one from outside his office during the whole day, in consequence of which the work of government, at least at high levels, would practically have come to a stop.

Reporting toward the end of the Eisenhower administration, Louis Koenig found that in addition to a personal White House staff of some 250 employees, there was a second circle consisting of powerful agencies such as the Bureau of the Budget, the National Security Council, the Council of Economic Advisers, the Office of Defense Mobilization, and the intelligence agencies, constituting a "sizeable bureaucracy." This group of employees alone, numbering more than a thousand, occupied 134,000 square feet of floor space in two buildings, *in addition* to the east and west wings of the White House itself. The presidential agencies, as they are called (to distinguish them from the White House staff), involved a budget outlay of no less than $5 million a year.[15]

When it is considered that the term "White House staff" was not even officially designated as such until 1939; that even as late as Herbert Hoover's day it consisted of only three secretaries, a military and a naval aide, and two-score clerks, the mushrooming since that time is a remarkable story. The turning point occurred shortly after the report of the so-called Brownlow Committee, when President

Roosevelt was given six presidential assistants, each "with a passion for anonymity." The trend reached its apogee during the two Eisenhower administrations, but apparently by the time President Kennedy was inaugurated in 1961 the excessiveness of the expedient had become clear. The new President announced that he would have none of this huge staff organization, that he would do his own masterminding. Simultaneously, the so-called Jackson Committee of the Senate, which had been studying top organization for policy decision for some time, came out with a resounding indictment of the excessive proliferation of staff agencies and other administrative machinery surrounding the President as good things that had been carried too far.[16]

Staff agencies are indispensable when used in moderation throughout an organization and not concentrated at the apex. Attempts since 1939 to reform and institutionalize the presidency show the fallacy of such a concentration. This apparent dismissal of an inglorious experiment does not, however, solve the underlying problem that gave rise to it in the first place.

The problem of assisting the President is now more urgent than ever, and the solution lies in a fundamental reform based on a cabinet government. When we compare the President's situation as it has been for the past twenty-five years with the vision of what it might be under a responsible cabinet government, it hardly seems possible that leaders of opinion would have any serious question as to where to throw their support.

The organization of the executive office is only one of the many problems, of course, in the complex of difficulties faced by the President of the United States. He cannot be sure of political backing, for example; under responsible government it would be imperative. He cannot rely on the support of Congress or even of his own party members in Congress; in cabinet government they would either support him or all would fall together. Because of congressional jealousy the President does not have control of all the executive machinery of the government, although Article II of the Constitution specifically states that "the Executive power shall be vested in a President" and that "he shall take care that the laws be faithfully executed . . ."; under responsible government, institutional jealousy would disappear because officials in both branches would be working together. The President has at least six major functions, any one of which constitutes a demanding full-time job for the ordinary mortal; under responsible government the fiction that the President, personally, must do everything would be abolished; and the managerial work of government would be organized so as to assure leadership and co-ordination.

Responsibility is action first, accountability second. Institutional balances are now so awry that action is constantly frustrated and in-fighting all too common. Accountability is side-tracked through congressional investigations that are often merely "fishing expeditions" to discover opportunities to expose derelict executive officials. Under responsible government, congressional committees would periodically confer with key executive officials, when need be summoning them to explain their actions before Congress itself; and would force the President to resign if he could not keep his own house in order.

Our strength as a nation depends more than anything on whether we can make our government a more effective instrument. There is no question what must be done: First, political parties must be made more responsible than they are; secondly, the President must be assured of the support of his congressional majority; and thirdly, he must have the help of an able executive team that will free him from the detailed work of administration, so that he may exercise his role as leader of the nation.

THIRTEEN

TOP-LEVEL ORGANIZATION

How to organize the top level of government is a fateful issue. Failure to secure the necessary planning and coordination could result in the collapse of the political economy, whereas success may assure a better way of life than this country has ever known.

Almost everyone agrees that whatever else the occupant of the White House may be, he can no longer be an amateur. "In its finest moments," says an experienced Washington correspondent, "the White House has been occupied by men of political genius—Lincoln, Wilson, Franklin Roosevelt."[1] The only respect in which a President may be "above politics" is in his devotion to the public interest. More than any office in the world, the presidency of the United States demands and rewards political mastery.

OPPOSING VIEWS

Two points of view are in conflict in the matter of top-level organization for the federal government. One holds that the President is of necessity a lonely leader; that he should have a charismatic personality; that he should concentrate power in his own hands, dominate his department heads, participate in all major decisions and many minor ones, and generally place his personal stamp on the government. He should try to keep all the guiding strings in his own hands, appoint technicians rather than political colleagues and independent executives, actively engage in the selection of their immediate lieutenants, be careful to maintain multiple sets of advisers on every problem, confide wholly in no one, and jealously guard his own personal decision on every issue.[2]

In business, where this is called the one-man show or the benevolent autocrat, the type is becoming increasingly rare. There are still some examples of outstanding accomplishment according to the strong-man formula, at least during the time he is in office. What happens after that is often a different matter.

The opposing approach to top-level organization wants a *team* of strong men, not merely one individual, however strong. This is not to disparage the importance of individual abilities as the basic ingredient of success, but it does place a greater emphasis on structure and on creating an institutional model that will carry on with a high degree of continuity, constantly becoming more effective, and avoiding the danger of collapse after a strong man leaves office.

Those who favor this institutionalized approach support it with arguments which seem to me unanswerable. We *must* come up with a unifying national purpose and a plan of action to achieve it if we are to match the direct-action methods of communism. The engine of American government has become so large and complex that no one individual can be expected to master it, much less dominate it. Foreign policy issues alone are now so time-consuming and awesome in their implications that any President, no matter how great his abilities, must of necessity delegate to subordinates great chunks of his authority in other matters.

Even the supporters of the strong-man formula agree that no President can do all that he is supposed to do. How then, in the name of common sense, can we expect him to do otherwise than delegate, fix responsibilities, and multiply himself by the number of trained executives (as against staff assistants) needed to do the total planning and decision-making job?

Hence, for mid-century America, a pattern for the presidency which is collegial in approach, a kind of board-chairman type of organization that is modeled also on the holding-company device, seems the realistic course, for it is more in line with tested concepts of how to run big institutions than the outmoded virtuoso theory. The chairman of the board, in effect, frees himself of all petty and medium-sized concerns and concentrates solely on the large ones.

Then he gives big jobs to big people, grants them an authority equal to their responsibility, and puts his own stress on big stakes, the confluence of many policies, and the coordination of the whole.

The bigger the institution becomes, the more must the chairman of the board concentrate on putting first things first. This does not mean that his personality is a secondary consideration. On the contrary, the more immediate and compelling he can make it felt, the better. The point is that he must not try to decide everything himself, do everything himself, or coordinate everything himself because as a reasonable man he knows that to extend himself in this way defeats its own purpose.

It is no valid objection to the board-chairman approach to point out that we have tried this system in the recent past and found it wanting. It is true that the Eisenhower administration was sometimes called the board type, but in fact it was not. It was merely an assistant-president-staff type of organization, for it did not divide executive responsibilities among a team of full-fledged executives, as the ordinary board does.

There have been just enough virtuosos in the history of the American presidency to encourage people, even scholars, to hope that the miracle will happen again. But it cannot be counted on, and even if it could, the size and complexity of modern government in Washington are such that the end product could not possibly be as effective as in the past. The problems confronting the President in the early 1960's, remarked a hard-bitten newspaper reporter, are more complicated, onerous, and somber than they were even fifteen years before, at the end of World War II. Today we are dealing with superpowers. The lessons of the past are not wholly reliable. Until fifteen years ago America was many things, but she was not one of two global superpowers nor the possessor of the hydrogen bomb.[3] A system in which a strong President works closely with strong subordinates and combines the intelligence and energy of half a dozen to a dozen people, is more rational than one that relies not only on the strengths but also on the human frailties of one man.

An implication of virtuoso rule is an inflated "kitchen cabinet," producing government by anonymity. The board-chairman type puts the emphasis on hard-hitting executives—production men, if you like. If the one-man myth fades, therefore, as I think it must, we may expect fewer policy advisers surrounding the President[4] and more policy executives dividing up the work and relieving him of his managerial load. This is the organization pattern of all large institutions and its effectiveness has been sufficiently tested so that from the pragmatic standpoint of results, it can now be called the best.

Instead, therefore, of judging alternative solutions by subjective evaluations of who was the better President—Franklin Roosevelt as an illustration of one type, for example, and Eisenhower of another —let us, more sensibly, consider top-level organization in big institutions on the basis of *all* the relevant information that can be secured.

A RECOMMENDED PLAN

The system that we have called in an offhand way the board-chairman type is based on a plural or collegial type of executive. The chief executive himself is ultimately responsible for what his colleagues do; hence, in a collegial arrangement he is considerably more than first amongst equals. The main emphasis, however, is on the division of total responsibility into several areas, so that each member of the collegium has a definite mandate, a workable span of concentration, and all the freedom needed to carry out his assignment. In addition, he is responsible for seeing that the work in his area is coalesced with that in all other areas, so that all members of the top team focus on the whole range of institutional policies and survival values. It is at this level that the chief executive principally operates. A main reason for releasing his time is to allow him to concentrate on survival and grand strategy.

The collegial holding-company pattern of organization suggested here is not a committee as that term is usually understood, because the roles of committee members are rarely so clearly defined and there is less need for hierarchy. Nor is the proposal exactly the board type of organization as conventionally known. Boards are often exclusively policy groups or, if their role is also operational, the work is frequently so compartmentalized that board members work in virtual isolation from each other. The collegial pattern—or what might also be called the inner executive group pattern—that is favored in many large corporations and in governments in other nations vests ultimate authority and responsibility in the chief executive, subordinates the subchiefs to the top executive, provides clear areas of responsibility for each subchief, and requires concentration on the aggregate of policy by the whole group.

Combined with the board pattern there should also be elements of the holding-company type of organizational thinking. The President and his subchiefs should design grand strategy, make top policy and political decisions, provide the signals and the coordination for the government as a whole, and do everything in their power to facilitate the work of action programs in the departments and in the field services. Then the departments and agencies do the work.

The holding-company analogy is appropriate for yet another reason. The federal government already serves the states and great urban centers in a variety of ways. It passes legislation that is state administered, assists state and local programs through the federal-aid formula, and acts as banker to the cities in matters of housing and public works. If decentralization through regional governments should eventuate, as envisaged elsewhere in this book, the holding-company role of the federal government would become even more pronounced than it is today.

Under the collegial type of organization for the federal government, the President and his subchiefs would be mainly responsible for two things. First, they would conduct foreign relations along safe and sound lines. Secondly, they would also emphasize the domestic role of government, which is to keep the economy in balance and on an even keel by the skillful use of policy controls having to do with money, credit, public works, and conservation in order to prevent recessions and depressions. The point cannot be made too often that if recessions are to be avoided, if the standard of living is to rise and to be justly distributed, and if the profit system is to be maintained by making community needs as well as corporate profits assured in an over-all way, then the federal government must do the job because no other institution can.

As the federal government is now set up, the executive branch has holding-company responsibilities, but lacks the organization and the structure to perform its political economy tasks satisfactorily. In theory, the President is general manager, but even the strongest President cannot actually put his mind to management policy and decision making as much as the need requires. His enormous staff does far more cogitation than can ever be communicated to him. When, as under President Eisenhower, this problem was tackled through what was in effect an Office of Assistant President, the differing points of view were winnowed out at lower levels instead of reaching the President directly, as they would have, had a collegial executive group met with him. Under the assistant-president pattern the President runs the risk of getting only half the story.

Then, to make things worse, there are ten major federal departments, each including a multitude of different and sometimes unrelated activities and each operating in more or less watertight compartments. An exception is when, as occasionally happens, a cabinet or interdepartmental committee is created to study a particular problem. But these committees often confuse responsibilities, usually lack the power and the inclination to come up with recommendations for decisive action, and generally become moribund before someone remembers to abolish them.

Topping the whole thing off, there are upward of a hundred detached agencies of all kinds: from commissions regulating main sectors of the economy, such as labor relations and industrial monopoly; through government corporations spending billions of dollars, such as the Commodity Credit Corporation and the Tennessee Valley Authority; all the way down to little known programs having to do with battle monuments and the affairs of the city of Washington. No one thinks the President can do much, if anything, about this vast mélange of federal activity, and yet everyone assumes that in theory he should. Especially for that part of the federal bureaucracy which, like regulatory commissions and government corporations, is at the heart of political economy decision making.

Unfortunately, the picture is not overdrawn. And although three major reorganizations have been undertaken since 1937, the situation is not markedly improved because the decisive issue has been avoided: the President has more than he can do and needs the assistance of subexecutives instead of large staff organizations.

A practical plan of organization would be to reduce the number of the President's assistants to four or five and provide that none should have executive responsibilities over departments or agencies; they should be *personal* assistants to the President and not in the direct line of authority between him and the operating programs.

Then, there should be an inner executive or collegial group of eight men. One of these would be responsible generally for coordinating foreign affairs and the other generally for coordinating domestic affairs. Under them, the other six members of the group would handle major areas of the economy, in some cases having more than one program, now called a department, under them.

Together, this group of two top coordinators and six subexecutives would constitute the top management team directly under the President. Their duty would be to see that the work of the government as a whole, in behalf of the President, was properly planned, energized, and coordinated. They would think as a team, as a collectivity, and not segmentally.

Under this plan of organization there might be more than the present number of departments (ten) if it were decided, for example, to create new ones for transportation, urban and housing affairs, and natural resources. A responsible top-management group would make this kind of flexibility possible as the need appeared.

In addition to the inner executive group, there would also be the cabinet in the pattern of most other national governments where there is a large cabinet and a small inner cabinet. The large cabinet here might run to twenty or thirty top executives (in recent years cabinet meetings have often been attended by this many officials), while the inner cabinet would consist only of the eight men of the top executive group.

Under this plan, the larger cabinet would not meet nearly so often as it has in recent years, and it would deal only broadly with policy and objectives. The inner group, on the other hand, might meet as often as twice a week, as any small directing group frequently must. Being an executive body, moreover, it would meet only when it needed to and not on a fixed schedule. This kind of rigidity usually results in meetings that are merely *pro forma* and generally regarded as uninspiring and a waste of a busy man's time.

Of the staff officials and agencies now attached to the White House or the Executive Office of the President, many would be transferred to one or another of the two key coordinators for foreign and domestic affairs or to one of the major departments. The work now done by the National Security Council, for example, would be attached to the coordinator in charge of foreign affairs. The Bureau of the Budget, which now reports directly to the President, should be attached to the Treasury Department, as it is in most other national governments.

Finally, the so-called independent agencies (regulatory commissions, government corporations, and other units not in the regular departments) would be tied into the central structure of policy and execution either by assignment to one of the major departments in a formal or liaison capacity, or, in exceptional cases, by assignment directly to one of the members of the inner executive group.

To help to visualize this plan, I have drawn two alternative diagrams to show how federal organization would look, first, if the existing departmental framework were not changed, and secondly, if the structure of the economy were made the dominant consideration in an ideal assignment of responsibilities.

Certain features are common to both plans: The President would be relieved of most of his day-to-day attention to coordination. All domestic and foreign affairs would be pulled together under single coordinators. Not all departments would be included in the inner executive group, but all functions would be. Although details have not been supplied in the diagrams, independent agencies would be tied into the central framework. And finally, the major planning agencies, such as the Bureau of the Budget and the National Security Council, would be tied into the coordinative machinery *below* the President's office instead of being a part of it.

Other features in common are that a large part of the duty of the coordinator for domestic affairs would be to create conditions favorable to economic growth and stability, and in this connection the Council of Economic Advisers would report directly to him. Similarly, the coordinator for foreign affairs would coordinate foreign and defense policy, and the National Security Council, or its successor, would report directly to him. This seems more sensible than to try to make the Secretary of State, in effect, superior to the Secretary of Defense in matters of policy, as some exasperated individuals have recommended. The State Department would be relatively small so as more easily to concentrate on diplomacy and constructive solutions to world tensions. And because technical assistance and foreign aid should be offered without strings attached, they would be administered not by the State Department but by a separate agency reporting to the coordinator for foreign affairs.

The success of the coordinator plan would depend largely on the degree to which these two officers kept their machinery small and avoided the temptation to appoint assistants and assistants to assistants. What these two men must do can be done only by them personally, for they must consult frequently with each other and with the President on how to tie foreign and domestic policy together in an over-all plan and strategy.

The only real difference between the two alternative diagrams, therefore, is the departmental structure. If present departmental designations were unchanged, as shown on Diagram 1, the departments represented directly within the eight-man group would be State, Defense, Treasury, Commerce, Labor, and Agriculture, with Interior and Post Office tied in through Commerce; with Health, Education, and Welfare represented through Labor; and Justice reporting through the Attorney General directly to the coordinator for domestic affairs. To have every department represented in the inner group would clearly make it too large. The Post Office Department has few major policy issues to decide or interests of the economy to cope with as large as those of the other departments. Health, Education, and Welfare is an admixture of functions poorly rationalized by calling them "welfare," and since labor had more to do than any other group with creating them in the first place, they and Labor belong together.

As for Justice, if the Antitrust Division were transferred to Commerce, as recommended in a previous chapter, the remaining police function of the Justice Department would not involve many important economy-wide policy decisions. Since the Attorney General,

DIAGRAM 1– ORGANIZATION OF THE FEDERAL GOVERNMENT FOR MANAGEMENT LEADERSHIP:
With Existing Departments

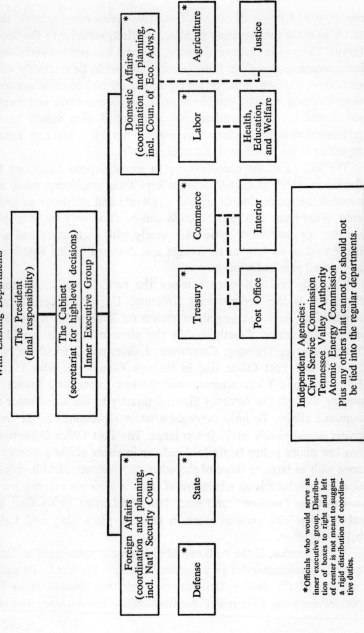

*Officials who would serve as inner executive group. Distribution of boxes to right and left of center is not meant to suggest a rigid distribution of coordinative duties.

DIAGRAM 2—ORGANIZATION OF THE FEDERAL GOVERNMENT FOR MANAGEMENT LEADERSHIP:
With Reorganized Departments

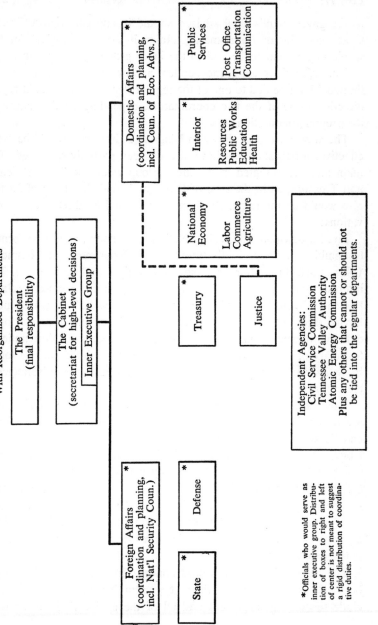

The President
(final responsibility)

The Cabinet
(secretariat for high-level decisions)

Inner Executive Group

Foreign Affairs
(coordination and planning,
incl. Nat'l Security Coun.) *

State *

Defense *

Domestic Affairs *
(coordination and planning,
incl. Coun. of Eco. Advs.)

Treasury *

National
Economy *

Labor
Commerce
Agriculture

Interior *

Resources
Public Works
Education
Health

Public
Services *

Post Office
Transportation
Communication

Justice

Independent Agencies:
Civil Service Commission
Tennessee Valley Authority
Atomic Energy Commission
Plus any others that cannot or should not
be tied into the regular departments.

*Officials who would serve as
inner executive group. Distribution of boxes to right and left
of center is not meant to suggest
a rigid distribution of coordinative duties.

as the government's legal adviser, should in any case report directly to the coordinator for domestic affairs, it would be logical for the whole department to be tied to the inner group by that means.

Finally, on Diagram 1, independent and non-departmental agencies that could not be tied to one of the regular departments, should report directly to one of the two coordinators, depending on the nature of the program in question.

The alternative plan shown in Diagram 2, however, would be more effective, for reasons that have already been partially suggested. The main areas represented in the inner group would be State, Defense, and Treasury, as in the case of Diagram 1, and the status of Justice also would be the same. But then there would be three major innovations:

First, a new coalition, called National Economy, would be formed to combine duties presently found in the Departments of Commerce (plus antitrust), Labor (plus social security), and Agriculture. The interests and policies of these three groups are so closely related that they should be organizationally related as well. This would mean having three separate department heads (cabinet officers) as at present, but it would make possible much closer coordination under a Secretary of the National Economy. This plan is similar to one found in Switzerland, for example, that has produced the advantages I claim for it.

I realize that these three departments, and especially Agriculture, are now so large that bringing them together might be judged difficult, if not impossible.[5] But consider the following points: Industry, labor, and agriculture must find their common ground if economic policy is to be stable and sound; only under a common coordinator are they likely to find this common ground; and if the ideas regarding decentralization advanced in an earlier chapter are adopted, there would be a considerable reduction in the size of all three agencies—again, especially Agriculture—thus making them more manageable.

The second innovation would concern Interior. Its duties would be vastly more important than at present because they would include resource management and all of the engineering functions of government, such as public buildings and roads; and in addition, the department would take over public health, public education, and power resources, including their regulation.

The third innovation would be a new Department of Public Services, to include all of transportation, communications, and the Post Office. This formula would help to crack one of our major unsolved problems: where to put the regulatory commissions such as the Federal Communications Commission, the Interstate Commerce Commission, and the like. These agencies might not remain intact, but their functions should be taken over by a cabinet officer able to emphasize promotion in these areas as well as regulation. Finally, the remaining non-departmental agencies would be treated in the same manner as in Diagram 1.

An advantage of this over-all plan is to provide greater latitude for change than is possible under the existing system where Congress legislates regarding the principal questions of organization. Under the arrangement suggested here, independent agencies as well as bureaus within the departments could be shifted as experience indicated the need. No part of the organization would be fixed except the apex, the President and his team of eight executives. Suppose, for example, it turned out that social security would be better off in the Commerce Department instead of in Labor; the transfer could be made without disturbing working relationships with the coordinator in charge of domestic affairs. Or suppose it were found that soil conservation, now in Agriculture, would be better off if connected with Interior, which would be concerned with conservation broadly; this change also could be made without upsetting working relationships.

Further, a collegial type of executive organization might also prove advantageous at the departmental level in some of the larger departments, such as National Economy, Interior, and Public Services, serving better for these larger agencies than a Secretary aided by an undersecretary and assistant secretaries each working more or less in isolation. If so, there is no reason why the pattern could not be adopted in some agencies and not in others, for irrelevant uniformity is the foe of administrative efficiency and executive leadership.

SECURING CONTINUITY

If reorganization according to one of these plans could be effected, the next major objective of reform should be to provide continuity in a system that at present is dangerously weak in that respect. No private business could operate with a complete turnover of top personnel every four to eight years. Actually, it is worse than that in Washington because in recent years policy officials have been averaging only about two years in office. Since it takes the better part of a year to learn the intricacies of a top-level job, that leaves precious little time for an official to hit pay dirt during a single term of office.

Even more reckless is the discontinuity of national policy. With the best of good will and the most meticulous arrangements for the transfer of administration from one political party to the other, foreign nations become jittery or bellicose, and Wall Street and business reflect the fear caused by changing pilots even in smooth weather. The plague of troubles at the end of the Eisenhower administration and the commencement of the Kennedy administration is so recent as to need no further elaboration.

There are four ways by which continuity might be improved. The first is by regarding some of the top executive staff, including the inner executive group, as indispensable and carrying them over from one administration to the next; an example is Douglas Dillon, who served the State Department in the Eisenhower administration and became Secretary of the Treasury under President Kennedy. The second method is by making the undersecretaries of the regular departments career officials by tradition, so that they also could become a principal source of continuity during a changeover of administration.

The third method is by increasing the leadership opportunities for the permanent civil service, as mentioned in previous chapters. Even if the over-all structure were not strengthened to anywhere near the extent that it should be, this last improvement would make an enormous difference in the planning and decision-making effectiveness of the federal government and correspondingly in the effectiveness with which the political economy operates.

The fourth way to secure better continuity is to improve recruitment to the top executive ranks of government, especially at the coordinative, cabinet, and subcabinet levels; for unless outstandingly able men occupy these positions, there is little reason or incentive to carry at least some of them over from one administration to the next. Appointments at this policy level, of course, are the President's own because these men are members of his official household. Here, as in other areas of federal administration, however, the field is so vast that some kind of assistance to the President would be an improvement over the present system. Thus, among other sources of possible candidates available to the President, there might be maintained somewhere in the government—possibly in the Civil Service Commission—a roster of the best executive talent to be found anywhere in the nation: in industry, the universities, the labor unions, in state and city governments. The Civil Service Commission might also consult panels drawn from certain professional groups such as engineers, accountants, personnel experts, and professional public administrators.

A good many top government executives would be promoted from within, of course, but this practice should be flexible, with the needs of the job and acceptability to the President as the prime considerations. As at present, senatorial confirmation also should be required.

Men closest to the President, especially at the inner group and cabinet levels, would have to be temperamentally and generally attuned to work harmoniously with the President and with each other. An experienced executive, however, can usually work with others and be loyal to the top man's policies even when there is not full agreement in every detail. I believe that a better method of recruitment than at present and from a broader field would produce this type of man and that even loyalty to the President would be higher than it has sometimes been in the past.

The chief justification for the plan proposed here is that in the modern world, the programs of nations are viable only if all the threads of policy are woven together, and this takes appropriate organization. The Jackson committee has stated this need in the comment that "the line between foreign and domestic policy, never clear to begin with, has now almost been erased. Foreign policy and military policy have become more inseparable than ever. Today almost every department of our government and some eighteen independent agencies also, are involved with national security policy. Four government agencies and six international financial organizations work in the field of foreign economic aid alone."[6]

Coordination must bring these segmented policies into a workable unity. Then, the President must be on a level a little above them, except in the final stages of decision, to allow himself time to think and reflect on what constitutes ultimate policy designed to promote national security and economic well-being. Hence, he should not try to intervene in matters of detail; these should be handled by his management team.

These, then, are the outlines of a plan and a brief indication of the reasoning on which it is based. In the chapter that follows, I consider, by reference to analogous situations in other large-scale organization, public and private, the reasons that this pattern seems to be so widely preferred over any other.

FOURTEEN

PUBLIC AND PRIVATE MODELS

Canada has worked out an effective system of high-level planning and coordination in the confederation government,[1] and some features of it could well become part of our own reconstructed organizational set-up in Washington.

Thus, as in Britain and many other nations, there is in Ottawa a large cabinet consisting of all ministers designated for inclusion in that body. Then there is an inner executive group of cabinet ministers (also members of the Privy Council) consisting of the principal policy and coordinative officers of the government. Ordinarily they number around six, although the figure varies. This inner group deals with the economy as a whole, with foreign policy as a whole, and with the government as a whole. Its members take this organic view of their responsibilities and work together as a unity in over-all planning and coordination.

Each of the ministers of the inner cabinet is in charge of a large area of policy and administration, which ordinarily centers in his own department but is broad enough to include lesser programs that are functionally related. For example, Canada recently created a department of forestry because this had become a problem requiring special attention. But instead of including the new minister in the top governing group, his department was given a direct relation to the minister of the inner group who is broadly responsible for resources and development generally.

In this total pattern, political leadership and leadership in the civil service are tied together in a rather ingenious way. The top Canadian civil servant is the secretary of the Privy Council, whose members also constitute the inner cabinet. This civil servant, working with the ministers of the inner cabinet, formulates for the Prime Minister the most important matters of policy and legislation. And since each minister also holds the reins in the actual administration of affairs, the secretary of the Privy Council is tied in here, too.

Administrative coordination also takes place in Ottawa in the Treasury Board. Here, again, a top civil servant is the secretary of the board, and its members are drawn from the principal areas of the government and the economy, so that the group is a treasury board in name only. It is located in the Treasury, but takes a government-wide and economy-wide view of its business. Its function is to review every proposed expenditure of any magnitude (even though the monies have already been appropriated) from the standpoint of their time- liness, appropriateness, and consistency with over-all plans and ob- jectives, before the funds are actually made available.

In theory, of course, such a function could become a serious bot- tleneck and a brake on the plans of a progressive minister desiring to institute a new program. No doubt this sometimes happens. But the other side of the matter is that because of government-wide re- view by the best policy and executive personnel available, all pro- grams are likely to be soundly conceived and executed, and neces- sary coordination and higher strategy are facilitated.

In other words, working through a small inner group of top min- isters, and with coordination in the Privy Council and the Treasury Board, Canada is able to reconcile two necessary ingredients of po- litical economy. First, the organic, economy-wide view is maintained through the device of the small inner cabinet; and secondly, cabinet ministers and civil servants not included in this top group have plenty of opportunity for policy and executive leadership in an over- all plan where objectives are reasonably clear.

Britain's cabinet government works in a similar way. There is an inner group within the larger cabinet, and the Prime Minister is re- lieved of an overly heavy burden because his chief colleagues share the duties of policy decision making and executive leadership. The Prime Minister himself has no staff except for personal assistants. He looks to his cabinet ministers for all planning and decision making. The cabinet has a secretariat, and plans and decides as a group.

Among administrative agencies, only the Central Statistical Board reports directly to the cabinet, a device aimed at keeping it above suspicion and at guarding its integrity. As a result of these over-all arrangements, a remarkably small superstructure runs a world-wide government.

Also in the British government, the Treasury performs the chief housekeeping and budgetary functions and generally coordinates financial plans and expenditures. The Economic Section of the Treasury is the top policy planning staff for the government as a whole and reports to the Prime Minister through the Chancellor of the Exchequer.[2] Formerly this division, consisting of twelve top economists, was attached directly to the cabinet, but it was found that as a Treasury unit it received more support and its recommendations were more readily adopted.

This Economic Section, headed by a civil servant, deals broadly with stabilization on the domestic front. It prepares an annual economic survey, but ordinarily its reports are not made public. In its work it draws on other departments and agencies, as does our own Council of Economic Advisers. The device works well because the cabinet and the principal ministers act collegially and provide a unified leadership.

The Swiss Republic offers yet another interesting analogy. Like the United States, Switzerland is, of course, a federal republic. What in this country we call states' rights has always been a strong force in Switzerland; and, hence, government is closely controlled through the cantons, the use of the popular referendum, and the delegation of authority wherever possible.

The remarkable and distinctive feature of the Swiss federal executive branch is that it consists of a Federal Council for the management of the public business. The President of the Confederation, who is a member of the Federal Council, does not possess greater influence than any of his colleagues.[3] The seven equal members represent different political parties, as proportionately as possible, and no two members may be citizens of the same canton. Members are elected by the Federal Assembly from among private citizens or public officials for four-year terms, and the Council is entrusted with all the duties of a cabinet. Its chairmanship rotates each year; and the man who fills it, and who also by that means becomes President of the Confederation, has no unusual powers, such as the power to veto or to act as legislative leader.

Every fourth year all seats in the Federal Council must be filled, but in practice there is little turnover. Federal Councillors who wish to continue in office are customarily re-elected, so that one or at most two positions need be filled at any one time. Councillors continue to serve as long as they have the confidence of the legislature, which elects them in the first place, and service may be for twenty years or more. When a vacancy occurs, the other councillors may choose to transfer to it if they wish, but in practice most remain in their original jobs.

Federal Councillors have both policy and executive duties to perform. Although they are not permitted by the constitution to serve in the legislature (or to take any other employment, for that matter) they draft much of the legislation, either on request from the General Assembly or directly on their own initiative. Their major duties, however, are administrative, each having an area of government and the economy to look after. In all of this work, final decisions are collegially presented. Although each federal Councillor has his own department to administer and enjoys a considerable freedom therein, his relation to his colleagues is one of organic unity and shared responsibility for the public interest.

The procedure is that on any tough problem, a combination of two or three councillors will be formed, depending on the problem. A new trade agreement, for example, might involve the minister of foreign affairs, the minister of national economy, and the minister of the interior. These changing combinations are decided by the whole Council. When such a group has done its work, with the help of outside consultants if it wishes, the whole Council debates the recommendations that are made. In some cases the Federal Council has divided four-to-three on particular issues, but once the majority view has been ascertained, all minority members are bound by custom to maintain a united front, and any betrayal of previous opposition would result in the eclipse of a man's political career, so highly is sportsmanship regarded in this matter.[4] If he wishes, however, he may properly resign and oppose the measure as a private citizen.

It is interesting that this procedure resembles that of Standard Oil of New Jersey, as will be explained later. Indeed, some of the most interesting analogies to the plan proposed here for government in Washington come from the experience of our largest industrial corporations. Some political scientists deny the relevance of such evidence on the ground that the institutions of business and government are markedly different. I disagree. The purposes may be different—profit in one case and a non-profit service in the other; they may not be equally subject to law and constitutions; and government may be more political than business. When all this is admitted, the fact remains that the larger a business corporation becomes, the more does its managerial problems resemble those of the political state, which is what is in question here.

Some of the greatest oil companies, for example, are said to be integrated because they try by organization to coalesce and unify the different stages of production and distribution from the time a shaft is sunk until a motorist's tank is filled. This is an interesting datum for the organization scientist because one of government's greatest problems is just here: How to get a reasonable unity out of great complexity.

Like many other large undertakings, the oil companies also have administrative headaches similar to those of government and stemming in part from exceeding diversification. Thus, they operate shipping companies, by-product plants, foreign offices, insurance schemes, and much more, as well as specializing in old-fashioned petroleum geology. As diversification increases, so also do problems of policy, organization, and politics in corresponding ratio.

In Standard Oil of Indiana, for example, a few years ago there was a notorious proxy fight as a result of which the company's president was unhorsed. Thereafter, having had one experience with an authoritarian head, the company sought to avoid a repetition of the experience by creating an executive committee that virtually runs the business. It consists of four persons: the president, two executive vice-presidents, and a financial vice-president. The two executive vice-presidents are young—around forty or so—and much of the burden of administration is thrown on their shoulders.

In addition, a sharp line is drawn between the holding company, headed by the executive committee of four, and the integrated operating company. The role of the holding-company executives is to review and to assist. They review questions of policy and finance in which, as men of experience, they may see implications overlooked by operating officials. In general, however, the rule is to interfere as little as possible with operations so as to encourage energy in the operating executives.

"But," I asked, when studying this situation, "does not the fact of constant review tend to take the bloom off the peach? Would not the operating people get more satisfaction if you were not breathing down their necks?" To which the reply was, "I suppose so. *But in a large organization it can't be avoided.* We have a financial stake; errors must be avoided; even when you have good men there must be a lot of checking because the collective judgment of four good men is usually more reliable than the judgment of a single person, no matter how able he may be. We can only try to be as considerate of each other as possible and still be hardheaded."[5] I quote this because a similar organizational philosophy would be useful at the top levels of federal administration in Washington. It will not be forthcoming, however, unless there is first the structure to make it feasible.

Perhaps the most ingenious and successful method of top-level coordination is the system worked out by Standard Oil of New Jersey. This company has long been known for its progressiveness in management and personnel matters, so such a development is not surprising. The operation of the system is fairly complicated as to detail, but in general outline it is something like this:[6]

The president, of course, is top man. The real work of policy formulation and decision making, however, is the job of an executive committee consisting of the president, the chairman of the board, and four executive vice-presidents. To this group are added nine full-time directors, making a total top executive staff of fifteen. These are the men who constitute the high command of the holding company.

Affiliated with the holding company are two hundred companies operating all over the world. In Venezuela, the Middle East, and elsewhere they are plunged into international politics (although they try scrupulously to be politically neutral) to an extent resembling that of the State Department. As a matter of fact, Adolf Berle, a former official of that department, has said that most foreign offices could probably learn something by studying the foreign offices of the oil companies.[7]

In Jersey Standard's head office, the organizational structure is viewed as a major competitive weapon; its finer points are kept under wraps, and the company never publishes an organization chart. The key factors, however, are these:

A large organization must combine the best in centralization with the best in decentralization. The method is to push the execution of policy as far down as possible into the affiliated operating companies, and at the same time centralize policy determinations that bear upon survival. Much information comes to the top ranks of the holding company that the operating companies have less opportunity to receive; top people acquire a wider knowledge and experience than most operating officials. The role of the top, therefore, is to pass along to the operating companies any information that might be useful; and collectively to settle life-and-death matters of policy, for this is where the competitive edge is secured.

The underlying idea is to allow the two hundred operating companies to run their own day-to-day affairs and to grant them the maximum degree of freedom so long as their top managements have sound judgment, which is another term for survival sense. What, then, is the coordinative responsibility of the holding company? In the words of a Jersey official, it is "seeing that affiliates act in the best interests of Jersey as well as their own." Applying this rule to the federal government, it means seeing that the fractional interest also serves the public interest. In Jersey, the holding company is banker, executive personnel department, and management consultant. It sets basic policies; has the last word on proposals for capital investment; and selects, trains, and evaluates the officers and directors of the affiliates.

The original and exciting aspect of the work of the fifteen-man leadership group at the top is the manner in which its members maintain contact with one another to secure unity. The conventional system in most corporations and in most governments is to compartmentalize: a certain individual will be in charge of a company, a function, a geographical unit, or a staff activity. In Jersey it is different. Each member of the top team of fifteen has a variety of contact points, creating functional cross-checks. For example, one of the fifteen may be the specialist on production, serve as the number-two man for Latin American affairs, and have a special interest in executive development programs.

There are three major objectives: first, to use the best skills of the top fifteen in two or three relationships, not merely one; secondly, by this means to prevent stratification and encourage dynamic integration; and thirdly, by this system of skill admixture to get team judgment instead of one-man judgment.

There is no set formula for any job at this top level; each is tailored to the individual. The total work is analyzed and then partitioned, so that two or possibly three people are involved in each section, one as principal, the other or others as double-check. Not only does this provide a double check, but as a result of jumping boundaries in the work load, it also creates real organic unity and common thinking. "The problems we deal with today," the company president once remarked, "are so complex that two men's judgment is better than one's, and three are better still."

Needless to say, the six members of the executive committee have fewer specific responsibilities than the other nine directors for the simple reason that they are paid to scan higher elevations of policy and survival.

One of the keenest problems in any large organization is the choice between functional and geographic (areal) coordination. Whichever one is emphasized, the other suffers. With this in mind, Jersey divides its two hundred affiliates into six regions, such as Latin America or the Middle East, with a control director for each and a coordination staff for three. (There are no coordination staffs for American, Canadian, and Far Eastern operations because these are concentrated in three big companies, Humble, Imperial, and Standard-Vacuum.) Actually, each region has three directors assigned to it: a primary contact, an alternate if he is sick or away, and an advisory contact director on the executive committee. As in any government, when to consult and when not to consult is regulated partly by written directives and also, inevitably, by experience and judgment.

As large and world-wide as the Jersey system is, it seems to work well, partly because the fifteen key men are full-time and provide continuity, and partly because the best skills of each are used in a variety of contact relationships, thus promoting teamwork and collective judgment. Almost alone among major industrial corporations in the United States, Jersey officially has an inside board, self-perpetuating and self-controlling. This is not necessarily, nor even likely, the best system for an *operating* program, but there is much that suggests that it might be made to order for the *holding-company* functions of the top people who should be masterminding the operations of the federal government.

To take a hypothetical illustration in the federal government: the inner executive group member responsible for monetary and fiscal affairs might also serve as State Department consultant on Latin America, if that happened to be his experience. Or the Secretary of Commerce, in addition to running his own department, might be the alternate for technical assistance policy and the adviser on atomic energy—again, if these areas happened to be within the bounds of his practical experience.

I would be the last to insist that the federal government should ever go this far toward continuity, but that it should take some steps to secure more continuity than is now possible seems clear beyond doubt.

HOW THE PLAN WOULD WORK

If the plan suggested in the preceding chapter were put into effect, the decision-making process in the federal government would work something like this:

The President would continue to discharge all of his present functions, including the managerial function that is in question. But instead of maintaining the fiction that he is actually able to serve as general manager, and then, in effect, shunting off his responsibilities onto a large and variegated staff outside the channel of operations, the bulk of the managerial and decision-making load would be transferred to the suggested inner executive group. These eight men would carry out what in large-scale industry is called the holding-company function; what in Canada, Switzerland, and some other countries is the inner cabinet or the executive council.

Under the plan suggested here, the cabinet would have a much more important role than at present. It would include not only the eight who have been mentioned but also the secretaries of other departments and the heads of agencies such as the Atomic Energy Commission, TVA, and the like. The cabinet might also include one or more ministers without portfolio, so to speak—elder statesmen with an over-all viewpoint who would help to center policy discussion on areas of overlap and grand strategy. Fortunately, both the Truman and Eisenhower administrations laid the foundation for more effective cabinet operation by providing it with a secretary and a staff to arrange agenda; and, hence, the deliberations of that body were far more thorough and businesslike than had formerly been the case.

The proposed inner executive group of eight would meet with the President and the cabinet, but they would be considerably more than a cabinet committee. In effect, they would be the President's executive team, and many other members of the cabinet would be administratively answerable to them. This is not an unusual procedure in other large-scale enterprises because the top officers of the typical holding company almost always serve on both the board of directors and the executive committee.

There would still be individual advisers in the President's own office, of course, but they would operate in connection with his duties as chief of state, head of the dominant political party, and chief legislator—duties which, under the proposed arrangement, he should have more time to study. At the same time, the inner executive group and the cabinet would remain the seed bed of legislation sponsored by the President, for those best qualified to prepare legislative proposals are those with the fullest knowledge and with first-hand experience of the facts.

In effect, therefore, the President's role vis-à-vis general management would be much like that of the board chairman of a large corporation. He would be thinker, long-range policy formulator, public relations symbol, the man who tries to keep everyone reasonably happy and who concentrates on the survival of the institution and the prosperity of the business.

This is not to suggest that even so, the President's managerial job would automatically become completely manageable. He could spend all of his time on only the political function, for example, and still be busy; or he could concentrate exclusively on legislation or foreign policy or his ceremonial functions and still have a full daily schedule. The point is that by transferring the President's duties as general manager to a tested means of execution, we make certain that that job at least would be better done than if we continued to operate on the basis of the existing makeshift, which no experienced man would ever assume could be made to work properly.

The alternative to the arrangement proposed here would be to amend the Constitution to provide for an assistant president in charge of administration—a national variation on the city manager plan for cities. I doubt, however, that this would be an effective solution. The assistant president would soon find the job too big for one man. There is the danger that he and the President might have a falling out or that the President might become jealous and withhold his support of the executive vice-president. There is some of this last danger also in the collegial type of executive, but it is less of a problem because membership on the eight-man team could last only so long as the President willed it.

In addition, the American executive profile is a fine one, and nothing challenges such a man as a chance to work for his country in a position where he feels he has scope and is not frustrated. Hence, there should be little trouble in finding the right men for the top holding-company jobs—men who, because of temperament, judgment, demonstrated executive skill, and high motivation would soon become indispensable to America's future as a nation.

They would have to be good, and they would also have to enjoy a wide freedom to take decisive action. The only serious danger in the plan is the possibility of bottlenecks appearing at the top level. If all action had to clear through and be initialed by these eight men, matters would rapidly become intolerable. But this danger can be avoided, the best proof being that it is avoided in the analogous cases examined here. An experienced executive delegates authority to subordinates. He is also willing to take chances, but reduces the risk by having clear objectives and policies and by testing his subordinates before he increases their authority to act on their own.

To solve the problems of top federal management is no different in its essentials than to solve the problem of running Jersey Standard on a world-wide basis. The procedure is the same: analyze the total need; find the individual with the right combination of skills to work with other members of an executive group; give each member a clear mandate and define it so as to produce integration, not stratification; then, distribute staff activities at the *logical* points in the hierarchy instead of at the top, so that neither the President nor any line officer is overburdened with line-staff relationships.

With this top-level organization, the processes of policy formulation and decision making in the federal government would take place as they do in other large organizations. The smallest unit of organization in the field and the largest in Washington would both plan objectives, policies, budgets, and methods *simultaneously,* each for its own needs but with the other in mind. Policy and decision making would then rise vertically through the various levels from the field offices to the regional offices, the departments, the inner executive group, and finally to the President. At the same time, those at the top of the pyramid would not only be deciding on plans coming to them from the action areas, but would also be formulating long-range plans and policies for the government as a whole. These would then be communicated as quickly as possible downward, so that those who work at the lowest action levels would appreciate the over-all framework in which their detailed programs had a larger meaning.

An experienced executive knows that effectiveness and motivation depend on making planning and decision making a two-way traffic. An error of the one-man myth is its failure to take this fundamental truth adequately into account. Hence, even if the President *could* bear all the administrative burden that the myth assumes he must, the results would still be disappointing because one-way traffic in decision making cannot produce spirited administration. Top-level coordination secured through a collegial executive has a long record behind it to prove that energy can be developed by this means. With such a plan in effect in the federal government we should be able to place performance in the United States on a par with the best of any nation in the world. When that time comes we may breathe more freely about the future of our political economy and our posture in world affairs.

EPILOGUE

FIFTEEN

EDUCATING FOR GREATNESS

The goal of America's new political economy is the good life, which, however, is not a fixed terminus but an evolutionary process. The good life is not an either/or proposition but a blend of necessary ingredients at particular stages of national growth. It is not merely the good society but the outstanding individual as well. It is neither collectivism nor individualism, but both. It is not only intelligence in personal and community affairs, it is also humanitarianism and values. It is not merely a reliable economic system, it is also one that promotes the greatest opportunity for growth and innovation.

In short, based on a philosophy of political economy, the good life is not an iron-clad formula, valid for all time. Rather, it is a combination of ancient wisdoms and the critical judgments by which people and nations respond to given situations inhering in different stages of growth in the advance of humanity toward higher stages of adaptation and satisfaction.

Progress toward this desirable state of affairs is slow partly because of certain human idiosyncrasies, which in time we should be able to overcome. Education, for example, is now often regarded as the process by which an individual becomes familiar, largely through memorization, with accumulations of knowledge handed down from one generation to the next. It is that, but much more: Education makes it possible for people to analyze the challenges in each stage of national development and to respond in a way that will assure survival and progress toward higher goals. Lacking this kind of education we tend to emphasize glittering but obsolete generalizations and hypostatic terms such as capitalism, free enterprise, collectivism, and socialism, little appreciating their real meaning or questioning whether the assumptions formerly underlying them have any relevance to today's situations.

Scholars and men of average education alike when faced with a problem too often merely analyze opposing propositions in order to discard the one they like the least. The enlightened individual, on the other hand—he whose education has taught him to think in terms of the many relationships inhering in most problems—realizes that truth is most often a fusion of truths found even in seemingly opposing propositions. The uncritical belief that an economic system must be run wholly by individuals on the basis of the profit motive, for example, or as a collectivism on the basis of production for use, overlooks the fact that any system, from the simplest to the most complex, includes elements of both patterns. The problem, therefore, is not to favor one and reject the other but to determine the most appropriate blend for a particular time and purpose in order to achieve the evolutionary process which is the good life.

I submit, therefore, that all the problems dealt with in this book and all the roadblocks standing in the way of the good life and an effective political economy depend for their solution on a proper approach, on a rethinking of the philosophy and objectives of education. America is challenged to greatness but, as we have seen, is held back by biased attitudes toward government and by government's own structural weaknesses, which make it hard for public policy to respond as it should to the needs of a nation in a sophisticated stage of development. A strengthened system of education would make the political economy approach a main emphasis of America's educational philosophy and would produce public persons able to guide the nation toward the good life we all seek. Hence, this last chapter deals with the educational challenge and how it may be made to contribute to the strengthening of our attitudes, our values, and our institutions.

KNOWLEDGE IS INSTRUMENTAL

Surveying the hundred or so countries that are now members of the United Nations, one may wonder which are most likely to succeed in making the good life a reality for themselves and which to fail. In each case the basic problem is education: How can education advance fast enough to supply the men and women on whom the conduct of national affairs depends? How can one be sure that the program of education underlying the political economy is tailor-made for the country's stage of national development? Do we understand enough about these stages of development, about the responses that are needed, and about priorities and objectives, in both education and the political economy, to proceed with any assurance that we know what we are doing?

The first question to be asked, therefore, is: Knowledge for what? We usually know what the accumulation of knowledge is in any particular field; our difficulty is in knowing how to use it in a particular situation at a particular time in order that the necessary evolution may take place.

In Nigeria, for example, much knowledge is needed about agricultural production, about how to build roads, construct power dynamos, hook up telephone sets, build radio and television facilities. In the United States we already have that knowledge. In Nigeria there are not enough people with enough training and self-confidence to organize and administer the political, economic, and social institutions that are required by a nation at that stage of development. In the United States we have at least 5 million trained managers, probably more. Superficially, therefore, one might conclude that Nigeria lacks almost everything it needs while in the United States conditions are just the reverse. Not true. At least, it is not true so far as the United States is concerned.

The reason is that the United States is in a different stage of national development from that of Nigeria. We have mastered the skills and the organizing ability that have put the economic multiplier to work. Consequently, we have new and unprecedented problems due to the rapidity of our growth and our seeming inability to respond to change as quickly as needed. Unless we do respond to this challenge our peril is relatively as great as that of Nigeria, if not greater, for with us every element in the situation is larger and more powerful than it is in a less developed nation such as Nigeria. The situations in the two countries may seem different; in fact, in both of them the problem is how to respond to challenge and change in a way that will safeguard the nation's assets and make good its deficiencies, so that it can evolve toward a better life.

It might be said that there are two kinds of knowledge, that which goes into a universal storehouse and that which is relevant to a particular time, place, and stage of growth. The first type is static, like adding grain to an elevator. The second is instrumental, operational, dynamic. The test is relevance.

In *The Art of Scientific Investigation,*[1] W. I. B. Beveridge says that there are two kinds of intellect: on the one hand, the patient, thorough, fact-finding technician; and on the other, the brilliant, imaginative, innovative developer of new theories and solutions. The approach to instrumental knowledge is of this second type. It is managerial and pertains to the political economy; its successful purveyor needs skills which the patient fact-gatherer does not require to the same extent—imagination, ability to identify structure and sequence, ability to see things whole and in organic relation. The intelligence required of the political economist must enable him to get from here to there, to pick priorities, arrange them in workable order, and see in which direction knowledge must go as well as how it compounds itself.

Although there is a dichotomy here, it is equally true that every country in every stage of growth needs both the fact-gathering and the innovative, problem-solving type of person. It needs the inheritors of past knowledge, but it also needs catalysts with the operational skills of the political economist to keep the nation moving and on the alert for new adjustments to new situations. Knowledge seems to grow vertically into great piles until at last it becomes so stratified that relationships are more important than quantities of facts. The need to understand these relationships is especially acute when a nation passes over into the sophisticated stage where the United States finds itself today.

If we are to solve our problems and help less developed nations to solve theirs, we must know vastly more about the requirements of political economy and its educational implications than we now do. A few people combine what is best in both types of intellect—the fact-gathering and the innovative—and knowledge always seems to advance more rapidly when the number of these two-barreled intellects is plentiful. To develop this type of person should be the objective of a theory of education that is dynamic and responsive.

EDUCATIONAL RESPONSE TO STAGES OF GROWTH

In the nation as in the individual, the problems inhering in each stage of growth are solved through balance. The objective to be sought is the happiness of the whole man in an organic society. Necessary ingredients are moral philosophy and ethics. The best way to produce an effective individual or an effective political economy is through the process of natural maturation. And the results are best, when, if a choice is necessary, people are encouraged to master subject matter first, and to acquire managerial skills afterward.

The outstanding example of factually trained men today are scientists, and increasingly we find that they make first-rate political scientists and administrator-statesmen. They are analytical, objective, and systematic, and hence are apt to have good judgment and a predisposition to fairness in human relationships. Thus, they are more than a match for the type of administrator, who, having never been thoroughly trained in anything but technique, assumes management to be merely manipulation, in consequence of which aversions are created due to suspicions of insincerity and superficiality. As between these two types, the scientist can frequently acquire what he lacks, while the manipulator, having less to build on, never seems to develop beyond a certain point.

Irrespective of their training, administrators sometimes lack the mental qualities of the theoretician, which may be a nearly fatal weakness in the head of an institution. The person who cannot identify concepts is frequently unable to analyze and to synthesize complex relationships, nor is he especially effective in communicating a sense of mission to others. It is possible that theoreticians are the result of a combination of inheritance, temperament, and the fortunate confluence of personality and environmental factors. If this is so, a born theoretician is hard to discourage, while a person lacking these innate traits is almost impossible to train even if he spends a lifetime at it. The problem in education, therefore, is to spot these rare birds early, to offer them a degree of training compatible with their temperamental demands, to encourage flexibility, and always to keep in mind that thoroughness and genius go together.

America has gone too far in teaching the techniques required in particular fields, to the neglect of other factors that are at the very least equally important. We ought immediately to repair the balance and pay more attention to teaching substance. To be specific, instead of spending so much time teaching teachers to teach, we should recruit as teachers more of those whose love of their subject is so great that they can teach movingly to any grade from the primary through the graduate level. Most teachers' colleges should be converted into arts and sciences colleges, with training in the techniques of teaching offered at the tool and workshop level.

Similarly for schools of business administration and public administration, where currently much emphasis is on technique rather than on a basic knowledge of policy, engineering, finance, and other systematic subjects. I do not mean that human relations should be neglected. I simply urge that what is taught be taught as systematically and as thoroughly as possible and that the place to give the future executive-statesman specialized training in how-to-do-it organizational administration is in executive development programs. Except for an occasional course that treats these subjects philosophically and in terms of principle, little of this instruction is needed or even appreciated until a man has had practical experience. At that point—especially if he has never studied social science before—he is eager to learn and can understand references and relationships because of personal on-the-job experience.

I would also register a protest against the tendency in American education—impelled no doubt by a desire to compete with the USSR —to speed up the process by throwing more and more facts at students, increasing their workday, and adding to the length of the school year. This is a different issue from increasing the effectiveness of teaching. A certain superficial case can be made for the forced-feeding approach in the contention that in our educational methods we have not been sufficiently thorough, rigorous, and tough and that to give students more to do at a faster pace will "separate the men from the boys."

But this is only partially true. The student arrives at understanding and wisdom by a natural maturation process the speed of which
differs with the individual. The best students need time for reflection and self-instruction without which they are not likely to develop
the mental set and the quiet self-confidence that are prime assets in
innovation and management and for the role of the statesman-gov-
ernor. If it is true that to live successfully in the distributive age a
people must be independent and original, socially experienced,
laboratory-tested, and rough-and-tumble in their outlook, then these
qualities must be developed gradually in the formative student years.

THE MORAL PHILOSOPHY TRADITION

Whatever dangers are inherent in substituting thorough subject-
matter training for technique would be less if we faced up to the
present neglect of moral philosophy and ethics as subjects of study
and as emphases running throughout the whole curriculum. Having
passed into the distributive or statesmanship stage of national development, we must have leaders of wisdom and penetration, men and
women who see things in relation, whose conceptual and managerial
abilities enable them to analyze problems, to project solutions, and
to master the intricacies of institutional management while at the
same time skillfully engineering programs to ends that produce a
better way of life.

We need the type of leader whom I have called the public person,
the ideal individual,[2] whose importance was incidentally noted by
witnesses testifying before the Jackson committee in 1960. Thus,
"the position of the individual in government," it was said, "is being
constantly downgraded," whereas in fact, "the main source of policy
innovations is the contribution of the individual."[3]

The ideal individual combines the cutting edge of his own trained
intellect with the wisdom of past experience. He sees what society
needs and how to progress toward higher levels, but he knows that
in seeking change we must safeguard tested values. The ideal individual is sufficiently hard-headed to choose measures that will
work, but he seeks constantly for solutions that promote human

well-being and happiness. He knows how to get things done, which is sometimes considered the hallmark of the conservative, and at the same time he has the high aspirations and ethical standards that are associated with the liberal pattern. He believes in universal principles and has an incisive and catholic capacity to probe and to make connections in his thinking. He understands the theory of opposing forces and the need for balance, for specialization combined with integration. He recognizes the role of challenge and response in the various stages of institutional growth. He knows that these key ideas exist everywhere in the social sciences and the humanities, and especially in philosophy.

So far from producing this type of leader, our present academic weaknesses often turn out men and women who are superficial manipulators instead of stewards, narrow instead of cultivated, segmented between knowledge on the one side and values and character on the other. We need a revival of moral philosophy, a union of the social sciences into political economy, a partnership of business and government, a clearer definition of roles and areas of responsibility, the production of more public persons. How are we to produce this type of leader?

By rediscovering and then re-emphasizing moral philosophy, which was the forerunner of political economy. Moral philosophy is a body of knowledge and a set of mind that stresses relationships, interconnections, and the values and truths found in disparate areas of knowledge. It is a distilled, down-to-earth wisdom, emphasizing universal principles and values. It is an amalgamator, respecting the conventional specialized disciplines with their segmenting tendencies but going beyond their autarchical boundaries to the common principles that bind them together.

From moral philosophy comes the knowledge of the proper thing to do at the proper time, the workable thing to do when people and their universal urges and ambitions are involved, the survival thing to do if a nation's program and culture are to enjoy longevity and a degree of well-being. This is the area where the humanities, the physical sciences, the knowledge of men and institutions, and the skills of governors meet and fuse to become a mature philosophy. Without such a philosophy—whether in business, labor, government, the church, or the school—a nation is not likely to surmount the difficulties that inhere in the sophisticated stage of national development. This is the stage in which most of the material wants of man can be met if there is adequate analysis, planning, and execution based on worthy goals and tested values.

Political economists have often differed—as have political philosophers since Socrates—as to whether happiness is a goal sufficiently tangible to constitute the end of living. In recent times the so-called happiness principle has been said to be too hedonistic and subjective to be acceptable as a goal of society, that what is one man's meat is another's poison, and that happiness cannot constitute a practical goal because empirical experience shows that the harder and more deliberately one seeks it, the more elusive does it become.

These truths, however, do not dispose of happiness as a goal of education and of political economy. Indeed, as the utilitarians argued, happiness is a proper goal of society. Happiness can be achieved by recognizing the universal principles that help people and nations to live in sympathetic accord with the balances and expectations of nature. It also promotes happiness to combine ends and means, to equalize production and consumption, to find ways of translating human aspirations into reality, to avoid becoming overly introverted or excessively extroverted, to serve the interests of one's country and at the same time to promote the principle of reciprocity that gives other countries an equal chance.

The happiness of society depends also on the wide distribution of skills. In the United States, for example, there is an oversupply of lawyers and advertising experts and a shortage of teachers and preachers. Any society needs a variety of skills but always in the right proportions to achieve human goals and contribute to stability and contentment. Thus a nation that respects the farmer as well as the industrial worker has the edge over one that neglects the farmer. Switzerland is a good example of the desirable balance in this respect. The farmer is close to nature and controls many of the means of his own livelihood, factors which tend to make him stable and conservative in the best sense of these terms. The industrial worker, on the other hand, is usually several removes from the product he helps to fashion and, hence, has little of the satisfaction of craftsmanship.

He ordinarily controls nothing but his own strength and skills and easily feels insecure and exploited. When, therefore, we try to solve the farm problem by encouraging farmers to abandon agriculture for industrial employment, we are in effect weakening stability and conservatism in favor of chronic unrest and discontent which easily turn to isms for solutions.

In the United States, the moral philosophy tradition comes largely from Scotland, which may justly claim to be the home of political economy. Nowhere else, over so long a period, have so many books been written tackling political economy at its roots.[4] More than any other people, the Scots have realized the need for balance: materialism combined with idealism; rationality with sentiment; individualism with cooperation; planning with resourcefulness; social yearnings with hard-headed attention to detail; private fulfillment with social responsibility; power with trusteeship; production with distribution; profit with distributive justice; equality with reward; coercion with persuasion; public education with a fascinating array of individual differences. The Scots are idealistic, as in Adam Smith's *The Theory of the Moral Sentiments,* and canny and thrifty, as in his *The Wealth of Nations.* What latter-day economists seem to have forgotten and what Overton Taylor fortunately reminds us of is that like Smith himself, the Scots thought of these things together, not as separate entities poles apart.[5]

It is largely because of this homespun wisdom, which came to be called moral philosophy, that in both Britain and America there have been relatively more outstanding policy leaders in all fields of business and public life who trace their origins to Scotland than to any other country.

Until recently, moral philosophy was a dominant interest in the universities of Oxford and Cambridge. Combining with French rationalism and the ideas of the radicals and social reformers of the day, it produced the philosophy and passion of Thomas Jefferson and a host of his spiritual successors. Since Jefferson put the principles of moral philosophy into the Declaration of Independence they have enjoyed a continuous and hardy life, emerging resonantly, for example, in the philosophy and the public life of Woodrow Wilson and Franklin D. Roosevelt.

Moral philosophy still lives in the United States and appears in many places. In industry there is the type represented by Owen D. Young and Arthur Page; in education, by Harold Dodds and Robert Gordon Sproul; in government, by George Norris and George Aiken. Such men are in the moral philosophy tradition: they look for universal principles; they are balanced and wise; they combine idealism and workability; their every act and impulse is first to discover and then to promote the public interest.

But although the venerable universities in Scotland and Britain still bring together philosophy, politics, and economics to form a triad most likely to promote moral philosophy, the ancient wisdoms, and relevant solutions for our time, it must be admitted, as Sir Oliver Franks observed in his Reith lectures,[6] that moral philosophy is not as vigorous as it was a century or even a generation ago. In the United States, academic specialization has progressively demanded grudging compliance with specialization's dictates. Increasingly, only a full-fledged economist or a full-fledged political scientist is "respectable." In consequence, the political economist who epitomizes moral philosophy is regarded as a regrettably nonconformist and excessively individualistic relic of a past age.

But there is about to be a reaction. Moral philosophy is about to reassert itself, both in the United States and in Britain. We know that syndicalist knowledge has its place as intellectual masonry but that it will never provide the aplomb and the wisdom that are needed to overcome the subtle dispersiveness of forces latent in an affluent society. By means of moral philosophy and political economy we shall master our own future and provide a rapport that will call forth the respect of peoples struggling for self mastery and self-government in two thirds of the world.

TEACHING POLITICAL ECONOMY

A precondition, however, is that we consider political economy in the larger context of the reform of education, and especially the reform of higher education. In a wealthy nation such as ours we cannot afford narrow training, autarchy, segmentation, deep probing for more facts for their own sake, testing hypotheses—in a word, specialization and scientism—unless they occur within a larger, integrated context. Those who wish to specialize should realize that theirs is not the only relevant tradition, that there may be others alongside theirs that are equally relevant for other purposes in the total situation. Increasingly in our educational institutions we must have courses of instruction that will revive the moral philosophy tradition with its stress on relevance, timing, universal principles, challenge, and response.

Then there must be a revival of philosophy itself. Despite the insistence of some specialists and rigorous scientists that ethical considerations are irrelevant, everyone working with institutions today needs a reliable body of ethics that is operational because the ultimate problems of political economy are of that nature: What *is* the public interest? What *are* the values that we fix as targets? Under what circumstances, if ever, may questionable means be employed to achieve ends that are above reproach?

In late years philosophy has seemed to abdicate responsibility in these areas; hence, the fields of political science, law, engineering, and the other professions have had to pick up the burden. In the universities more knowledge and insight having to do with operational ethics is accumulating outside of the departments of philosophy than inside them, and this is not a desirable state of affairs. If philosophy were as dynamic and integrative as it once was, it would be attracting other fields to it for the philosophical insights they need, and the resulting interactions would be more useful than the present improvisations on the part of other disciplines.

If education is to respond to the challenges of each stage of national growth, and if there is always a need for two types of knowledge—the specialized and the instrumental—then the academic specialties of economics and political science need not be *replaced* by political economy as an integrative and operational field; rather, the two kinds of knowledge may properly exist together.

Specialization has advantages if it goes deeply enough into its subject. It is only when policy makers assume that the conclusions of specialists are the whole of the matter and, hence, constitute a reliable and sufficient basis for decision making that trouble begins.

Specialization is appropriate for partial analysis but cannot be the sole guide to action because many other factors are normally involved in the solution of most problems. Synthesis is made to order for the guidance of action, but it must be based on deep probings to be complete. Even those who rely heavily on intuition must also have facts at their command, and the more of fact there is, the better the solution.

Hence, I do not mean to disparage any academic specialty. I simply contend that in educational philosophy and curriculum content in the United States today political economy is almost wholly neglected; that both as an academic and a man-of-affairs subject, political economy has much to do with survival and the good life; that relatively, therefore, the universities should be giving more attention to political economy than to any specialty, important as these are for many purposes; and that consequently there is an urgent need for rethinking in institutions of higher learning so that *organizationally,* political economy will enjoy a prominence second to none.

In Canada this problem has been solved along sound lines. Almost without exception in Canadian universities, economics and political science are taught in departments of political economy. This is an old tradition and a good one, a pattern once found also in the United States and Great Britain and one to which we should return. The larger concentration of political economy is a kind of holding company within which the disciplines of economics and political science constitute faculties within larger faculties, autonomies within a larger synthesis. More than that, in many cases, as at the University of Toronto, political economy also embraces business administration (as an arts subject), sociology, anthropology, and the international relations concentration—in short, the whole of the social science emphasis. In the United States, by contrast, it is not uncommon to divide this same area among four to six distinct and competitive departments, the number depending on whether public administration and international relations are taught as separate subjects.

After first-hand study I found that the Canadian custom of keeping political economy together as a single faculty has had the following advantages:

1. Even when political science and economics are organizationally distinct within the larger synthesis (and this is not invariably the case), the two groups of specialists bring the two bodies of knowledge together in their teaching, writing, and consulting far more than is the case in most American universities.

2. Books, monographs, and articles published by Canadian political scientists and economists show a greater awareness and sophistication—more of a real synthesis of the political and the economic, the policy and the institution—than do similar publications in the United States.

3. The effect of this synthesis is seen in its product: first, in the men who assume leadership in Canadian affairs after having been exposed as students to a political economy emphasis; and secondly, in the research and consultative contributions of Canadian scholars to the conduct of affairs in government and in the large corporations which increasingly resemble government.

Thus, when Canadian political economists are asked to advise on the structure of government administration, for example, they automatically think also of the structure of the economy and how it must be served. When they deal with foreign trade they automatically consider the strengths and weaknesses of the Department of External Affairs, the International Bank, and the United Nations. These men merge the political and the economic, consider institutional and pragmatic factors alike, and hence are able to offer advice more nearly resembling that of the practicing executive than any which characteristically comes from American universities.

In our own country, by contrast, economists frequently know what *not* to do, and even what to do, but *qua* economists they automatically stop at the point where institutional feasibility and various forms of political resistance enter the picture. Political scientists, on the other hand, concentrate on these workaday institutional and practical matters but often with little understanding of the ideal goal as determined by economic principles and analysis. The result is that neither group can supply more than half the answer, and even that may be wrong when placed beside the other half.

Under the political economy pattern in Canada, the student gets the necessary synthesis at the outset. Thus he becomes more like the Scot, balancing the theoretical and the practical, the private and the public, the ideal and the feasible. It is this approach that the United States needs perhaps more than any other nation, because as a result of size and opulence, we entered the statesman-managerial stage of growth earlier than many others and consequently lack guiding precedents.

When I asked our Canadian colleagues how they explain the keeping together of economics and political science as political economy they were inclined to minimize factors such as tradition, common sense, and clairvoyance and to cite the circumstances of Canada's geography and history. Canadians are proud of their country, realize more than most that its governmental policies have largely determined its national well-being, believe that only a strong government can maintain a strong economy, and are apprehensive about the possible effect of the economic power of their neighbor to the south. There is a determination that economics and political science shall continue to work closely together to give Canada the good life—and the independence—that Canadians demand.

If that is not a naturalistic explanation of academic subject-matter grouping I have never heard one. The result is sound and irrefutable. If in the United States we are equally determined to survive and prosper, we too had better establish departments of political economy and stop this foolish splintering in which economists and political scientists hardly speak to each other and even have trouble reading each other's journals.

Our academic aim should be: (1) to give every college student—especially prospective mathematicians, scientists, and engineers—a year's course on political economy; (2) give those headed toward government and business the same course, but follow it with specialized instruction in subjects such as accounting, public finance, personnel, and the like; and (3) expect students in both the physical and the social sciences to take courses in the humanities and the arts, for these are the subjects that consider the question: What do we work for if not to grow in culture and happiness?

I believe the reason that business schools are now preferred by more students than any other is not that more money is to be made in business than elsewhere (although that may be so), but that business administration combines theoretical economics with institutional management (the forte of political science) and, hence, gives students something they need, which the artificial separation of economics and political science has tended to deny them. If these subjects were brought together in a working accord, there would be less need for separate business schools and the attendant danger that many will become merely trade schools.

I believe it would be possible to teach a basic two-semester course in political economy if something like the following outline were adopted:

1. Resources—human, physical, institutional, with comparisons to other countries
2. Needs—analysis of strengths and weaknesses, again involving comparisons
3. Structure of the economy—including power relationships, as well as the usual institutional factors, and something about the legal system and its assumptions
4. Principles of economics—in a condensed form, with emphasis on basic assumptions and interrelationships among areas such as price, demand, wages, and the like
5. Shortcomings of the economy—wants not adequately met, areas of unbalance, again involving comparisons
6. Adequacy of the governmental mechanism—what government is supposed to do, how well it does it, and the principles that apply
7. Main areas of public policy—based on the structure of the economy and dealing with promotion and control
8. Principles of public policy—a philosophical, economic, and political consideration of public policy and the public interest
9. Future needs of the country—criteria relating to defense, conservation, human welfare, institutions; much of this would deal with problems of large-scale administration
10. Problems of peace and stability—international trade and relations, foreign competition, the common factors in domestic and foreign policy.

This outline includes elements of what is now taught in four different courses: beginning economics, beginning government, business and government, and international relations. From such a combined course, future businessmen and public officials alike would get the solid schooling in the tough issues of public policy that today they are inadequately equipped to handle, as a survey in 1959 made abundantly clear.[7] What are these policy issues? They include an understanding of the concept of the public interest and of laws affecting business; short- and long-term calculations affecting institutional survival; determination of the point of diminishing returns in markets, prices, and institutional size; the handling of labor relations and human relations generally; the matter of incentives and morale; the promotion of innovation and discovery; problems of taxation, economic stability, foreign competition, and consumer psychology; and finally, the achievement of over-all managerial effectiveness.

THE FUTURE OF POLITICAL ECONOMY

It may be objected that the principles of political economy are lacking in scientific precision. Except in a narrow sense, this is not so. If happiness and survival are the goals, political economy is the basic science of mankind. It can be tested pragmatically, although not always by counting techniques alone. It is based on situations that recur and, hence, predictability is possible. The more we learn about the subject the more deeply are we able to probe into the universal principles that bind all fields of knowledge together.

We are sometimes told that to be precise we must banish all considerations of ethics from our minds. This may be true for the limited purpose of piling fact on fact or for testing unproved hypotheses, but it is not operationally sound for the man of affairs, the ideal political economist. His knowledge is deeper and more reliable than segmented knowledge and includes ethical and human considerations as well as those that are material. His knowledge is also relational, being concerned with problem-solving at a particular time and place, with as many as possible of the variables known, including those that are ethical.

Knowledge that best serves the happiness of mankind is a combination of experience, feeling, analysis of universal principle, and a creative thrust to overcome new combinations of factors and advance toward a higher norm. It can also be claimed, I think, that if we knew enough about the flow from universal principle to moral philosophy to political economy, we could produce a higher standard of both physical and emotional well-being than is now possible through specialized approaches and non-communicating disciplines.

The new American political economy will never, I think, harden into an unchanging body of principle. The purist will call it merely common sense, and he will be right; indeed, political economy would be derailed if it were not common sense. The emphasis will be on wholeness and on what works.

With this approach, furthermore, it is possible that eventually the present differences between ourselves and the USSR, which now seem insuperable, will greatly narrow. If I am right, it will not be because one system comes to dominate the other, but because both will have learned more than they now know about the universal factors of political economy, which in the long run are a more reliable guide to survival and the good life—irrespective of system—than the enunciations of Karl Marx or David Ricardo.

The successful way to compete with communism is not to imitate it but to be true to our own ideals, so long as these are based on tested principle and are not merely narrow conservatism or prejudice. Our values as expressed in our religious beliefs and our political faith are superior to materialism, as even communists are beginning to learn. Our aim should be to make most people property owners; to strengthen competition; to police prices but never to decree them; to pass the efficiencies of technology on to consumers and workers as well as to management and investors; to be able to boast that government does progressively less because people are growing in their ability to govern themselves and in their regard for the public interest.

Then, if we improve some of our tastes, so as to recognize quality and appreciate art and beauty and all else that adds to man's cultural enjoyment and growth; if we remember that power must be widely distributed; if we keep in mind that much truth is still to be discovered and that we should encourage the searchers for it no matter how wrong we may think them to be; if we can do all these things, then I believe that communism will continue to swing toward our way of life. As the people of the Soviet Union become individually more prosperous they will want more personal property, for this urge is universal. As they reach a higher standard of living they will want the consumer's goods which only private enterprise can effectively offer; and as their new class turns out to be merely oligarchy in another guise, they will want to reject a class society run by a minority elite.

If this optimism is to prove well-founded, however, we must remember that the best way to compete with communism is to strengthen our own way of life, to do our own job better than we have done it before.

FOOTNOTES · SUGGESTED READING · INDEX

FOOTNOTES AND SUGGESTED READING

FOOTNOTES TO CHAPTER I

1. On this crucial issue, see Alexander Leighton, *The Governing of Men* (Princeton: Princeton University Press, 1946), pp. 343 ff.
2. This idea is more fully developed in my book, *A Philosophy of Administration* (New York: Harper, 1958).
3. On recent trends in Soviet administration, see my article on a comparison of Soviet and American administration in *Public Administration Review,* Summer 1960. This article was based largely on observations made during the summer of 1959, when nine American governors visited the USSR to study administration at the state and local levels.
4. This is spelled out more fully in my book, *Business and Government* (New York: Holt, Rinehart & Winston, 4th ed., 1961).
5. On the Scottish tradition, see A. L. Macfie, "The Scottish Tradition in Economic Thought," *Scottish Journal of Political Economy,* Vol. II, pp. 81–103; an address delivered at the annual general meeting of the Scottish Economic Society, March 24, 1955.
6. See, for example, Arthur T. Hadley, "The Relation between Economics and Politics," *Economic Studies,* American Economic Association, February 1899, this being the Association president's annual address.

FOOTNOTES TO CHAPTER II

1. Dealt with by a number of recent authors, but see especially Robert L. Heilbroner, *The Future as History* (New York: Harper, 1959), pp. 159–184.
2. For an excellent discussion of the requirements of voluntarism, see John M. Clark, *Economic Institutions and Human Welfare* (New York: Knopf, 1957), pp. 36 ff.
3. Thorstein Veblen, *The Instinct of Workmanship* (New York: Macmillan, 1914), *The Theory of the Leisure Class* (New York: Viking, 1931), and *The Place of Science in Modern Civilization* (New York: Huebsch, 1919). Also, John A. Hobson, *Work and Wealth* (New York: Peter Smith, 1914).
4. Donald S. Watson, *Economic Policy: Business and Government* (Boston: Houghton Mifflin, 1960), pp. 12, 14, and 91.
5. On the American tradition and how it is influenced by earlier traditions, see Henry Steele Commager, *The American Mind* (New Haven: Yale University Press, 1950); Robert L. Heilbroner, *The Future as History* (New York: Harper, 1959); and Max Lerner, *America as a Civilization* (New York: Simon and Schuster, 1957). On the origins of the liberal-democratic philosophy, the best source is Vernon L. Parrington, *Main Currents in American Thought* (New York: Harcourt, Brace, 1927–30).
6. Alexander Pope, *An Essay on Man,* Epistle 3.
7. *Ibid.,* Epistle 4.

8. Stuart Chase, *Democracy Under Pressure* (New York: Twentieth Century Fund, 1945), Chap. II.
9. Wesley McCune, *Who's Behind Our Farm Policy* (New York: Praeger, 1956), pp. 6–7.
10. "Do Businessmen Want Good Government?," *National Municipal Review,* January 1931, pp. 31–37.
11. Overton Taylor, *A History of Economic Thought* (New York: McGraw-Hill, 1960), Chaps. 3 and 4.
12. Francis X. Sutton *et al., The American Business Creed* (Cambridge: Harvard University Press, 1956), p. 184.
13. This viewpoint is illustrated in Harold D. Lasswell, *Politics: Who Gets What, When, and How* (New York: McGraw-Hill, 1936) and in David B. Truman, *The Governmental Process* (New York: Knopf, 1951).
14. See my book that has the subtitle, "A Study of the Creative State": *Modern Politics and Administration* (New York: American Book, 1937).
15. Knight, a former colleague of mine, has stated this orally on numerous occasions. For a fuller exposition, see his books *The Ethics of Competition* (New York: Harper, 1935) or *Freedom and Reform* (New York: Harper, 1947).
16. Robert A. Gordon and James E. Howell, *Higher Education for Business* (New York: Columbia University Press, 1959), pp. 61, 81–84; cf. Frank C. Pierson, *The Education of Businessmen* (New York: McGraw-Hill, 1959).
17. Clark, *op. cit.,* p. 16.
18. Taylor, *op. cit.,* p. 285.
19. Clark, *op. cit.,* p. 5.

SUGGESTED READING: CHAPTERS I AND II

For anyone wishing to investigate any of these subjects further, the following annotated bibliography may prove useful.

On the American dream, some of the best sources are Vernon L. Parrington, *Main Currents in American Thought* (New York: Harcourt, Brace, 3 vols., 1927–30); Dennis Brogan, *The American Character* (New York: Knopf, 1944); H. S. Commager, *The American Mind* (New Haven: Yale University Press, 1950) and *America in Perspective* (New York: Random House, 1947); Merle Curti, *The Growth of American Thought* (New York: Harper, 1943); Richard Hofstadter, *Social Darwinism in American Thought* (Boston: Beacon, 1955); Ralph Gabriel, *The Course of American Thought* (New York: Harper, 1943); Louis Hacker and Helene Zahler (eds.), *The Shaping of the American Tradition* (New York: Columbia University Press, 2 vols., 1947); Max Lerner, *America as a Civilization* (New York: Simon and Schuster, 1957); William Orton, *America in Search of a Culture* (Boston: Little, Brown, 1933); Ralph Barton Perry, *Characteristically American* (New York: Knopf, 1949); and Alexis de Tocqueville, *Democracy in America,* Reeves trans. (London: Longmans, 1889).

One of the best discussions of the old attitude of business toward government is Francis X. Sutton *et al., The American Business Creed* (Cambridge: Harvard University Press, 1953). A more critical view is Marquis Childs and

Douglas Cater, *Ethics in a Business Society* (New York: Harper, 1954). The two best critical essays in recent years, centering on power and ethics, are Adolf A. Berle, Jr., *The 20th Century Capitalist Revolution* (New York: Harcourt, Brace, 1954) and Walter Lippmann, *The Public Philosophy* (Boston: Little, Brown, 1955). The mature reflections of a great economist, John Maurice Clark, are found in his book, *Economic Institutions and Human Welfare* (New York: Knopf, 1957).

Among the recent books that show an increasing sympathy with the moral philosophy approach, the following may be mentioned: Paul Appleby, *Morality and Administration in Democratic Government* (Baton Rouge: Louisiana State Univerity Press, 1952); Howard Bowen, *Social Responsibilities of the Businessman* (New York: Harper, 1953); Sidney Fine, *Laissez Faire and the General Welfare State* (Ann Arbor: University of Michigan Press, 1956); George Graham, *Morality in Politics* (New York: Random House, 1952); Robert A. Gordon and James E. Howell, *Higher Education for Business* (New York: Columbia University Press, 1959); George A. Steiner, *Government's Role in Economic Life* (New York: McGraw-Hill, 1953); Donald Watson, *Economic Policy* (Boston: Houghton Mifflin, 1960); Willard Thorp (ed.), *American Issues* (Chicago: Lippincott, 2 vols., 1941–44); A. Dudley Ward (ed.), *Goals of Economic Life* (New York: Harper, 1953); and E. Ronald Walker, *From Economic Theory to Policy* (Chicago: University of Chicago Press, 1943).

Some of the books that deal with the policy function and with public policy in particular are Kenneth E. Boulding, *Principles of Economic Policy* (Englewood Cliffs: Prentice-Hall, 1958); Marshall E. Dimock, *Business and Government* (New York: Holt, Rinehart & Winston, 4th ed., 1961); Clair Wilcox, *Public Policies Toward Business* (Homewood, Ill.: Irwin, 1955); Vernon A. Mund, *Government and Business* (New York: Harper, 2d ed., 1955); William D. Grampp and Emanuel T. Weiler (eds.), *Economic Policy* (Homewood: Irwin, rev. ed., 1956); Robert A. Dahl and Charles E. Lindblom, *Politics, Economics, and Welfare* (New York: Harper, 1953); and Daniel Lerner and Harold D. Lasswell (eds.), *The Policy Sciences: Recent Development in Scope and Method* (Palo Alto: Stanford University Press, 1952).

FOOTNOTES TO CHAPTER III

1. Adam Smith, *The Wealth of Nations,* Canann ed. (London: Modern Library, 1905, originally published 1776) and *The Theory of the Moral Sentiments* (London, 6th ed., 1790). For a modern commentary, see Overton Taylor, *A History of Economic Thought* (New York: McGraw-Hill, 1960), Chap. IV.

2. Alfred Marshall, *Principles of Economics* (London: Macmillan, 8th ed., 1922). See also Taylor, *op. cit.,* Chap. XIII, "Marshallian Economics."

3. Kenneth E. Boulding, *The Skills of the Economist* (Cleveland: Howard Allen, 1958), pp. 9 and 10.

4. Paul A. Samuelson, *Economics* (New York: McGraw-Hill, 2d ed., 1951), pp. 13–15.

5. Sismondi and Saint-Simon, for example. See Charles Gide and Charles Rist, *A History of Economic Doctrines, From the Time of the Physio-*

crats to the Present Day. Second English edition, B. Richards. (Boston: Heath, 7th ed., 1947).

6. Among the best known of Thorstein Veblen's books are *The Instinct of Workmanship* (New York: Macmillan, 1914), *The Engineers and the Price System* (New York: Huebsch, 1921), and *The Theory of the Leisure Class* (New York: Viking, 1931). The best one-volume evaluation of Veblen that I have found is Abram L. Harris, *Economics and Social Reform* (New York: Harper, 1958), Chap. IV.

7. C. Wright Mills, *The Sociological Imagination* (New York: Oxford, 1959), pp. 6-7.

8. *Ibid.*, p. 174.

9. In general, see Quesnay's *Droit Naturel* or Henry Higgs, *The Physiocrats* (London and New York: Macmillan, 1897); Gide and Rist, *op. cit.;* or Taylor, *op. cit.*

10. Donald S. Watson, *Economic Policy* (Boston: Houghton Mifflin, 1960), p. 137.

11. Clair Wilcox, "Economic Theory and Economic Policy," *American Economic Review,* May 1960, pp. 27-33.

12. Mills, *op. cit.*, p. 168.

13. *Ibid.*, p. 9.

14. *Ibid.*, pp. 9-10.

15. *Ibid.*, p. 168.

16. Jacob Viner, *The Long View and the Short* (Glencoe: Free Press, 1958).

17. Peter Drucker, *The Practice of Management* (New York: Harper, 1954), p. 88; see also Ordway Tead, *The Art of Administration* (New York: McGraw-Hill, 1951).

SUGGESTED READING: CHAPTER III

There is a definite swing toward political economy in the United States, and the following are symptomatic: Kenneth E. Boulding, *Principles of Economic Policy* (Englewood Cliffs: Prentice-Hall, 1958); Walton Hamilton, *The Politics of Industry* (New York: Knopf, 1957); Donald S. Watson, *Economic Policy* (Boston: Houghton Mifflin, 1960); Howard R. Bowen, *Toward Social Economy* (New York: Rinehart, 1948) and *Social Responsibilities of the Businessman* (New York: Harper, 1953); W. W. Rostow, *The Stages of Economic Growth* (Cambridge, Eng.: Cambridge University Press, 1960); Arthur H. Cole, *Business Enterprise in its Social Setting* (Cambridge, Mass.: Harvard University Press, 1959); Sidney Fine, *Laissez Faire and the General Welfare State* (Ann Arbor: University of Michigan Press, 1956); A. Dudley Ward (ed.), *Goals of Economic Life* (New York: Harper, 1953); John Maurice Clark, *Economic Institutions and Human Welfare* (New York: Knopf, 1957); William D. Grampp and Emanuel T. Weiler (eds.), *Economic Policy* (Homewood: Irwin, rev. ed., 1956); Robert A. Dahl and Charles E. Lindblom, *Politics, Economics and Welfare* (New York: Harper, 1953); George A. Steiner, *Government's Role in Economic Life* (New York: McGraw-Hill, 1953); and Clair Wilcox, *Public Policies Toward Business* (Homewood: Irwin, 1955).

Also, A. Ronald Walker, *From Economic Theory to Policy* (Chicago: University of Chicago Press, 1943); Gunnar Myrdal, *The Political Element in the*

Development of Economic Theory (Cambridge: Harvard University Press, 1954), original in Swedish, 1928; J. P. Hicks, *The Social Framework of the American Economy* (New York: Oxford, 1955); Calvin B. Hoover, *The Economy, Liberty, and the State* (New York: Twentieth Century Fund, 1959); Sidney S. Alexander *et al., Economics and the Policy Maker* (Washington: Brookings, 1959); Abram L. Harris, *Economics and Social Reform* (New York: Harper, 1958); Paul A. Baran, *The Political Economy of Growth* (New York: Monthly Review Press, 1957); Harry Gunnison Brown, *Basic Principles of Economics and their Significance for Public Policy* (Columbia, Mo.: Lucas, 2d ed., 1947); and Emmette S. Redford, *Administration of National Economic Control* (New York: Macmillan, 1952). I could greatly extend the list if I were interested in inclusiveness.

I also recommend reading the discussion of economics' aims in *American Economic Review,* May 1960.

Among the older books I have found particularly worthwhile are Eli F. Heckscher, *Mercantilism,* Shapiro trans. (London: Allen & Unwin, 2 vols., 1935), original Swedish edition, 1931; John R. Commons, *Institutional Economics* (Madison: University of Wisconsin Press, 2 vols., 1959); all of Thorstein Veblen's books; A. C. Pigou, *The Economics of Welfare* (London: Macmillan, 4th ed., 1948); Gustav Cassel, *The Theory of Social Economy,* Barron ed. (New York: Harcourt, Brace, 1932); Thomas C. Leslie, *Essays in Political and Moral Philosophy* (London: Longmans, Green, 1879); Henry Sidgwick, *The Elements of Politics* (London: Macmillan, 1883); J. E. Cairnes, *Essays in Political Economy* (London: Macmillan, 1873); Anders Chydenius, *The National Gain,* Schauman trans. (London: Ernest Benn, 1931), originally published in 1765; Richard T. Ely, *An Introduction to Political Economy* (New York: Chautauqua, 1889); Thomas Nixon Carver, *Principles of Political Economy* (Boston: Ginn, 1919); J. Shield Nicholson, *Principles of Political Economy* (New York: Macmillan, 1898); J. R. McCulloch, *The Principles of Political Economy* (Edinburgh: William Tate, 1843); William Roscher, *Principles of Political Economy,* Lalor trans. (Chicago: Callaghan, 1882); Frederick List, *National System of Political Economy,* Matile trans. (Philadelphia: Lippincott, 1856); and David Hume, *Enquiries Concerning the Human Understanding and Concerning the Principles of Morals,* Selby-Bigge, ed. (Oxford: Clarendon, 1902) and *Theory of Politics,* Watkins ed. (London: Nelson, 1951).

FOOTNOTES TO CHAPTER IV

1. Francis Bowen, *Principles of Political Economy, Applied to the Conditions, the Resources, and the Institutions of the American People,* first published in 1856 (Boston: Little, Brown, 3rd ed., 1863), pp. 17 and 19.

2. From his book, *Utilitarianism.* Overton Taylor has a good critique of this issue in *A History of Economic Thought* (New York: McGraw-Hill, 1960), pp. 223–227.

3. Said Dean Harlan Cleveland, in an address given at the sixteenth Conference on Science, Philosophy and Religion in their Relation to the Democratic Way of Life (New York City, August 29, 1960, mimeo): "No, for any individual in any situation, the public interest must ultimately be what he thinks it is. If this seems a peculiarly American

answer to the question, 'What *is* the public interest?,' perhaps the answer
demonstrates what free men we Americans really are."

4. *The Power of the Democratic Idea,* Special Studies Project, Report VI,
Rockefeller Brothers Fund, America at Mid-Century Series (Garden
City: Doubleday, 1960), p. 21. Italics added.
5. *Ibid.,* p. 11.
6. *Ibid.,* pp. 5–14.
7. *Ibid.,* p. 14.
8. *Ibid.,* p. 16.
9. *Ibid.,* p. 43.
10. *Wealth of Nations,* Canaan ed. (New York: Modern Library, 1937), p.
862.
11. J. R. McCulloch, *The Principles of Political Economy* (Edinburgh:
William Tate, 1843), p. viii.
12. See the following: *An Autobiography* (London: Hodder & Stoughton,
1929); *Higher Nationality* (New York: Dutton, 1913); *Conduct of
Life and Other Addresses* (London: Murray, 1914); *Education and the
Empire* (London: Murray, 1902); also evaluations of his influence in
Public Administration (London), October 1928.
13. Mary Dewing, "Lord Haldane's Contributions to the Theory of Public
Administration" (Master's thesis, University of Chicago, 1937).
14. Leslie Lipson, *The Great Issues of Politics* (Englewood Cliffs: Prentice-
Hall, 2d ed., 1960).
15. *Ibid.,* pp. 4, 11, 20, 22, 58, 150, 207, and 410.
16. *Ibid.,* pp. 67, 70, and 71.
17. *Ibid.,* pp. 14–16.
18. Donald S. Watson, *Economic Policy: Business and Government* (Boston:
Houghton Mifflin, 1960).
19. *Ibid.,* pp. 94–105.
20. *Ibid.,* p. 106.
21. *Ibid.,* p. 39.
22. *Ibid.,* p. 126.
23. *Ibid.;* see especially pp. 106–107.

SUGGESTED READING: CHAPTER IV

America's concern for goals resulted in the appearance of no less than three
thoughtful volumes on this subject in 1960. The first of these, *The Power of
the Democratic Idea,* by The Rockefeller Brothers Fund, has been extensively
discussed in the text above. The second, *The National Purpose* (New York:
Holt, Rinehart & Winston, 1960), is a compendium taken from *The New
York Times* and *Life.* The third, *Goals for Americans* (Englewood Cliffs:
Prentice-Hall, 1960), is the report of the President's Committee on National
Goals. All of these center on the meaning to be attached to the public interest.

Many books on economics, political science, and philosophy must reckon
with the general-welfare function before they are through. Among the recent
ones that deserve mention are Howard R. Bowen, *Social Responsibilities of
the Businessman* (New York: Harper, 1953); Leslie Lipson, *The Great Issues of Politics* (Englewood Cliffs: Prentice-Hall, 2d ed., 1960); Donald S.

Watson, *Economic Policy: Business and Government* (Boston: Houghton Mifflin, 1960); J. P. Hicks, *The Social Framework of the American Economy* (New York: Oxford, 1955); Calvin B. Hoover, *The Economy, Liberty and the State* (New York: Twentieth Century Fund, 1959); and I. M. D. Little, *A Critique of Welfare Economics* (Oxford: Oxford, 2d ed., 1957).

G. H. Sabine, *A History of Political Theory* (New York: Henry Holt, rev. ed., 1950), is a convenient place to check the political philosophers. Equally, Overton Taylor, *A History of Economic Thought* (New York: McGraw-Hill, 1960) centers on the theme of liberalism and the public interest.

A symposium of John Stuart Mill's works, including *Utilitarianism, Liberty,* and *Representative Government* (New York and London: Everyman's Library, 1914) is a convenient means of securing the pith of Mill's thought. The best insight into Marxist theory is provided by Paul M. Sweezy, *The Theory of Capitalist Development* (New York: Oxford, 1942). The ideas of many other economists, as they center on the issues of this chapter, are found in J. A. Schumpeter, *History of Economic Analysis* (New York: Oxford, 1954).

FOOTNOTES TO CHAPTER V

1. Set forth in David Easton, *The Political System* (New York: Knopf, 1953).
2. Philip Buck, *The Politics of Mercantilism* (New York; Holt, 1942), pp. 101 and 121.
3. *The Positive Philosophy of Auguste Comte,* Martineau trans. (London: Chapman, 1853), Preface, p. 5.
4. W. W. Rostow, *The Stages of Economic Growth* (Cambridge, Eng.: Cambridge University Press, 1960), p. 149.
5. On this general contention, see Leslie Lipson, *The Great Issues of Politics* (Englewood Cliffs: Prentice-Hall, 2d ed., 1960), pp. 20–21.
6. Dealt with in my book, *Administrative Vitality: The Conflict with Bureaucracy* (New York: Harper, 1959).
7. Adam Smith, *The Theory of the Moral Sentiments* (New York: Duyckinch, Long *et al.,* 1822), p. 2.
8. Martin J. Hillebrand, *Power and Morals* (New York: Columbia University Press, 1949), p. 44.
9. V. W. Bladen, *An Introduction to Political Economy* (Toronto: University of Toronto Press, 1948), p. 49.
10. Gardiner C. Means, "The Distribution of Control and Responsibility in a Modern Economy," in Benjamin E. Lippincott (ed.), *Government Control of the Economic Order* (Minneapolis: University of Minnesota Press, 1935), p. 8.
11. Abram L. Harris, *Economics and Social Reform* (New York: Harper, 1958), pp. xiv, 150, and 153.
12. Paul R. Harbrecht, *Pension Funds and Economic Power* (New York: Twentieth Century Fund, 1959).
13. *Ibid.,* pp. 278–280.
14. C. Wright Mills, *The Sociological Imagination* (New York: Oxford, 1959), p. 41.
15. Hillebrand, *op. cit.,* pp. 33 and 35.

16. Adolf A. Berle, Jr., *The 20th Century Capitalist Revolution* (New York: Harcourt, Brace, 1954), Chap. V; and Walter Lippmann, *The Public Philosophy* (Boston: Little, Brown, 1955), Chaps. X ff.
17. Berle, *op. cit.,* pp. 45 and 172.

SUGGESTED READING: CHAPTER V

The subject of statecraft is so vast that is is obviously impossible to suggest all of the background sources. This would include all of the classics, such as Plato, Aristotle, Aquinas, Dante, Machiavelli, Hobbes, Locke, Montesquieu, and others. It would surely suggest *The Federalist Papers,* the writings of Thomas Jefferson, John Stuart Mill, Jeremy Bentham, James Bryce, Woodrow Wilson, Charles A. Beard, Charles Merriam, and of many now living, such as Robert MacIver, Arthur Holcombe, and Arnold Brecht.

Two books by Charles A. Beard are especially relevant to this chapter: *The Economic Basis of Politics* (New York: Knopf, 1934) and *Current Problems of Public Policy* (New York: Macmillan, 1936). See also Ernest Barker, *Principles of Social and Political Theory* (Oxford: Clarendon, 1951); Thomas Nixon Carver, *Essays in Social Justice* (Cambridge: Harvard University Press, 1932); G. D. H. Cole, *Essays in Social Philosophy* (London: Macmillan, 1959); Walton Hamilton, *The Politics of Industry* (New York: Knopf, 1957); Robert A. Dahl and Charles E. Lindblom, *Politics, Economics, and Welfare* (New York: Harper, 1953); Robert M. MacIver, *Democracy and the Economic Challenge* (New York: Knopf, 1952); and two presidential addresses given before the American Economic Association: Morris A. Copeland, "Instituionalism and Welfare Economics," *American Economic Review,* March 1958, and George W. Stocking, "Institutional Factors in Economic Thinking," *American Economic Review,* March 1959.

My own point of view is perhaps best seen, in evolution, in *Modern Politics and Administration: A Study of the Creative State* (New York: American Book, 1937); *A Philosophy of Administration* (New York: Harper, 1958); and *Administrative Vitality: The Conflict with Bureaucracy* (New York: Harper, 1959; London: Heinemann, 1960). I have also drawn heavily on John Maurice Clark, *Economic Institutions and Human Welfare* (New York: Knopf, 1957); Oberton Taylor, *A History of Economic Thought* (New York: McGraw-Hill, 1960); Leslie Lipson, *The Great Issues of Politics* (Englewood Cliffs: Prentice-Hall, 2d ed., 1960); C. Wright Mills, *The Sociological Imagination* (New York: Oxford, 1959); W. W. Rostow, *The Stages of Economic Growth* (Cambridge, Eng.: Cambridge University Press, 1960); Adam Smith, *The Theory of the Moral Sentiments* (New York: Duyckinch, Long *et al.,* 1822); Abram L. Harris, *Economics and Social Reform* (New York: Harper, 1958); Robert L. Heilbroner, *The Future as History* (New York: Harper, 1959); Auguste Comte, *The Positive Philosophy,* Martineau trans. (London: Chapman, 1853); Walter Lippmann, *The Good Society* (Boston: Little, Brown, 1943) and *The Public Philosophy* (Boston: Little, Brown, 1955); and Adolf A. Berle, Jr., *The 20th Century Capitalist Revolution* (New York: Harcourt, Brace, 1954).

If this appears as a strange admixture of historians, lawyers, economists, political scientists, anthropologists, and sociologists, I can only confess that

I agree with C. Wright Mills that "the social sciences are becoming the common denominator of our cultural period, and the sociological imagination our most needed quality of mind."

FOOTNOTES TO CHAPTER VI

1. Martin Wells, "The Survival Game," *The Listener* (London), January 5, 1961, p. 15.
2. For an indication of what needs to be done, see Charles McKinley, *Uncle Sam in the Pacific Northwest* (Berkeley: University of California Press, 1952); C. Herman Pritchett, *The Tennessee Valley Authority* (Chapel Hill: University of North Carolina Press, 1943); and Charles E. Merriam, "The National Resources Planning Board," *American Political Science Review,* October 1944.
3. "Management in the USSR—Comparisons to the United States," *Public Administration Review,* Summer 1960, pp. 139–147.
4. See National Resources Planning Board, *Regional Factors in National Planning and Development* (Washington, D.C.: Government Printing Office, 1935); John M. Gaus was chairman of the committee. See also Howard W. Odum, *Southern Regions of the United States* (Chapel Hill: University of North Carolina Press, 1936).
5. The best single source is Joint Federal-State Action Committee, *Final Report,* February 1960 (Washington, D.C.: Government Printing Office, 1960); this report was to the President of the United States and the Chairman of the Governors' Conference.
6. Interview with Brevard Crihfield, Executive Director, Council of State Governments, Chicago, Illinois, January 17, 1961. Also, interview with Robert Matteson, Executive Director, American Society for Public Administration, Chicago, Illinois, January 21, 1961.
7. J. K. Galbraith, *American Capitalism: The Concept of Countervailing Power* (Boston: Houghton Mifflin, rev. ed., 1956).
8. Walter Adams and Horace M. Gray, *Monopoly in America* (New York: Macmillan, 1955).
9. W. C. Allee, *The Social Life of Animals* (Boston: Beacon, rev. ed., 1958), originally published in 1938.
10. *Ibid.,* pp. 16, 21, 24, 28, 30, 74–75, and 94.
11. *Ibid.,* pp. 122, 134, and 185.
12. *Ibid.,* pp. 100, 122, and 134.

SUGGESTED READING: CHAPTER VI

The Rockefeller Study Group in their series, *America at Mid-Century,* has put out a seventy-eight page plan entitled *The Challenge to America: Its Economic and Social Aspects* (Garden City: Doubleday, 1958). This should be read along with another volume in the same series, *The Power of the Democratic Idea* (Garden City: Doubleday, 1960). The number of books presenting bold and clear plans for a better America diminished considerably after the 1930's and 1940's, which may show something about the state of our national morale. However, in the last few years there has been a deep, though largely unrequited, interest in the subject on the part of the public. President Eisenhower appointed a Commission on National Goals under the chairmanship of the former president of Brown University, Henry M. Wriston. The Commission's report appeared in 1960 as *Goals for Americans* (Englewood Cliffs: Prentice-Hall, 1960). At about the same time a number of essays by Archibald MacLeish, James Reston, Walter Lippmann, Adlai Stevenson, and others, which had previously appeared in *Life* and *The New York Times,* were brought out in book form under the title, *The National Purpose* (New York: Holt, Rinehart & Winston, 1960). Useful as these studies are, they are not very concrete; but perhaps public opinion is not yet ready for that.

Books of a more scholarly nature are A. Dudley Ward (ed.), *Goals of Economic Life* (New York: Harper, 1953), which was in the Series on the Ethics and Economics of Society; also, the various reports of the Council of Economic Advisers to the President, created under the Employment Act of 1946. Other useful books are H. A. Innis, *Political Economy in the Modern State* (Toronto: Ryerson, 1946); Donald S. Watson, *Economic Policy* (Boston: Houghton Mifflin, 1960); and Kenneth E. Boulding, *Principles of Economic Policy* (Englewood Cliffs: Prentice-Hall, 1958). A book that succeeded in capturing the progressive mood of the 1930's was George B. Galloway (ed.), *Planning for America* (New York: Holt, 1941). This volume still contains many suggestions that are germane to the discussion in this chapter. However, possibly the best single source is National Resources Planning Board, *Annual Report, 1934* (Washington, D.C.: Government Printing Office, 1934), where the philosophy of resources development was spelled out. In fact, all the publications of this agency, whose life span was 1933–1943, will repay the reader's attention, especially the study on regionalism (1935), referred to in the note 4 to this chapter.

On the issues of monopoly, transportation, public utilities, income tax, and other similar matters, probably the most convenient source is one of the following: Clair Wilcox, *Public Policies Toward Business* (Homewood: Irwin, 1955); Vernon A. Mund, *Government and Business* (New York: Harper, 2d ed., 1955); Harold Koontz and Richard W. Gable, *Public Control of Economic Enterprise* (New York: McGraw-Hill, 1956); Dudley E. Pegrum, *Public Regulation of Business* (Homewood: Irwin, 1959); Merle Fainsod, Lincoln Gordon, and Joseph C. Palamountain, Jr., *Government and the American Economy* (New York: Norton, 3d ed., 1959); Melvin Anshen and Francis D. Wormuth, *Private Enterprise and Public Policy* (New York: Macmillan, 1954); or my own book, *Business and Government* (New York: Holt, Rinehart & Winston, 4th ed., 1961).

FOOTNOTES TO CHAPTER VII

1. See, for example, Edward S. Mason, *Economic Concentration and the Monopoly Problem* (Cambridge: Harvard University Press, 1957). Mason has always stood for competition, but especially in the early part of this book he expresses the recent doubts that have arisen. Of course, the classic in the field is David Lilienthal, *Big Business, A New Era* (New York: Harper, 1953).

2. John Stuart Mill, *Principles of Political Economy,* Ashley ed. (London: Longmans, Green, 1923), p. 90; originally published in 1848.
3. *Ibid.,* p. 210.
4. Thornstein Veblen, *The Theory of the Leisure Class* (New York: Viking, 1931), conveniently evaluated in Abram L. Harris, *Economics and Social Reform* (New York: Harper, 1958), Chap. IV.
5. See, for example, Oskar Lange and Fred M. Taylor, *On the Economic Theory of Socialism* (Minneapolis: University of Minnesota Press, 1938); B. P. Beckwith, *The Economic Theory of a Socialist Economy* (Palo Alto: Stanford University Press, 1949); Paul Sweezy, *Socialism* (New York: McGraw-Hill, 1949); W. A. Robson (ed.), *Problems of Nationalized Industries* (New York: Oxford, 2d ed., 1952); A. H. Hanson, *Public Enterprise and Economic Development* (London: Routledge, 1959); and W. Friedmann, *The Public Corporation* (Toronto: Carswell, 1954).
6. John Jewkes *et al., The Sources of Invention* (New York: St. Martin's Press, 1958).
7. See my book, *Administrative Vitality, The Conflict with Bureaucracy* (New York: Harper, 1959), especially Part III.
8. Paul A. Samuelson, *Economics* (New York: McGraw-Hill, 2d ed., 1951), pp. 644–650.
9. Adolf A. Berle, Jr., *The 20th Century Capitalist Revolution* (New York: Harcourt, Brace, 1954).
10. W. C. Allee, *The Social Life of Animals* (Boston: Beacon, 1958), p. 94.
11. David Cushman Coyle, "The Big Cannot Be Free," *Atlantic Monthly,* June 1947, p. 74 (italics added).
12. George J. Stigler, "Competition in the United States," *Five Lectures on Economic Problems* (New York: Macmillan, 1950), pp. 46–65.
13. Donald S. Watson, *Economic Policy* (Boston: Houghton Mifflin, 1960), p. 101.
14. George Romney, President of American Motors, before Senate Sub-committee on Antitrust and Monopoly of the Committe on the Judiciary, February 7, 1958 (privately printed, Detroit), pp. 13–18.
15. Watson, *op. cit.,* pp. 211–214.

SUGGESTED READING: CHAPTER VII

As stated in an earlier chapter, possibly the best work on competition is still Alfred Marshall, *Principles of Economics* (London: Macmillan, 8th ed., 1922). One of the best recent presentations is the whole of Overton Taylor, *A History of Economic Thought* (New York: McGraw-Hill, 1960), but especially Chapter 16. The best treatments of monopoly and competition in recent years are by George W. Stocking and Myron W. Watkins, *Monopoly and Free Enterprise* (New York: Twentieth Century Fund, 1951); Corwin D. Edwards, *Maintaining Competition* (New York: McGraw-Hill, 1949); and Clair Wilcox, *Public Policies Toward Business* (Homewood: Irwin, 1955), especially Chapter 9, "Enforcement of Antitrust." The book that more than any other shows how mistakes in public policy contribute to monopoly is Walter Adams and Horace N. Gray, *Monopoly in America* (New York: Macmillan, 1955). A book that deals with the problem broadly and which includes labor is Fritz Machlup, *The Political Economy of Monopoly: Business, Labor, and Government Policies* (Baltimore: Johns Hopkins Press, 1952); in fact, this is one of the best books from the political economy point of view ever to appear in the United States. See also Frank H. Knight, *The Ethics of Competition* (New York: Harper, 1935); and Henry Simons, *A Positive Program for Laissez Faire* (Chicago: University of Chicago Press, 1944).

The trend toward a revision of the theory of competition was started by Edward Chamberlin in *The Theory of Monopolistic Competition* (Cambridge; Harvard University Press, 1933) and Joan Robinson, *The Economics of Imperfect Competition* (London: Macmillan, 1933). It was carried forward by J. K. Galbraith, *American Capitalism: The Concept of Countervailing Power* (Boston: Houghton Mifflin, rev. ed., 1956), originally published in 1952. Public attitudes toward this question are reflected in Burton R. Fisher and Stephen B. Withey, *Big Business as the People See It* (Ann Arbor: University of Michigan Press, 1951). Some proposals for reform written by a former businessman are found in T. K. Quinn, *Giant Business: Threat to Democracy* (New York: Exposition Press, 1953). The implications of excessive economic power are explained by Adolf A. Berle, Jr., *The 20th Century Capitalist Revolution* (New York: Harcourt, Brace, 1954); and the best defense of concentration is David Lilienthal, *Big Business: A New Era* (New York: Harper, 1953). An approach to the "new economics" is provided in Eugene V. Rostow, *Planning for Freedom: The Public Law of American Capitalism* (New Haven: Yale University Press, 1959). A. D. H. Kaplan has written *Small Business: Its Place and Problems* (New York: McGraw-Hill, 1948), and the Committee for Economic Development has published *Meeting the Special Problems of Small Business* (New York: CED, 1947). One of the best books on how the socialists hope to get around the problem of non-competition is Oskar Lange and Fred M. Taylor, *On the Economic Theory of Socialism* (Minneapolis: University of Minnesota Press, 1938), p. 65 ff.

FOOTNOTES TO CHAPTER VIII

1. See *The Mid-Century Challenge to U. S. Foreign Policy, Foreign Economic Policy for the Twentieth Century,* and *International Security: The Military Aspect* (Garden City: Doubleday, 1958 and 1959).

2. *The National Purpose* (New York: Holt, Rinehart & Winston, 1960); see especially the essays by John K. Jessup, Adlai Stevenson, John W. Gardner, and James Reston.

3. The turning point occurred in 1960 at the meeting of the United Nations General Assembly, when President Eisenhower announced this country's decision to funnel more of its aid through United Nations channels and to support that body down the line.

4. James Reston, "How to Win a Battle and Lose a War," *The New York Times,* April 7, 1961.

5. *The New York Times,* June 24, 1960. For background, see "A Chro-

nology of U. S. Statements on Spy Plane Flight," *Chicago Sun-Times,* May 17, 1960; Hanson W. Baldwin, "Post-Mortems on U-2," *The New York Times,* June 12, 1960; and James Reston, "The Political Consequences Following the U-2," *Ibid.,* May 13, 1960.

6. *The New York Times,* June 6, 1960.
7. *The National Purpose,* p. 6 (italics added).
8. *The Secretary of State and the National Security Process,* Senate Committee on Government Operations, Subcommittee on National Policy Machinery, 87th Cong., 1st sess., January 28, 1961.
9. See Clair Wilcox, *Public Policies Toward Business* (Homewood: Irwin, 1955), Chap. 27.
10. The best short treatment of this subject is Adolf A. Berle, Jr., *The 20th Century Capitalist Revolution* (New York: Harcourt, Brace, 1954), Chap. 4, where he compares the foreign office of a large corporation to our own State Department.

SUGGESTED READING: CHAPTER VIII

There is a vast bibliography on international relations, but the number of books written from an economic viewpoint are few. The reason is that economists *qua* economists have shown little concern for the subject, except as it deals with international trade. This seems unfortunate, but there will probably not be much change in the situation until, or unless, large numbers of economists become political economists.

The principles of economics and international trade are dealt with in Paul Samuelson, *Economics: An Introductory Analysis* (New York: McGraw-Hill, 4th ed., 1958), Part V. The public policy aspects are considered in my own book, *Business and Government* (New York: Holt, Rinehart & Winston, 4th ed., 1961), Part V; also Chapter 26, "The Foreign Economic Policy of the United States," in Donald S. Watson, *Public Policy* (Boston: Houghton Mifflin, 1960). See also William Y. Elliott (ed.), *The Political Economy of American Foreign Policy* (New York: Holt, 1955); this book, sponsored by the Woodrow Wilson Foundation and the National Planning Association, is clearly a step in the right direction. Another good book is Wilson E. Schmidt, *International Economics* (New York: Rinehart, 1957). See also Clarence B. Randall, *Foreign Economic Policy for the United States* (Chicago: University of Chicago Press, 1954).

Quincy Wright has written *A Foreign Policy for the United States* (Chicago: University of Chicago Press, 1947) and *A Study of War* (Chicago: University of Chicago Press, 2 vols., 1942), this last dealing with the economic factor, among others. The Brookings Institution, annually since 1954, has brought out *Problems of United States Foreign Policy: A Study Guide* (Washington, D.C.: Brookings, 1954). A readable book on foreign policy is that of Lawrence H. Chamberlain and Richard C. Snyder, *American Foreign Policy* (New York: Rinehart, 1954). See also Robert A. Dahl, *Congress and Foreign Policy* (New York: Harcourt, Brace, 1950).

The Rockefeller Brothers Fund, in their symposium, *America at Mid-Century,* produced three first-rate studies of foreign policy in 1958–1959: *International Security: The Military Aspect, Foreign Economic Policy for the*

Twentieth Century, and *The Mid-Century Challenge to U. S. Foreign Policy,* all of them published in Garden City by Doubleday.

A number of books have appeared in recent years on technical assistance. Three recent ones that are of interest are Gerald M. Meier and Robert E. Baldwin, *Economic Development* (New York: Wiley, 1957); Charles P. Kindleberger, *Economic Development* (New York: McGraw-Hill, 1958); and Edward S. Mason, *Economic Planning in Underdeveloped Areas: Government and Business* (New York: Fordham University Press, 1958). Among contemporary political economists who succeed in combining the political and the economic is the Britisher, W. Arthur Lewis; his books, *The Theory of Economic Growth* (London: George Allen & Unwin, 1955) and *The Principles of Economic Planning* (London: George Allen & Unwin, 1949) are uniquely applicable to this chapter. The story of international negotiations relating to the control of cartels is told in Clair Wilcox, *A Charter for World Trade* (New York: Macmillan, 1949).

FOOTNOTES TO CHAPTER IX

1. Hal Borland, reviewing *The Balance of Nature,* by L. J. and Margery Milne, *The New York Times,* October 23, 1960.
2. David Cushman Coyle, *Waste: The Fight to Save America* (New York: Bobbs-Merrill, 1936), pp. 21 and 82.
3. All the above reported in *The New York Times* for 1960: August 20, October 30, and December 11, 12, 13, 14, and 18.
4. *Ibid.,* August 14, 1960.
5. *Ibid.,* December 11, 1960.
6. *Ibid.,* October 28, 1960.
7. J. Frederic Dewhurst and Associates, *America's Needs and Resources, A New Survey* (New York: Twentieth Century Fund, 1955), pp. 767–772.
8. Charles A. Scarlott, "Changing Energy Scene," *The Scientific Monthly,* May 1957, pp. 221–228.
9. Best set forth in W. C. Allee, *The Social Life of Animals* (Boston: Beacon, 1958), p. 154.
10. *The New York Times,* March 6, 1960. See also Charles McKinley, *Uncle Sam in the Pacific Northwest* (Berkeley and Los Angeles: University of California Press, 1952).
11. H. G. Wells, *The Work, Wealth and Happiness of Mankind* (New York: Doubleday-Doran, 2 vols., 1931), pp. 344–347.

SUGGESTED READING: CHAPTER IX

A number of excellent books on conservation have appeared during the past few years, and their influence is one reason for optimism that something may be done. Vance Packard's best-seller of 1960, *The Waste Makers* (New York: McKay, 1960) not only presents many facts but deals also with deliberate and built-in obsolescense as a policy of industry and with the general shoddiness that may result from high-pressure consumerism. Three years earlier, David Cushman Coyle, one of America's most distinguished authors, published *Conservation: An American Story of Conflict and Accomplishment* (New Brunswick: Rutgers University Press, 1957), which is perhaps the most authentic work in this area. Nevertheless, his earlier book, *Waste: The Fight to Save America* (New York: Bobbs-Merrill, 1936), is a classic. The Malthusian problem is well presented in William Vogt, *The Road to Survival* (New York: Sloane, 1948) and in his more spectacular recent book, *People! Challenge to Survival* (New York: Sloane, 1960).

For factual material on resources, see J. Frederic Dewhurst and Associates, *America's Needs and Resources, A New Survey* (New York: Twentieth Century Fund, 1955); the President's Materials Policy Commission, *Resources for Freedom* (Washington, D.C.: Government Printing Office, 6 vols., 1952); Hoover Commission on Organization of the Executive Branch of the Government, *Department of the Interior* and *Task Force Report on Natural Resources* (for both: Washington, D.C.: Government Printing Office, 1949).

On the politics of conservation, see Norman Wengert, *Natural Resources and the Political Struggle* (Garden City: Doubleday, 1955); Gifford Pinchot, *Breaking New Ground* (New York: Harcourt, Brace, 1947); Charles McKinley, *Uncle Sam in the Pacific Northwest* (Berkeley and Los Angeles: University of California Press, 1952); Arthur Maas, *Muddy Waters* (Cambridge: Harvard University Press, 1951); and B. Lyons, *Tomorrow's Birthright: A Political and Economic Interpretation of Our Natural Resources* (New York: Funk & Wagnalls, 1955). Some of these, especially McKinley's book on the Pacific Northwest, are excellent examples of how the political and economic elements must be fused to become political economy.

FOOTNOTES TO CHAPTER X

1. Interview with Merrill E. Kilby, Consultant, General Electric Management Training Course, Crotonville, New York, December 12, 1960.
2. My own book, *Administrative Vitality: The Conflict with Bureaucracy* (New York: Harper, 1959), reviews the state of knowledge in this field.
3. *The New York Times,* May 29, 1960.
4. *Political Science Quarterly,* June 1887; reprinted in same journal, December 1941, pp. 481–506.
5. See especially *The Art of Administration* (New York: McGraw-Hill, 1951) and the books and articles on leadership and democracy by the same author.
6. This is my language, not the official statement of the school. For an appraisal of the Henley experiment, which was started in 1948, see Sir Noel Hall, *The Making of Higher Executives: The Modern Challenges* (New York: School of Commerce, Accounts, and Finance, New York University, 1958), Lecture II, "The Henley Experiment"; or my own article, "The Administrative Staff College," *American Political Science Review,* March 1950.

SUGGESTED READING: CHAPTER X

Among the books which were prophetic in their comprehension of the requirements of a new outlook and the need for a *rapprochement* between business and government, the following are outstanding: Beardsley Ruml, *Tomorrow's Business* (New York: Farrar & Rinehart, 1945); Walton Hamilton, *The Politics of Industry* (New York: Knopf, 1957); Arthur H. Cole, *Business Enterprise in Its Social Setting* (Cambridge: Harvard University Press, 1959); Thomas C. Cochran, *The American Business System* (Cambridge: Harvard University Press, 1957); Peter F. Drucker, *Concept of the Corporation* (New York: John Day, 1946) and *The Practice of Management* (New York: Harper, 1954); and Merver H. Bernstein, *The Job of the Federal Executive* (Washington, D.C.: Brookings, 1958). Two recent books of my own are also relevant: *A Philosophy of Administration* (New York: Harper, 1958) and *Administrative Vitality: The Conflict with Bureaucracy* (New York: Harper, 1959).

The personal skills needed by administrator-statesmen in the future are succinctly stated in Robert A Gordon and James E. Howell, *Higher Education for Business* (New York: Columbia University Press, 1959). The ideal qualifications are set forth in the concluding chapters of Walter Lippmann, *The Public Philosophy* (Boston: Little, Brown, 1955) and Adolf A. Berle, Jr., *The 20th Century Capitalist Revolution* (New York: Harcourt, Brace, 1954). There is much sound sense also in John W. Gardner's essay, "Can We Count on More Dedicated People?" in the symposium, *The National Purpose* (New York: Holt, Rinehart & Winston, 1960).

FOOTNOTES TO CHAPTER XI

1. See W. W. Rostow, *The Stages of Economic Growth* (Cambridge, Eng.: Cambridge University Press, 1960); also W. Arthur Lewis, *The Theory of Economic Growth* (London: George Allen & Unwin, 1955) and *The Principles of Economic Planning* (London: George Allen & Unwin, 1949).
2. Professor Samuel H. Beer, reviewing Paul T. David, Ralph M. Goldman, and Richard C. Bain, *The Politics of National Party Conventions* (Washington, D.C.: Brookings, 1960) in *Science,* July 8, 1960, p. 80.
3. James McGregor Burns, "Inside View of the Big Powwow," *The New York Times Magazine,* July 10, 1960.
4. If it would help us to think rationally about this problem, perhaps a substitute phrase could be found for the term "cabinet government," which some people seem to regard as "foreign" and, hence, less acceptable than our "native" variety. It might, for example, be called "buckle government," to describe the manner in which the legislative and executive branches are bound together. I would hope, however, that this semantic difficulty would not distress too many people and that we might rely on our national boast that "As an American, I am for anything that works."
5. Clinton Rossiter, "The Democratic Process," in *Goals for Americans* (New York: The American Assembly, 1960), p. 66.

SUGGESTED READING: CHAPTER XI

Woodrow Wilson's *Congressional Government* (Boston: Houghton Mifflin, 15th ed., 1913), which first appeared in 1885, is still foremost for its insight into what is needed to strengthen American government. Another landmark is W. Y. Elliott, *The Need for Constitutional Reform* (New York: McGraw-Hill, 1935), which in its boldness and grasp has not been equaled since. See also Charles E. Merriam, *The Written Constitution and the Unwritten Attitude* (New York: R. R. Smith, 1931).

Pendleton Herring, *Presidential Leadership* (New York: Farrar & Rinehart, 1940) provides a penetrating essay on the strengths and weaknesses of this office. See also Edward S. Corwin and Louis W. Koenig, *The Presidency Today* (New York: New York University Press, 1956); Clinton Rossiter, *The American Presidency* (New York: Harcourt, Brace, 1956); Louis Brownlow, *The American Presidency* (Chicago: University of Chicago Press, 1949); Edward S. Corwin, *The President: Office and Powers* (New York: New York University Press, 4th ed., 1958); Sidney Hyman, *The American Presidency* (New York: Harper, 1954); and Harold D. Laski, *The American Presidency* (New York: Harper, 1940).

Four major studies have been made of top organization and functioning in the federal government since 1937: President's Committee on Administrative Management (Brownlow Committee), *Problems of Administrative Management* (Washington, D.C.: Government Printing Office, 1937); Commission on Organization of the Executive Branch of the Government (first Hoover Commission) *General Management of the Executive Branch* (Washington, D.C.: Government Printing Office, 1949); Commission on Organization of the Executive Branch of the Government (second Hoover Commission), *Report* (Washington, D.C.: Government Printing Office, 1955), which consists of twenty volumes and nineteen task force reports dealing with the functions of government as well as with their organization; and Senate Committee on Government Operations, Subcommittee on National Policy Machinery, whose reports began to appear in 1960. The second Hoover Commission reports are especially relevant, since they deal with functions as well as with machinery.

One of the fairest comparisons of presidential and cabinet government is J. A. Corry, *Elements of Democratic Government* (New York: Oxford, 1947). See also a debate between Harold D. Laski and Don K. Price, *Public Administration Review*, Autumn 1944. The issue is also objectively dealt with in Thomas R. Adam, *Elements of Government: An Introduction to Political Science* (New York: Random House, 1960).

The need for responsible party government is set forth in a report of the Committee on Political Parties, American Political Science Association, *Toward a More Responsible Two-Party System* (New York: Rinehart, 1950).

FOOTNOTES TO CHAPTER XII

1. *The New York Times,* September 6, 1959.
2. Sidney Hyman, "Kennedy and Congress: Power vs. Power," *The New York Times Magazine,* January 1, 1961.
3. The most eloquent presentation of this position is to be found in Pendleton Herring, *Presidential Leadership* (New York: Farrar & Rinehart, 1940).
4. James Reston, "Inquiry at its Best," *The New York Times,* February 2, 1960.

5. *The Need for Constitutional Reform* (New York: McGraw-Hill, 1935), pp. 31 ff.

6. Professor Herman Finer, of the University of Chicago, has recommended that the President be given eleven executive vice-presidents; see his book, *The Presidency: Crisis and Regeneration* (Chicago: University of Chicago Press, 1960).

7. Peter F. Drucker, "The Almost Secret Art of Being an Effective President," *Harpers Magazine,* August 1960.

8. This is a review by Rexford G. Tugwell in *Science,* July 22, 1960, p. 215. The four books are by Walter Johnson, *1600 Pennsylvania Avenue* (Boston: Little, Brown, 1960); Richard Neustadt, *Presidential Power* (New York: Wiley, 1960); Richard F. Fenno, Jr., *The President's Cabinet* (Cambridge: Harvard University Press, 1959); and Joseph N. Kane, *Facts about the Presidents* (New York: Wilson, 1959).

9. The reference here is to Louis Koenig, *The Invisible Presidency* (New York: Holt, Rinehart, & Winston, 1959) and, with Edward S. Corwin, *The Presidency Today* (New York: New York University Press, 1956).

10. Wilfred E. Binkley, *President and Congress* (New York: Knopf, 1947), p. 297.

11. Louis Brownlow, *The President and the Presidency* (Chicago: Public Administration Service, 1949), pp. 19, 21, and 52–53 (italics added).

12. *Ibid.,* p. 54.

13. *Ibid.,* p. 62.

14. Herring, *op. cit.,* p. 63.

15. Koenig, *The Invisible Presidency,* pp. 16–17.

16. See *Organizing for National Security: Super-Cabinet Officers and Superstaffs,* Senate Committee on Government Operations, Subcommittee on National Policy Machinery, 86th Cong., 2d sess., Committee Print, November 16, 1960. For comment, see Holmes Alexander, "Superstaffs Debunked: Kennedy Dooms Pomp and Props," *The Boston Herald,* November 30, 1960.

SUGGESTED READING: CHAPTER XII

There have been few first-rate books on responsible government since Woodrow Wilson's *Congressional Government* in 1885, although some brilliant essays have played around the fringes of it. I refer to books by Herring, Rossiter, Corwin, and others that are listed in Chapter XIV and are referred to frequently in the footnotes. W. Y. Elliott, *The Need for Constitutional Reform* (New York: McGraw-Hill, 1935) still repays careful reading. So, too, does a recent book by Thomas R. Adam, *Elements of Government* (New York: Random House, 1960).

A short but good book that has a concrete plan is Thomas K. Finletter, *Can Representative Government Do the Job?* (New York: Reynal & Hitchcock, 1954). Herman Finer also comes up with a plan in *The Presidency: Crisis and Regeneration* (Chicago: University of Chicago Press, 1960). See also Henry Hazlitt, *A New Constitution Now* (New York: McGraw-Hill, 1942).

Harold J. Laski and Don K. Price have compared the presidential and cabinet plans of government in *Public Administration Review,* Autumn 1944.

W. Ivor Jennings writes on parliamentary government authoritatively, as does Frederic A. Ogg in *English Government and Politics* (New York: Macmillan, 2d ed., 1936). One of the best brief discussions in recent years is George B. Galloway, *Congress and Parliament: Their Organization and Operation in the United States and the United Kingdom* (Washington, D.C.: National Planning Association, 1955). Among the classics are A. Lawrence Lowell, *The Government of England* (New York: Macmillan, 1908); Walter Bagehot, *The English Constitution* (London & New York: Oxford, 2d ed., 1952); Sidney Low, *The Governance of England* (New York: Putnam, 1914); and Ramsay Muir, *How Britain is Governed* (Boston: Houghton Mifflin, 1935).

FOOTNOTES TO CHAPTER XIII

1. Tom Wicker in a book review, "Politicians Preferred," *The New York Times,* December 18, 1960.
2. See "The Lonely Leader," by William V. Shannon, in *The New York Post,* January 5, 1961.
3. *Ibid.*
4. "Kennedy to Take Direct Approach to Policy Matters," *The New York Times,* November 22, 1960.
5. I was not sure of the wisdom of this proposal until I had interviewed Frederich Wahlen, President of the Swiss Confederation and also minister in charge of the Department of Public Economy, at Berne, April 21, 1961.
6. *Super-Cabinet Officers and Superstaffs,* Senate Committee on Government Operations, 86th Cong., 2d sess., November 16, 1960.

FOOTNOTES TO CHAPTER XIV

1. Interviews with various government officials in Ottawa and with experts on public administration in a number of Canadian universities.
2. Interview with W. A. B. Hopkin, Assistant Director, Economic Section, British Treasury, London, February 16, 1961.
3. Consult William E. Rappard, *The Government of Switzerland* (New York: Van Nostrand, 1936), and "Les Conditions de la Prosperité Helvétique," an address presented on the occasion of the seventy-fifth anniversary of the Société Suisse des Industries Chimiques, August 29, 1957; Carl J. Friedrich and Taylor Cole, *Responsible Bureaucracy: A Study of the Swiss Civil Service* (Cambridge: Harvard University Press, 1932); Christopher Hughes, *The Federal Constitution of Switzerland* (Oxford: Clarendon Press, 1954); Sir Francis Adams, *The Swiss Confederation* (London: Macmillan, 1889); Hans Huber, *How Switzerland Is Governed,* Hottinger trans. (Zurich: Schweizer Spiegel, 1946); and André Siegfried, *La Suisse: Democratie-Témoin* (Neuchatel: A la Braconniére, 1948).
4. Interview with Hermann Böschenstein, political journalist of Berne, March 26, 1961.

5. Interview with Samuel Montgomery, vice-president, Standard Oil of Indiana, Chicago, Illinois, December 10, 1960.
6. The best single article on the subject is called "Standard of Jersey's New Plan of Realignment," *Business Week,* August 6, 1960. There are also two good articles in *Fortune,* October and November, 1951. My principal source of first-hand information is A. C. Reiners, assistant secretary of the company.
7. Adolf A. Berle, Jr., *The 20th Century Capitalist Revolution* (New York: Harcourt, Brace, 1954).

FOOTNOTES TO CHAPTER XV

1. W. I. B. Beveridge, *The Art of Scientific Investigation* (New York: Norton, 1957).
2. There is a first-rate discussion of this subject in the Rockefeller Brothers Report, *The Pursuit of Excellence: Education and the Future of America,* in the series, *America at Mid-Century* (Garden City: Doubleday, 1958).
3. *The National Security Council,* Senate Committee on Government Operations, Subcommittee on National Policy Machinery, 86th Cong., 2d sess., December 12, 1960; and *Ibid., Hearings,* Part I, p. 30.
4. The outstanding names are Hutcheson, Hume, Smith, and the two Mills. In a surrounding ring of satellites are many others: Lauderdale, Rae, McCulloch, Nicholson, Gray, Heatherington, Macfie, and Cairncross, for example. In his article on "The Scottish Tradition in Economic Thought," A. L. Macfie remarks that there is a unique Scots method, or approach, which is as individual as any personal approach. It can be called philosophic or sociological. It reached its peak development in the eighteenth century with the writings of Hutcheson, Hume, and Adam Smith. These writers gave political economy its "unique bite and flavour," though the flavor depends on the Scottish soil and the qualities and propensities of the people. His article is found in *Scottish Journal of Political Economy,* Vol. 11, pp. 81–103; see also A. L. Macfie, "Adam Smith's Moral Sentiments as Foundation for his Wealth of Nations," *Oxford Economic Papers,* New Series, October 1959 (Oxford: Clarendon Press, 1959).
5. Overton Taylor, *A History of Economic Thought* (New York: McGraw-Hill, 1960), Chaps. 3 and 4.
6. Sir Oliver Franks, *Britain and the Tide of World Affairs* (London: Oxford, 1955).
7. Robert A. Gordon and James E. Howell, *Higher Education for Business* (New York: Columbia University Press, 1959). This and Frank C. Pierson, *The Education of American Businessmen* (New York: McGraw-Hill, 1959) are discussed and the educational needs evaluated in Leonard S. Silk, *The Education of Businessmen,* Committee for Economic Development, Supplementary Paper No. 11 (New York: CED, 1960). The author gives special attention to the size and complexity of firms, the separation of ownership and management, rapid scientific and technological change, human and labor relations, innovation and profitability, and expanding areas of knowledge needed.

SUGGESTED READING: CHAPTERS XIII, XIV, AND XV

The best source of detailed information on the organizational problems dealt with in these chapters is the reports of the Senate Subcommittee on National Policy Machinery, headed by Senator Henry M. Jackson, which began to appear early in 1960 in several volumes. The most rewarding are these: *Super-Cabinet Officers and Superstaffs* (November 16, 1960), which condemned the use of excessive staff apparatus and advocated a managerial approach, and was analyzed in *The New York Times,* November 22, 1960; *The National Security Council* (December 12, 1960); *Interim Report* (January 12, 1960); *The Secretary of State and the National Security Process* (January 28, 1961); *National Policy Machinery in the Soviet Union* (January 20, 1960); *National Policy Machinery in Communist China* (January 1, 1960); *Resolution Expressing Concern of Senate over Turnover in Administrative and Policymaking Posts* (June 28, 1960); and *A Bibliography* (December 15, 1959). All of the *Hearings,* which run into several volumes, are also well worth reading. Among the best are Robert A. Lovett, Part I, pp. 12 ff; Roger Jones, Part III, pp. 434 ff; and John Corson, Part III, pp. 518 ff. For an evaluation, see James Reston, "Inquiry at its Best: Jackson's Study of Policy-Making Is a Scholarly and Objective One," *The New York Times,* February 26, 1960. See also Jackson's own article, "Organizing for Survival," in *Foreign Affairs,* April 1960.

Recent books bearing on this subject are Richard E. Neustadt, *Presidential Power: The Politics of Leadership* (New York: Wiley, 1960); Ernest R. May, *The Ultimate Decision: The President as Commander in Chief* (New York: George Braziller, 1960); Rexford G. Tugwell, *The Enlargement of the Presidency* (Garden City: Doubleday, 1960); Don K. Price (ed.), *The Secretary of State* (Englewood Cliffs: Prentice-Hall, 1960); Herman Finer, *The Presidency: Crisis and Regeneration* (Chicago: University of Chicago Press, 1960); Francis H. Heller, *The Presidency: A Modern Perspective* (New York: Random House, 1960); and Louis Koenig, *The Invisible Presidency* (New York: Holt, Rinehart & Winston, 1959). For the background of the extensive staff apparatus surrounding the President, see Edward H. Hobbs, *Behind the President* (Washington, D.C.: Public Affairs Press, 1954).

One important aspect of discontinuity is dealt with comprehensively in Laurin L. Henry, *Presidential Transitions* (Washington, D.C.: Brookings, 1960).

Leads to analogous problems in comparative governments, in large corporations, and in education will be found in chapter footnotes.

INDEX

Adams, Sir Francis, 239n
Adams, Sherman, 218
Adams, Walter, 109
Administration, *see* Government, *and* Presidency
Agriculture, a new look at, 192
Aiken, George, 82, 263
Alexander, Holmes, 219n
Alfred P. Sloan Foundation, xi
Allee, W. C., 111–112, 125–126, 164n
Ambition, incentives to, 46–47; political economy objective, 43, 46ff
America, *see* United States
Antitrust, enforcement, 128–129
  evasions, 108–109
  international competition, 148–149
  revision, 105, 124, 127, 128
Aristotle, 190

Bain, Richard C., 197n
Balance, competitive, 114ff
  through decentralization, 99–100
  in economic life, 41, 45
  in government, 82–83
  in growth, 40
  and institutions, 79–80
  political economy concept, 36, 43, 49–50
  and the public interest, 56–57, 59, 70
  structural, 77ff
Baldwin, Hanson W., 143n
Bart, Peter, 180
Beckwith, B. P., 118n
Beer, Samuel H., 197n
Berle, Adolf A., Jr., 49–50, 88, 90, 109, 122, 148n
Beveridge, W. I. B., 256
Bigness, *see* Size
Binkley, Wilfred E., 215n
Bismarck, Otto von, 77
Bladen, V. W., 84
Borland, Hal, 154n
Böschenstein, Hermann, 240n

Boulding, Kenneth, 44
Bowen, Francis, 55
Brownlow, Louis, 215–216, 217, 218
Buck, Philip, 73
Bureaucracy, in American institutions, 176
  effects of, 7, 30, 109
  increases in, 50
  and regionalism, 100
Burns, James McGregor, 197
Business, attitude toward government, 5–6, 28–29, 64, 178–179
  and cabinet government, 212–213
  conspiratorial, 121–122
  defined, 11
  education for, 33
  freedom and competition, 30
  a government institution, 1, 10, 11, 18, 23, 177
  leadership qualities needed, 12, 72, 181ff
  needs of, 179
  new attitude toward government, 175ff
  in politics, 179–180
  relationship to government, 11–12, 73–74
  small, encouragement of, 126–127
  top organization patterns, 241ff
  values of, 110

Cabinet government, *see* Government
Cairncross, Alexander K., 262n
Canada, the business-government relationship, 73–74
  moral-philosophy tradition, 33
  party responsibility, 196
  political economy teaching, 12–13, 265ff
  top organization pattern, 237–238
  transportation policy, 107, 108
Centralization, advantages and hazards, 86–87
Change, and growth, 39ff

297

Chase, Stuart, 27
Clark, John M., 17n, 30, 33n, 34
Cleveland, Harlan, 58n
Cole, Taylor, 239n
Commager, Henry Steele, 24n
Commons, John R., 44, 49
Competition, advantages, 115
    balance in, 114ff
    bases of, 115
    and collectivism, 5–6
    and concentration, 87
    degrees of, 42
    encouragement of, 126ff
    government's role, 121, 123–124
    imperfect, 120
    international, 145ff
    objections to, 117, 122–123
    and oligopoly, 122
    political economy concept, 32, 36
    preservation of, 30
    and the public interest, 56–57
    public opinion's role, 124–125
    in the USSR, 117–118, 119
    and values, 133–134
    weakened by government, 109
Comte, Auguste, 57, 74
Concentration, economic, and competition, 117
    and decentralization, 98ff
    degree of, 126
    encouraged by government, 109
    government's role, 123–124
    and innovation, 119
    tax remedy, 130–131
Confucius, 9
Conservation, abuse of resources, 155–156
    citizen support, 164, 166–167
    costs, 165
    federal department of, 166
    forests, 159ff
    history of, 157
    interrelationships, 154, 160–161, 163–164
    legislation for, 164–165
    minerals, 162–163
    the national heritage, 53
    parks, 161
    people, 168, 169–170
    political economy concept, 36, 43

Conservation (*cont.*)
    a positive program, 157, 163ff
    resource, 31, 154ff
    soil, 161–162
    values needed, 159, 171
    water, 157ff
Consumer sovereignty, 46, 56
Consumers, standard of living, 45
Control, political economy concept, 36
    and power, 87–88
Coolidge, Calvin, 197, 215
Cooperation, political economy concept, 36
Coordination, in government, 195ff
    political economy concept, 32, 36
Corporations, and antitrust, 127
    and bureaucracy, 177
    federal incorporation, 127
    as governing institutions, 10, 11, 18, 23
    government, as antitrust measure, 127
        for transportation, 108
    and institutional balance, 79–80
    size limits, 130–131
Corwin, Edward S., 215n
Coyle, David Cushman, 126n, 157
Crihfield, Brevard, 102n

David, Paul T., 197n
Decentralization, and entrepreneurship, 50–51
    governmental, 192–193
    industry and labor, 98–99, 106
    through legislation, 105ff
    problems of, 100ff
    regional, 97ff
    and survival, 113
    in USSR, 8
Decision making, organization for, 20
    policy base, 17ff
    political economy concept, 32, 36
    training for, 12–13
Democracy, advantages of, 81–82
    in new nations, 136–137
    testing ground of, 4–5
Democratic idea, power of, 60ff
Dewhurst, J. Frederic, 162n
Dewing, Mary, 65n

Dillon, C. Douglas, 198, 234
Diminishing returns, and balance, 42
  political economy concept, 36
Dimock, Gladys Ogden, xi
Dodds, Harold, 263
Douglas, Lewis, 198
Douglas, Paul, 82
Drucker, Peter, 53, 214

Easton, David, 73n
Ecology, and political economy, 49
Economic concentration, *see* Concentration, economic
Economic policy, goals of, 68
Economic stabilization, governmental priority, 191
Economics, and human values, 68–69
    limitations of, 266
    and political economy, 264–265
    and the public interest, 56, 66–67
    separation from political science, 4, 13–14, 121, 264–265, 268
    traditional concerns, 51
Economy, national, decentralization of, 98–99, 105ff
    elements of vitality, 17–18
    and foreign policy, 140
    and international competition, 145ff
    revitalization of, 95ff
    stabilization of, 43, 51–52
Education, and conservation, 164
    economics and political science separated, 4, 13–14, 121, 264–265, 268
    future of political economy, 269ff
    for greatness, 253ff
    instrumental knowledge, 254ff
    kinds of knowledge, 256
    kinds needed, 257–258, 270
    for leadership, 3, 12ff, 183ff, 269
    misconceptions about, 253–254
    moral-philosophy aspects, 260–261
    moral-philosophy tradition, 259ff
    national growth stages, 257ff
    new emphasis needed, 258
    the outstanding individual, 257–258
    political economy approach, 12ff
    for political economy, 263ff, 267

Education (*cont.*)
    political economy course outline, 268–269
    for public persons, 259–260
    re-examination of, 254
    specialization, 263–264, 264–265
Efficiency, meaning of, 131–132
    political economy concept, 36
    and size, 131–132
    and wealth, 41
Eisenhower, Dwight D., 141n, 143, 218, 219, 223, 224, 226, 234
Elliott, W. Y., 211
Entrepreneurship, and innovation, 50–51
    political economy concept, 36

Farm organizations, as governing institutions, 10, 11, 18, 23
Federal aid, variations and effects, 103–104, 104–105
Federal incorporation, antitrust measure, 127
Fenno, Richard F., Jr., 214n
Finer, Herman, 212n
Follett, Mary Parker, 151
Ford Foundation, x–xi
Foreign aid, bases of, 140–141
    and international competition, 145ff
Foreign policy, *see* Policy, foreign
Foreign service, characteristics needed, 145
Franks, Sir Oliver, 263
Free Enterprise, and collectivism, 5–6
Freedom, in business, 179
    and competition, 115
    meaning of, 47–48
    and the public interest, 57–58, 58–59
    and public policy, 60
Friedmann, W., 118n
Friedrich, Carl J., 239n

Galbraith, J. K., 106, 190
Gardner, John W., 137n
Gaus, John M., 100n
Gide, Charles, 45n, 49n
Gladstone, William, 189
Goldman, Ralph M., 197n
Gordon, Robert A., 33n, 269n

Government, administration and policy, 21, 80
  administrative continuity, 198, 234ff
  assisting the President, 199ff
  balanced, 82–83
  broad view, 29
  bureaucracy, 109
  cabinet, in Canada, 237–238
    in Great Britain, 80, 238–239
    need for, 142, 198, 210, 219
    possibility of, 212–213
    procedure under, 211–212
  coordination strengthened, 195ff
  costs of weakness, 179
  decentralization, 101–102, 191–192
  decision making at top, 245ff
  defined, 11
  departments realigned and increased, 232–233
  determining priorities, 189ff
  functions added and terminated, 194
  functions devolved to regions and states, 191–192
  in a generic sense, 73–74
  growth of, 38
  growth stages, 190
  leadership qualities needed, 12, 181ff
  legislative-executive relations, 197–198
  management improvement, 201
  minimum reform program, 187ff
  nature of, 185–186
  organizational lessons from business, 241ff
  and power, 25, 67
  practical administrators needed, 182
  private and public, 10–11
  proposed reorganization, departments and agencies, 228ff
  public attitudes toward, 64
  and the public interest, 61, 63–64
  reform plan, 188–189
  regional, 98
  relation to business, 11–12, 73–74, 175ff
  responsibility weakness, 203–204

Government (*cont.*)
  role of, 29, 39–40, 65, 66, 84–85, 121, 187–188, 190–191
  same needs as business, 179
  securing responsibility, 203ff, 210
  state, 100, 102
  statesmen needed, 109
  strengthening execution, 30–31
  top management confusion, 206
  top organization, 221ff
    models, Canada, 237–238
      Great Britain, 238–239
      private enterprise, 241ff
      Switzerland, 239–240
  world, 151ff
Gray, Sir Alexander, 262n
Gray, Horace M., 109
Great Britain, business-government relations, 73–74
  leadership training, 184–185
  moral-philosophy tradition, 33, 263
  party responsibility, 196
  political economy education, 12–13
  revenues decentralized, 103
  top organization pattern, 238–239
  transportation policy, 108
Greatness, national, building for, 1ff
  education for, 253ff
Greeley, Horace, 207
Growth, and change, 39ff
  institutional decay, 78
Guizot, François, 89

Hadley, Arthur T., 13n
Haldane, Lord, 64–65
Hall, Sir Noel, 185n
Hamilton, Walton, 49, 88, 109
Hansen, Alvin, 51
Hanson, A. H., 118n
Happiness, goal of political economy, 270
  goal of society, 58, 261–262
  values, 5–6
Harris, Abram L., 86n, 116n
Harbrecht, Paul R., 87–88
Harding, Warren, 204
Heatherington, Sir Hector, 262n
Herring, Pendleton, 205n, 217
Heilbroner, Robert L., 17n, 24n, 167

Hillebrand, Martin, 83, 89
Hobbes, Thomas, 74
Hobson, John A., 18
Hoover, Herbert, 197, 218
Hopkin, W. A. B., 239n
Howell, James E., 33n, 269n
Huber, Hans, 239n
Hughes, Christopher, 239n
Hume, David, 9, 262n
Hutcheson, Francis, 262n
Hyman, Sidney, 203, 204n

Ickes, Harold, 166
Innovation, and competition, 119
    and entrepreneurship, 50–51
Interest groups, *see* Pressure groups
Interest, public, *see* Public interest
International competition, *see* Foreign
    aid
International relations, *see* Policy, for-
    eign
Interrelatedness, in conservation, 154,
    160–161, 163–164
    among human institutions, 190
    in political economy, 36, 57, 69
Institutions, growth and decay, 78

Jackson committee, vii–viii, xi, 145,
    219, 235–236, 259
Javits, Jacob K., 143
Jefferson, Thomas, 49, 57, 262
Jessup, John K., 137n, 145
Jewkes, John, 50, 119n
Johnson, Walter, 214n

Kane, Joseph N., 214n
Kefauver, Estes, 82
Kennedy, John F., x, 203, 219, 234
Keynes, John Maynard, 44, 51
Kilby, Merrill E., 176n
Knight, Frank, 32
Koenig, Louis, 215n, 218

Labor, organized, decentralization of,
    98–99, 106, 125, 194
    encouragement of, 30
    as governing institution, 1, 10,
        11, 18, 23
    review of legislation, 129
    state responsibility, 192
Laissez faire, a positive program, 124ff

Lange, Oskar, 118n
Lasswell, Harold D., 29n
Lauderdale, James M., 262n
Legal profession, and the public in-
    terest, 108–109
Leighton, Alexander, 6n
Lerner, Max, 24n
Lewis, W. Arthur, 190n
Liberty, *see* Freedom
Lilienthal, David, 114n
Lincoln, Abraham, 221
Lippmann, Walter, 49–50, 90, 207
Lipson, Leslie, 65ff, 77n
Littman, Robert, xi
Lockwood, Henry C., 210

Macfie, A. L., 13n, 262n
Machiavelli, Niccolò, 27, 74
MacLeish, Archibald, vii
Macmillan, Harold, 214
Madison Avenue, false images created,
    97
    influence of, 27, 46
    and manipulation, 89
    values of, 110
Man, natural and artificial, 75ff
Managerial approach, to political
    economy, 36ff, 39ff
Managerial élan, 37
Management, *see* Government, *and*
    Presidency
Manipulation, poverty of, 88ff
Mansfield, Mike, 143
Marshall, Alfred, 41, 42, 56
Marx, Karl, 56, 76, 85–86, 270
Mason, Edward S., 114n
Matteson, Robert, 102n
Maximization, and competition, 120–
    121
Mayo, Elton, 77
McCulloch, J. R., 64, 262n
McCune, Wesley, 27
McKinley, Charles, 98n, 166n
Means, Gardiner, 49, 85, 88
Mercantilism, business attitudes, 73
    concerns of, 44, 52, 55
    main tenets, 56
    senile stages, 138
Merriam, Charles E., 98n
Metternich, Prince de, 138
Mill, James, 262n

Mill, John Stuart, 13, 44, 56, 58, 64, 116, 262n
Mills, C. Wright, 30, 47–48, 50, 51, 88, 90–91
Milne, L. J., 154n
Milne, Margery, 154n
Mitchell, Wesley, 51
Monopoly, *see* Concentration, economic, *and* Antitrust
Monson, Diane, xi
Montgomery, Samuel, 242n
Moral philosophy, revival of, 260–261
  in Scotland, 262
  in the United States, 33–34, 262–263

National debate, vii–viii, 14
National heritage, preservation of, 52ff
Natural law, and the public interest, 57
Natural resources, *see* Conservation
Neustadt, Richard, 214n
New York University, x–xi
Nicholson, Harold, 141
Nicholson, J. Shield, 262n
Norris, George, 82, 205, 263

Odum, Howard W., 100n
Organization, for decision making, 20, 221ff, 245ff
  models, public and private, 237ff
  political economy concept, 32, 36

Page, Arthur, 184, 263
Parrington, Vernon L., 24n
Peace, causes of war, 52
  political economy objective, 43, 51–52
  see also Policy, foreign
Phillips, Cabell, 203
Philosophy, role of, 65
  moral-philosophy tradition, 259ff
  revival needed, 264
  Scottish tradition, 262
  see also Moral philosophy
Physiocrats, 49, 56, 57
Pierson, Frank C., 33n, 269n
Pinchot, Gifford, 157
Planning, governmental priority, 191
  and statecraft, 79

Policy, and administration, 21, 80
  and consistency, 21–22
  generally plural, 20
  generic term, 23
  interrelationships in, 20–21, 22–23
  meaning of, 19ff
Policy, foreign, coexistence, 149ff
  forthright diplomacy, 141–142
  guidelines to, 135ff
  governmental priority, 191
  international law, 152
  moral aspects, 136–137, 150–151
  political economy as base, 135ff
  principles of, 139ff
  reform needed, 144–145
  responsibility in, 142ff
  traditional approach, 138
  world government, 151ff
Policy, public, Adam Smith's views, 28
  areas of, 68
  bases for decision making, 17ff
  defined, 19
  economic stability, 51
  formulation, 22
  and freedom, 60
  impact of pressure groups, 27
  issues of, 4–5, 30–31, 269
  political economy concept, 32, 36
  need for responsibility, 195–196
  securing continuity, 234ff
Political economy,
  approach,
    in business, 181
    need for, 9–10, 31
    potentialities, 10, 11–12
  concepts, viii, 5
  course outline, 268–269
  defined, viii–ix, 5, 7–8, 9 .
  determining governmental priorities, 190
  foreign policy guide, 135ff
  future of, 269ff
  goals, 7–8, 43ff, 253
  governmental reform, 187
  growth and change, 39ff
  interdependence and predictability, 57
  key terms, 32
  leadership training, 183–184
  the managerial approach, 36ff

Political economy (*cont.*)
objections to, 6–7
the public interest, 55ff
sentiment, 22–23
a synthesis, 122
teaching of, 262ff
unifying concept, 5ff
values, viii–ix, 7–8, 22–23
Political science, limitations of, 266
and political economy, 264–265
separation from economics, 4,
13–14, 121, 264–265, 268
Political scientists, views on public
policy, 29
Politics, and administrative continuity,
198
and business, 179–180
democracy and pressure groups,
63
foreign policy, 143–144
future issues of, 208–209
meaning of, 66
party system reform, 25–26, 31,
196–197, 208ff
and responsibility, 206
and statecraft, 77–78
Pope, Alexander, 25
Power, and the American credo, 25
balance, 49–50
centralization, 86–87
content of, 85ff
control of, 36, 49–50, 87–88
of the democratic idea, 60ff
excesses, 51, 95–96
to govern, 2, 7
and government, 67, 177
increases in, 18
manipulation of, 88ff
meanings and connotations, 49,
88–89
overemphasis on, 85–86
political economy concept, 32, 36
separation of, 80–81
and society, 30
Predictability, and political economy,
57
President, assistants to, 227
demands on, 199–200, 204–205,
215ff, 226
help for, 199ff, 222–223
human limitations, 199–200

President (*cont.*)
managerial responsibility, 216–
217
national symbol, 216
virtuoso rule, 223–224
Presidency, attempted improvements,
218–219
board-chairman plan, 224ff
cabinet functions, 227, 246
division of responsibilities, 225
holding-company plan, 224–225
an inner executive group, 212,
227, 246
how it would work, 245ff
qualities needed, 247
institutionalizing the office, 215ff
shared administrative power, 205
staff agencies, 228
organization, 200–201, 218–
219
top organization models, 237ff,
241ff
variety of functions, 219–220
views of the office, 221–222
Pressure groups, and competition,
126–127
freedom of, 30
history of, 27–28
impact, 27, 108, 187–188, 213–
214
methods of, 27, 121–122
and the public interest, viii, 26ff,
60
Price, and competition, 42
and the consumer, 46
market, 36, 42, 116–117
Pritchett, C. Herman, 98n
Public assistance, abuses, 213–214
hazards, 169
Public interest, issues of, 66–67
legal profession's influence, 108–
109
meaning of, 58–59, 60, 69ff
political economy view, 36, 66ff
President to promote, 215
and private interests, 62, 70–71
problem of political economy,
55ff
protection of, 63–64
recognition of, 53, 71
and the selfish interest, viii, 63ff

Public opinion, and antitrust, 129
  and conservation, 159, 164, 166–167
  maintaining competition, 124–125
  a responsible press, 207
Public ownership, as antitrust measure, 127
Public persons, characteristics of, 168–169, 259–260
  knowledge needed, 269
  need for, 82, 168ff, 170–171
Public policy, *see* Policy, public
Public relations, and corporation policy, 80

Quesnay, Pierre, 49, 57

Rae, John, 262n
Rappard, William E., 239n
Regionalism, defined, 100
  problems of, 100ff
Regions, decentralization through, 98ff
  for governmental functions, 192–193
Reiners, A. C., 242n
Relm Foundation, xi
Resources, natural, *see* Conservation
Responsibility, in government, *see* Government
Reston, James, 137n, 142, 206, 207
Revenue, *see* Taxes
Ricardo, David, 27–28, 270
Rist, Charles, 45n, 49n
Robson, William A., 118n
Rockefeller Brothers Fund, vii, 60, 61, 63, 68, 135, 259n
Rockefeller, Nelson, 214
Romney, George, 127, 130
Roosevelt, Franklin D., 77, 109, 197, 198, 221, 224, 262
Roosevelt, Theodore, 137–138
Rossiter, Clinton, 200
Rostow, W. W., 76, 190

Saint-Simon, Claude Henri, 45n, 56
Samuelson, Paul, 44–45, 120
Scotland, business-government relationship, 64
  moral-philosophy tradition, 33, 262

Scotland (*cont.*)
  political economic education, 12–13
Sentiment, in political economy, 9, 22–23
Shannon, William V., 222n, 223n
Shinner Foundation, xi
Siegfried, André, 239n
Silk, Leonard S., 269n
Simplicity, objective of statecraft, 75
Sismondi, Jean Charles, 45n, 56
Size, control of, 30, 125, 127–128, 129
  through taxation, 130–131
  effect of, 25, 31–32
  and efficiency, 42, 125–126, 131–132
  excesses, 95
  governmental, 98, 102–103
  optimal, 111–112
Smith, Adam, 9, 13, 27, 28, 41–42, 44, 48, 49, 56, 57–58, 64, 83, 91, 115, 121, 140, 262
Social sympathies, American, 24ff
Society, optimal size, 111–112
  stages of growth, 190
  values, needs, aspirations, 61–62
Socrates, 9, 261
Sombart, Werner, 56
Sproul, Robert Gordon, 263
Stabilization, economic, *see* Economy, national
Standard of living, political economy objective, 36, 43, 45–46
Standard Oil of Indiana, organizational pattern, 241–242
Standard Oil of New Jersey, organizational pattern, 242ff
Statecraft, cohesiveness and belonging, 83ff
  consistency, 78–79
  knowledge of power, 89–90
  meaning of, 72, 91
  need for, 72
  objectives, 75–76
  requirements of, 73–74, 77–78
  test of, 77
States, *see* Government
Statesmanship, political economy concept, 32, 36
  training for, 183–184
Stavisky, Nellie, xi

Stevenson, Adlai, vii, 137n
Stimson, Henry L., 109, 198
Stigler, George J., 126
Structure, importance of, 51–52
  and political economy, 36, 40
Survival, and decentralization, 113
  hazards to, 96
  values of, 111–112
Sutton, Francis X., 28n
Sweden, the business-government relationship, 73–74
  public policy support, 128
Sweezy, Paul, 118n
Switzerland, balance of skills, 261
  business-government relationship, 73–74
  federal-state relations, 192–193
  forestry control, 160
  legislatures and the press, 207
  revenue decentralization, 104
  top organization pattern, 239–240

Taxes, and concentration control, 130–131
  and conservation, 165
  and government decentralization, 101–102, 103–104
  revised income tax, 99, 106–107
  revised state and federal, 193
Tarzian, Carol, xi
Taylor, Fred M., 118n
Taylor, Frederick W., 9
Taylor, Overton, 28n, 30, 33, 49n, 58n, 262
Tead, Ordway, xi, 183
Toynbee, Arnold, 167
Transportation, problem of, 98, 107
  remedies, 108
Truman, David B., 29n
Tugwell, Rexford G., 210, 214n

Union of Soviet Socialist Republics, coexistence with, 149ff
  cultural struggle, 76
  and competition, 115, 117–118
  competition with, 270–271
  and concentration, 130–131
  and conservation, 165
  the consumer, 45
  deconcentration, 125
  income-tax policy, 106

Union of Soviet Socialist Republics (*cont.*)
  influences on, 184
  management in, 7, 8
  narrowing differences with capitalism, 270
  needs practical businessmen, 181–182
  revenue decentralization, 104
  strength of people, 139
  U-2 incident, 20, 143
United States, American beliefs, 24ff
  assets of, 1–2, 4–5
  cause and dream, 3–4
  characteristics, 6
  missing concept, 1–2, 10
  moral-philosophy tradition, 262–263
  policy weaknesses, 21, 22
  prestige loss, 137, 195–196
  public policy issues, 4–5, 30–31, 269
  shortcomings, 18–19, 25–26, 31–32
  social sympathies, 24ff
  and underdeveloped nations, 2, 3–4
  values, 24ff, 33, 62–63, 83, 110–111

Values, the American credo, 24ff
  America's needs, 33
  and behavior, 10
  and competition, 133–134
  and conservation, 159, 171
  the consumer, 45
  in economic life, 41, 68–69
  in a free society, 62–63
  and human happiness, 5–6, 261–262
  leadership training, 184
  and the political economy approach, viii–ix, 7–8, 22–23, 32, 36
  power, 86
  the public interest, 59, 60–61
  public policy, 108
  social and human, 75–76, 110–111
  strengthening of, 83
  survival, 111–112

Veblen, Thorstein, 18, 44, 47, 56, 98, 116
Viner, Jacob, 53
Voluntarism, need for, 193–194
    by public persons, 168–169
    a vital economy, 17–18

Wahlen, Frederich, 232n
War, causes of, 52, 139–140
Watson, Donald S., 22n, 49, 68–69, 126n, 133

Welfare state, definitions, 48
Wells, H. G., 170
Wells, Martin, 96n
Whyte, William H., 76
Wicker, Tom, 221n
Wilcox, Clair, 50, 148n
Wilson, Woodrow, 182, 198, 205, 210, 217, 221, 262
Work, views of, 47, 70

Young, Owen D., 184, 263